CINEMATICALLY SPEAKING

The Orality–Literacy Paradigm for Visual Narrative

THE HAMPTON PRESS COMMUNICATION SERIES
Media Ecology
Lance Strate, supervisory editor

Mediating the Muse: A Communications Approach to Music, Media, and Cultural Change
Robert Albrecht

Valuation and Media Ecology: Ethics, Morals, and Laws
Corey Anton (ed.)

Bookends: The Changing Media Environment of the American Classroom
Margaret Cassidy

Biotech Time-Bomb: The Side-Effects are the Main Effects
Scott Eastham

Parodox Lost: A Cross-Contextual Definition of Levels of Abstraction
Linda G. Elson (*Alan Ponikvar,* ed.)

Of Ong and Media Ecology: Essays in Communication, Composition and Literary Studies
Thomas J. Farrell and Paul A. Soukup (eds.)

Walter Ong's Contribution to Cultural Studies: The Phenomenology of the Word and I-Thou Communication Revised Edition
Thomas J. Farrell

An Ong Reader: Challenges for Further Inquiry
Thomas J. Farrell and Paul A. Soukup (eds.)

The Power of Metaphor in the Age of Electronic Media
Raymond Gozzi, Jr.

Constant Motion: Ongian Hermeneutics and the Shifting Ground of Early Modern Understanding
Jerry Harp

Perspectives on Culture, Technology and Communication: The Media Ecology Tradition
Casey Man Kong Lum

ScreenAgers: Lessons in Chaos from Digital Kids
Douglas Rushkoff

Echoes and Reflections: On Media Ecology as a Field of Study
Lance Strate

The Legacy of McLuhan
Lance Strate and Edward Wachtel (eds.)

Language, Culture and Identity
Sara van den Berg and Thomas Walsh (eds.)

CINEMATICALLY SPEAKING

The Orality–Literacy Paradigm
for Visual Narrative

Sheila J. Nayar

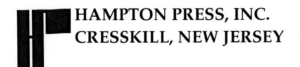

HAMPTON PRESS, INC.
CRESSKILL, NEW JERSEY

Printed in the United States of America

Library of Congress Cataloging-in-Publication Data

Nayar, Sheila J.
  Cinematically speaking : the orality-literacy paradigm for visual narrative / Sheila J. Nayar.
       p. cm. — (Hampton Press communication series. Media ecology)
  Includes bibliographical references and indexes.
  ISBN 978-1-57273-964-2 (hardbound) — ISBN 978-1-57273-965-9 (paperbound)
  1. Motion pictures—Philosophy.   2. Motion picture plays—History and criticism.   I. Title.
  PN1995.N372 2010
  791.4301—dc22

                                                            2010028038

Hampton Press, Inc.
23 Broadway
Cresskill, NJ 07626

Two birds, deepest of friends,
Live on the same tree.
One eats the sweet fruit.
The other, without eating, watches.

—Abhinavagupta, 10th century

Contents

Preface

Chances are good that when you sit down to watch a movie, whether Wong Kar-wai's moody *In the Mood for Love* or a crime drama-cum-martial-arts comedy like Stephen Chow's *Kung Fu Hustle*, the last thing you think about is reading and writing. More likely you sit down pleased at the prospects of indulging in something *visual*, in an optical language whose "literacy" derives from a different set of competencies.

This book proposes quite the opposite. That is, it enunciates a new and, according to some scholars, already controversial theory about cinematic literacy (Yaeger, 2008, p. 11). Its premise is simple: The reading and writing that you *think* you are escaping may in fact have had an integral role in contouring the film with which you are engaging—and, in turn, your ability to engage with that film. As a new theoretical way of thinking about visual storytelling, *Cinematically Speaking* problematizes the very notion of film as an autonomous mode of storytelling construction.

Under no circumstances would I claim that the cinematic medium does not have significant influence on shaping story (or "the message," in McLuhanesque parlance). However, in taking account of several millennia of storytelling forms—from the ancient Greek epics to James Joyce's playful deformation of Homer's odyssey in *Ulysses*—this project demonstrates that film narrative, not unlike these literary works, has fundamental ties to how *alphabetic literacy* has (or, in some cases, hasn't) shaped narrative. Or more accurately, the theoretical claims made in this book about film emerge largely from its consideration of the structuring principles behind both the oral epic *and* the modernist novel. Somewhat oddly then, perhaps, I trace this project's genesis to a pirated video of a 1990s Bollywood film, which my impoverished Hindi at the time did nothing to discourage as a viewing experience.

Storytelling, in order to be accessible, must "fit" with its participants' cognitive capacities, and these capacities are significantly shaped by those participants' relationship to reading and writing and print, both over the historical long term (phylogenetically) and also within the span of our own lives (ontogenetically). This may sound suspect, even discomfiting, to readers who have never had to contemplate the extent to which their consciousness has been shaped by such social skills and practices. But much like private property, reading or writing only appears "as a 'natural' object, typically denying the determinants of its productive process" (Eagleton, 1976, p. 101). (I will simply remind readers of the roughly 10 to 20 years of daily inculcation through schooling that it takes for an individual to master this "natural" state.) What follows, then, is an in-depth and systematic explanation of how the skills bound up with alphabetic literacy shape visual narrative—and how an unavailability or dismissal of these skills fundamentally shapes visual narrative, too.

In order to demonstrate alphabetic literacy's sway on film narrative, I will have to traverse, somewhat unorthodoxly, the boundaries that traditionally delineate a discussion of film narrative. Perhaps that is fitting; for, in some respects, *Cinematically Speaking* is the organic consequence of my proclivity for seeking out similarity rather than difference. This is a route of investigation no longer particularly in vogue. Scholars these days are, for understandable reasons, more comfortable anatomizing for distinction. But is it not possible that we have, in our intense scrutiny of the localized moment or the historically bracketed, missed some broader schemata of the visually experiential? I say this with a certain trepidation, knowing the difficulty that lies ahead of me in terms of my being able sufficiently to persuade readers. But as a preliminary teaser—or perhaps a forewarning—know that I frequently reference stories like the *Iliad* in order to talk about Bollywood (the Hollywood of Bombay), or the *Mahabharata* to explicate a film like Alain Resnais' *Last Year at Marienbad* (1961). I will adjoin under a single theoretical umbrella an Indian curry-western like *Sholay* (*Flames*, 1975) and Ingmar Bergman's *Persona* (1966); Italian peplums and Italian neorealism; kitsch and Kurosawa; as well as shed light on some of the etiological reasons for the Deleuzian movement-image and time-image. In this way, *Cinematically Speaking* hopes not only to offer a partial clarification regarding how and why filmic narratives take the shapes they do, but as well as to articulate and, perhaps most constructively, to complicate what is commonly referred to as the "high art–popular culture divide."

Of course every society brings to its popular film forms "its own special history and traditions, its own cultural stamp, its own quirks and idiosyncracies," as Arjun Appadurai and Carol Breckenridge (1988, p. 5) write, just as every auteur seeks to bring the same to his or her latest release. But even *these* differentiae are connected, this volume contends, by the human capacity for verbal language and by the technologies that have allowed that language to be nested in diverse forms. Through means such as writing, we have shaped our communications with each other, but we also have incontrovertibly been shaped by those means. As a result, I suggest that bards like Homer would have been flummoxed by Joyce's modernist masterpiece, and Bergman's *Persona* would most certainly have bombed in ancient Greece—but I do think the Indian blockbuster *Sholay* would have been a personal favorite of Homer's, with James Cameron's *Titanic* (1997) possibly coming in a close second.

I style *Cinematically Speaking* as a historical poetics, which, as David Bordwell (1989) succinctly outlines, attempts in the academic field of film studies to answer two broad questions:

1. What are the principles according to which films are constructed and by means of which they achieve particular effects?
2. How and why have these principles arisen and changed in particular empirical circumstances? (p. 371)

In attending to these questions, I hope to broaden the current parameters of film-narrative studies. Perhaps, too, if my framework is sufficiently coherent, I will be able to illumine some of sociology's bearing on poetics, and, perhaps most productively, to open up a new film-studies field of inquiry that does not derive exclusively from a Western intellectual tradition.

Poetics is of course a lofty term, as also is *theory*; and any book that begins by pronouncing itself both is no doubt setting itself up for a fierce critical demolishing. But if we think about the roots from which these terms derive—*poein* for poetics (to make or compose); *theōria* for theory (a viewing, a "looking at")—then what is offered in the forthcoming pages is hardly lofty, and certainly not theoretically grand. It is rather an attempt to draw out how composers, whether bardic or Bressonian, need, like their stories, to be "looked at" on the basis of the technologies that have inflected them through historical time.

Acknowledgments

I owe a great debt to Walter J. Ong, not only for serving as a scholarly mentor, but for being a generous human being, reading through my first foray into this field and unexpectedly initiating an encouraging correspondence. I thank Lance Strate, who took faith in the idea of *Cinematically Speaking* in advance of the manuscript's readiness for public scrutiny, and who, along with its blind reviewer, quite literally compelled this book into its current shape. I am also indebted to the *PMLA* Editorial Board, who, in suggesting changes to my article "*Écriture* Aesthetics" (2008), forced me to reconsider the theoretical framework for this project. Fortunately, in doing so, they helped me to avoid straitjacketing my own material before it ever saw the light of day. My colleagues at Greensboro College, past and present—especially Dan Burns, George Cheatham, Judy Cheatham, Val Gnup, Jillian Haeseler, Charles Hebert, Kathy Keating, Denise Kohn, Kevin Rippin, and Joyce Traver—grew listless no doubt with my constant quipping about orality and literacy, but they have continuously provided encouragement and a salutary critical sounding board.

I must also acknowledge the college generally for providing me with grant money to pursue part of this project's writing, and to Paul Leslie specifically for permitting me a course release in order to complete its revision. Jennie Hunt's skills as a reference librarian allowed me to engage with films and published materials that were not always easy to acquire, yet were somehow deftly obtained (and sometimes from surprisingly far-flung places). Gratitude also is owed to the participants of the 1999 University of Hawaii at Manoa/East-West Center N.E.H. Institute on India and to its organizers, Vrinda Dalmiya and Arindam Chakrabarti. In many respects, it was during that summer while studying the philosophies, religions, and cultures of India that the ideas in this book first took coalescent form. As well, Andrei Simic of the University of Southern California warrants recognition for unwittingly shepherding me into the world of Hindi popular film through a summer seminar on visual anthropology at the University of California, Berkeley. Two film professors, now retired, were especially seminal to my appreciation of film *qua* film, Marc Gervais, S.J., of Concordia University, in Montreal, and Roger Greenspun, of Columbia University. Without them, the seeds of this project may never have been sown.

I thank my husband, Thomas Weadock Shields, who has endured—even enjoyed—many, many hours of Bollywood film viewing, and who has been unflagging in his patience and intellectual support. Readers whose comments have kept me clear-headed and committed, and friends who have kept me intellectually alert, include Yonatan Abranyos, Amy Goldman, Amanda Hamilton, Anna Reisman, Joti Sekhon, and Jean Shields. No one, alas, has read through more of this material and commented more rigorously on it than my parents. They have served through the years as role models, both intellectually and humanistically. My father, Baldev Raj Nayar, sent me countless articles on Hindi film, which he culled with tenacious conviction from Indian newspapers and magazines while doing his own research. And my mother, Nancy Ann Nayar, a specialist in South Indian religion, one day informed me, in an unsuspecting act of prescience, that I might find Walter Ong's *Orality and Literacy* an interesting read. How could this book not be dedicated to them?

1

Orality, Literacy, and an Epistemic Approach to Visual Narrative:

An Introduction

We are the most abject prisoners of the literate culture in which we have matured. Even with the greatest effort, contemporary man finds it exceedingly difficult, and in many instances, quite impossible to sense what the spoken word actually is.

—Walter J. Ong (1967, p. 19)

This book introduces a new paradigm for understanding how, on a particular plane, visual narrative "works." Following Michel Foucault, it proposes that there is an *epistemic* explanation for contemporary conventions of visual storytelling—no matter whether one is speaking of that canonically prized species known as art-cinema narration, or those mass-oriented films that critics like Adorno and Horkheimer have denounced for their tendency toward formula, recycling, and preschematization (Carroll, 1998, p. 77). In fact, these are precisely the sorts of narrating systems that this book meticulously parses in order to assemble its narratological scaffolding and theoretically make its case.

Several prominent studies have, of course, already investigated these two systems of storytelling. David Bordwell (1985) scrupulously dissects the attributes of art cinema in *Narration in the Fiction Film*. (Indeed, I use his work as a scaffold for my own in Chapter 3.) Noël Carroll (1988) throws down the gauntlet to contemporary film theorists (especially those deploying semiotic, psychoanalytic, and Althusserian models) via his alternative unpacking of commercial movies on the

1

basis of their pictorial "intelligibility." Both these scholars operate from the vantage point of cognitivism, a self-described stance that "seeks to understand human thought, emotion, and action by appeal to processes of mental representation, naturalistic processes, and (some sense of) rationalist agency" (Bordwell & Carroll, 1996, p. xvi). Although a philosophical extension of these authors' commitments, *Cinematically Speaking* operates from the demonstrable presupposition that technologies significantly impact these processes. In that sense, its approach is decidedly media ecological; that is, it works from the assumption that media technologies can give "form to a culture's politics, social organization, and habitual ways of thinking" (Postman, 2000, p. 10).[1] Specifically, it proposes that the ways in which people are able to engage with storytelling—both as a spectatorial and generative act—are fundamentally contoured by their capacity to engage with the *written word*.

Other narratological studies have also offered valuable critical insight into the workings of fiction narration. However, like the aforementioned, they have not as of yet, in their pursuit of a poetics, been able persuasively to bridge the semantic gap between art films and mass entertainment. Sometimes this is a result of approach, as in the case of Branigan (1992), who privileges linguistic analogies, or of Chatman (1978), who splits off story (events) from discourse (treatment). Other times, it is because of the abandonment of a belief that was popular in narratology's formative stages—namely, that much *ought* to be made "of the autonomy of narrative structure, of its independence from any medium" (Herman, 1999, p. 315).

Often what happens in feature-film analysis is that *parts* of the whole of visual storytelling, or its visual coding, are extracted for study: the nature of causality, for instance, or the Lacanian functioning of the gaze. These can be valuable probes into the workings of the genre; however, they are also, as extractions, the least capable of commenting on (although neither are they particularly inclined toward analyzing) storytelling as a particular way of thinking, as a discursive system whose norms or tendencies may actually derive from a particular *source*.

In the case of this volume, that envisioned source is the human mindset as shaped (or not) by *alphabetic literacy*. This is a position no previous film theorist has ever paradigmatically taken, and so I must rely on a non-filmic tradition to make my case, on scholars like Walter J. Ong, Eric Havelock, Jack Goody, Marshall McLuhan, and Elizabeth Eisenstein, who have, from their various disciplinary vantage points, sought to uncover how writing as a technology has impacted social, cultural,

---

1. For a comprehensive overview of the interdisciplinary field of media ecology, see Lance Strate's (2006) *Echoes and Reflections: On Media Ecology as a Field of Study.*

and personality structures. (Christine Nystrom refers to this process as "'the invisible metaphysics' of technology" [cited in Postman, 1982, p. 69].) There are certainly scholars, such as Ruth Finnegan (1988), who consider the technology argument a case of overdeterminism. Fortunately the debate over levels of technological impact on social domains is not really pertinent here, as this project in no way proposes that the acquisition of literacy is not complexly facilitated by, and intertwined with, other "enabling" factors, such as capitalism (Gough, 1968). Nor does *Cinematically Speaking* suggest that literacy can even be isolated from other variables such as schooling (Street, 1984).[2] But salient to my project's argument is something that all the aforementioned scholars, including Finnegan, agree on, and that is that human consciousness is not an intrinsic quality. In A.R. Luria's words, the human has the capacity to "make and use tools [which] not only radically change his conditions of existence, they even react on him in that they effect a change in him and his psychic condition" (cited in Cole, 1990, p. 91).

In a sense, this project seeks to *redirect the narratological argument* and, in doing so, positions itself as a modeling practice between the scientist who "tends to underplay the extent to which raw experience is shaped by interpretation" and the humanist who "tends to ignore the external phenomena that interpretations are constructed from" (Lippert, 2000, p. 279). Readers conversant in film theory can probably already gauge how different this project is from the grammar-oriented approach to film that Christian Metz (1974a, 1974b, 1982) takes, and which follows from the work of linguist Ferdinand de Saussure. Rather than treating film as a language that can be syntagmatically parsed, *Cinematically Speaking* excavates the reticulate norms that our collective capacity for reading and writing has engendered—norms that call, by default, for a particular way of knowing, for a special ability narratively "to look at things" (Foucault, 1997, p. 211).

Such an emphasis on the technology of *writing* may appear paradoxical given the project's focus on the visual medium of film. Then again, earlier critics and theorists did intuit the significance of writing to visual narrative. The associations they made were often amorphous, but certain critics did shrewdly grasp the sway of writing over film. In coining the term *la caméra-stylo* (camera as pen) in the 1940s, Alexandre Astruc foresaw a cinema of *écriture* (writing style), an imaginative and expressive rendering of thought as an alternative to surrendering to spectacle and the visually anecdotal (Neupert, 2002, p. 48). This was followed by Bazin's (1967) joyous proclamation in the 1950s that, with the coming of

---

2. See, for example, R. Narasimhan (1991) on how, in the case of ancient India, social and religious restrictions on the word resulted in the literate tradition continuing to exhibit the psychosocial aspects of an oral society.

sound, the director was finally the equal of the novelist: The higher degree of realism afforded to the sound image meant that now film could have "at its disposal more means of modifying reality from within" (p. 40). More recently, we might turn to Jean-François Lyotard (1986), who maintained that cinematography was "a writing with movements" (p. 349), and to Metz (1974b), who compared cinema with writing, only to decide this analogy was not completely fruitful.

This project obviously suggests that drawing a relationship between writing and cinema *is* fruitful—but only once one is willing to forego these more analogical approaches. Still, we can take our lead from Metz, who declared that "the cinema for its part is not writing, but *what writing makes possible*" (p. 285, emphasis added). Metz's statement seems flexible enough to permit that an analysis of cinema's language might take place on a writing-related plane *other* than that which is semiotically negotiable. Such an analysis seems especially worthwhile in light of the numerous scholars across literary studies, classical studies, anthropology, and social psychology who have demonstrated that writing has the capacity to *restructure our consciousness*; that it has made possible our phylogenetic move toward an "increasingly articulate introspectivity" and opened up "the psyche as never before not only to the external objective world quite distinct from itself but also to the interior self against whom the objective world is set" (Ong, 1982, p. 105). The "literate," in other words, is not simply housed in *text*, just as the "oral" is not simply housed in *speech*. Meaning-making itself has been historically transformed by writing and print—and continues to be by those fortunate enough to be ontogenetically equipped.

The oral—or *orality*, as it is referred to when designating a state or mindset uninfluenced by writing—is thus the other focal point of this project. For, a move *toward* literacy invariably implies the abandonment of, or departure from, some other locale. In this case, that locale is less a place than a *mentalité*, a communal grid of thoughts, values, and awareness; or what Norman Simms (1992) describes as a "mind/brain process by which humans think, feel, and experience the world about them," in concert with the "the structure of language/culture that forms the contours, as well as the contents, of the reflective space of self-awareness that we call human consciousness" (p. 32). In contemplating an oral *mentalité*, one might want, for instance, to attend to the distinct pressures placed on a story's shape, content, and delivery, owing to its deliverer's incapacity to transmit that story *except by word of mouth*. Imagine, in other words, a narrative that can only be spoken—and must be so from memory, no less. Some of the most renowned narrative works were of course conceived under these conditions (Homer's *Odyssey*, for example, the anonymous epic *Gilgamesh*), and they attest to storytelling talents lost to many of us today, given our heavy reliance on the written word. We, more likely, think of stories as words on a page, whether paper or Web, "to be reproduced aloud only under special circumstances" (Lakoff, 1982). In oral societies, however, where narrative fixity does not have the potential to exist, members must "learn to abstract, to get to the gist of ideas, to discover what, in a list of items or a work of art, is crucial and unchangeable, and what can be altered and embroidered at will" (p. 258). How texts narratively unfold, in other words, what they say—how they can even say what they say—are all significantly impacted by their means of transmission, as well as by structures of consciousness that foster such transmission. When envisioned this way, the "what" of narrative (its story) cannot so easily be disassociated from the "way" of narrative (its discourse). One must take a more complex, gestalt approach.

No doubt the reader is guardedly wondering how oral narrative could possibly have anything to do with movies. After all, the medium of film came into being at the turn of the 20th century, and so was from its inception the offspring of a literate age. And yet, what I am about to contend and empirically demonstrate is that visual storytelling has not only been significantly contoured by the resources that literacy has made available to human consciousness, but, in some cases, by the lack of those resources. The implication of course is that orality cannot be ascribed to a precursory or "primitive"—and certainly not "tribal"—way of thinking, let alone to a worldview frozen in time. Sometimes orality may even be the *favored* mode of engagement in literate communities, reproducing as it does our more spontaneous, and perhaps more "natural," mode of human articulation.

The reader also may be skeptical about the pragmatics of a language-based theory being applied to a semantics of imagery. But if we think of narrative as a form of cultural knowledge (Geertz, 1973), then immediately we shed the assumption that film narrative needs to be studied exclusively *as* film, that it cannot additionally be investigated as a form of knowledge housed *in* film. If language is a social fact, one should "reasonably expect verbal activity"—here imagined as the telling of a story—"to form such a *symbolic* structure" (Crick, 1976, p. 66). Images that a film projects rely on an individual's internal schema to *make sense* of the discourse (Varadhan, 1985, p. 102), and thus the interpretation of those images should not be taken as merely optically based. They are fundamentally contoured and constellated by oral (or literate) exigencies of mind, just as *any* story unavoidably is. As Walter J. Ong (1982) states, "The interaction between the orality that all humans are born into and the technology of writing, which no one is born into, touches the depths of the psyche" (p. 178).

Assertions like these are no doubt one of the reasons that Ong—one of the scholars on whom this project liberally draws—is sometimes accused of unhealthily positing a "great cognitive divide," of reproducing a binary logic that forecloses any possibility of a "conceptual middle ground" (Coleman, 1996, p. 5; see also Finnegan, 1988; Gough, 1968; Graff, 1979; J. Langer, 1987; Olson, 1994; Olson & Torrance, 2001; Scribner & Cole, 1981; Tannen, 1987). Critics have sometimes further charged Ong with insinuating reductively—and only metaphysically and abstractly—that, when it comes to the evolution of the literate mindset, technology overrides all: culture, societal relations, and even enabling (or potentially disenabling) institutional forces. But these are, in many respects, myopic simplifications of Ong's overarching position—or, in some cases, convenient misreadings of his work. As Ong (1977) himself states, his thesis concerning technology is "sweeping, but it is not reductionist"; he does "not maintain that the evolution from primary orality through writing and print to an electronic culture . . . causes or explains everything in human culture and consciousness" (p. 9). Nor does he dismiss the presence of a middle ground. In fact, in the last paragraph of *Orality and Literacy*, his best known work, Ong pays explicit tribute to an "orality-literacy dynamics" (p. 179).

Cinematically Speaking follows the lead of both Ong *and* his critics. For, although I postulate two epistemic systems apropos storytelling, one oral, the other literate, in no way do I recommend that these are exclusive systems. (As Foucault, 1972, reminds us, "such a field is inexhaustible and can never be closed," p. 191.) Nor do I contend—as doubtless Ong would not—that the literate system is the polar opposite of the oral, but rather only evidence of a discursive system that has emerged from the human capacity to *depart* from a particular way of knowing. Without identifying these two systems in their most incongruent and contrasting forms, however—as a narrative sheet and a narrative crystal, as Deleuze might have it—I would not be able to disinter the "total set of relations" (Foucault, 1972, p. 191) that gives rise to various formalized systems of visual narrative. For the sake of excavation, then, orality and literacy must here function as poles, but they should not be envisioned under any circumstances as polarities.

As I already intimated, this project ultimately points to the theoretical inadequacy of calling orality *pre*modern or of proposing a cultural shift from orality to literacy, with all its mistaken connotations of a gradual extinction of the former. Instead, it proposes that multiple storytelling epistemes can coexist and even interact. In this way, it corresponds with the viewpoint of those post-Ongian scholars who stress that "in most societies there is an overlap and a 'mix' of [oral and literate] modes of communication" (Street, 1984, p. 110). Hence, the conjoint possibility, and even practicability, of an orality-literacy *paradigm* for visual narrative, as such a paradigm makes space for variously inflected storytelling forms. To call this paradigm monolithic would be misplaced, though, for as a theoretical construct it recognizes that cinematic story-telling spaces exist for multiple speakers, interpreters, and voices, and are, as such, eternally in flux.

That sometimes a palpable cleft *does* exist in spectatorship practices, however, should not be discounted or wholly ignored merely for the sake of political correctness. If there are measurable oral-to-literate vari-ances in storytelling form, it seems senseless, even politically hazardous, to overlook or repress them for fear of being misread as projecting a di-chotomy or of appearing revisionist as an enterprise. After all, only the literate are able to read this book—or engage, for that matter, with any written work (and perhaps even with the concept of political correct-ness[3]). In that sense, 774 million adults worldwide (UNESCO, 2009) are automatically cut off from critical engagement—just as they are alien-ated from species of film narrative that have been contoured by a literate way of knowing, or, what Foucault calls an *episteme*.

I have already cited Foucault several times, but perhaps some elabo-ration of his concept of the episteme is warranted.

Foucault rejects the notion that one can historically disinter ideal knowledge as truth. Instead, he fashions himself as an archaeologist in-terested in what has made different knowledges possible (Macdonell, 1986). What distinguishes his philosophy of knowledge is its commit-ment to connecting knowledge's existence "to the *processes of historical practice*" (Foucault, 1972, p. 192). As Sara Mills (2004) explicates, Fou-cault demonstrates how, within certain periods, there is a tendency to "structure thinking about a subject in a particular way and to map out certain procedures and supports for thinking" (p. 51). In other words, the episteme should not be mistaken for a worldview, which "assumes a coherence and cohesiveness to a set of ideas" (p. 51). The episteme may be suspected of being such, as Foucault (1972) himself points out, but that type of view

> imposes on each [branch of knowledge] the same norms and postu-lates, a general stage of reason, a certain structure of thought that the men of a particular period cannot escape—a great body of legislation written once and for all by some anonymous hand. By *episteme*, we mean, in fact, the total set of relations that unite, at a given period, the discursive practices that give rise to epistemological figures, sciences, and possibly formalized systems; the way in which, in each of these discursive formations, the transitions to epistemologization, scien-tificity, and formalization are situated and operate; the distribution of these thresholds, which may coincide, be subordinated to one another, or be separated by shifts in time. (p. 191)

---

3. Such concepts are typographically formed, says Ong (1980), "dependent on a feel for a mass of knowledge which . . . demands print" (p. 148).

Foucault's attempt to articulate the episteme may appear intricate, even knotty, possibly by virtue of the episteme's own nature. Perhaps he (1977) articulates his position most accessibly when he states in *Power/ Knowledge* that his own interest was always in "ascertain[ing] the sets of transformations in the regime of discourses necessary and sufficient for people to use these words rather than those, a particular type of discourse rather than some other type, for people to be able to look at things from such and such an angle and not some other one" (p. 211). That is, in effect, what this volume does: It excavates the interpenetrated attributes of two distinct discursive structures operating within the visual narrative arena, and speculates on how some percipients may be—for expressly *epistemic* reasons—able to look at cinematic storytelling (or desirous of looking at it, or restricted from looking at it) from "such and such an angle and not some other one."

This excavation is not founded on abstract philosophizing, however. Rather, the mapping of these epistemes proceeds from a close scrutiny of two extant species of film, Hindi popular film and art-cinema narration, as well as from a gathering of narrative phenomena and epiphenomena persistently reflected in—and inflecting—film. Hopefully the volume's dense referencing will redress its admitted lack of a sanctioned, or even familiar, disciplinary framework. Alas, there is no official school or movement of orality-literacy studies (Ong, 1982), and so one has little recourse but to pull from across the humanities and social sciences in order to make an informed argument. In its defense, *Cinematically Speaking* pulls much less for the sake of inventing a new theory or storytelling model than for the sake of disinterring what is already tangibly in circulation. In this way, its main interest is admittedly in line with that of structural analysis, which, as Christian Metz (1974a) expresses, privileges "being able to find what was already there, of accounting with more precision" for something that already may have been unsystematically divined (p. 17).

To be sure, narratives that can be styled as either epistemically oral or literate are mutually inflected by sundry other factors, such as culture, politics, personal taste, a particular pedagogical practice, or even an idealization of certain oral or literate attributes that get grafted onto culture. Literacy, moreover, is a protean process and practice, shifting and altering at the hands of time and technology. In this sense, it might be more prudent of me to refer to *a* literate episteme or to *an* oral episteme, in order to avoid accusations of absolutism. At the same time, the broad cross-cultural applicability of these two epistemes—frequently pointed to in the ensuing pages—suggests that they reflect systems of knowledge that are not merely lodged in a single nation or demonstrable of two discrete types of cinemas (or, thinner yet, two types of genres). Of course one is free to ignore the paradigm in pursuit of other factors that condition film narrative, but only in the same way that one can speak about language and disregard morphemes. Certainly disregarding a language's grammatical units in pursuit of other interests does not imply that such units are not structurally fundamental.

Despite the caveats I have offered thus far, the one-to-one mapping that a pair of storytelling epistemes (correctly) implies may appear still to bifurcate and totalize orality and literacy. But it seems to me that only in acknowledging that such epistemic extremities of storytelling might exist—largely because much film scholarship *does not* acknowledge this—will we be able to avoid the perpetuation of "an unconscious chirographic [handwriting] and typographic [print] bias" (Ong, 1980, p. 145). As Ong notes, the failure of even the most sophisticated literary criticism to take into account "depth structures or oral noetics and the subsequent technological transformations of the word by writing, print, and electronics can result in blind spots" (p. 147). Recognizing the historical ramifications of writing and how writing influences thought—and so, too, the creative expression *of* that thought—can only enrich the study of visual narrative, as well as constructively problematize the supposedly neutral waters in which critical activities take place.

Importantly (although perhaps only to me), I did not set out to locate forms that satisfied the elicitation of a new paradigm. Rather, that journey was the fortuitous byproduct of my having studied the box-office hits and "superhits" of Bollywood (the Hollywood of Bombay)—especially those films produced between the 1970s and 1990s. Often these films are referred to as *masala*, or spice-mix, films, on account of their formulaic blending of singing, dancing, fights, melodrama, romance, and more. Because I limited my scope to box-office successes, over time I internalized the norms of the *masala* genre but *only for when that genre was spectatorially successful*. This was especially important in the Indian context given that most Hindi popular films aren't even popular. In fact, 80% fail dismally at the box office, frequently procuring the cringeworthy label of "flop" (or "superflop") (Virdi, 2003). Had I evaluated films indiscriminately, or on the basis of critical acclaim, I might have lost sight of those norms that constituted a socially sanctioned form of storytelling, at least as determined by the viewing public.

Only upon my reading Ong's *Orality and Literacy*, however, did the etiology of those Hindi-film formula norms fall into place. The correspondence between those traits that typified Bollywood success and what Ong was articulating apropos oral psychodynamics and performativity was overwhelming, and it resulted for me in an immediate intellectual paradigm shift. Here, after all, was a national popular cinema whose hybrid, politically thorny, psychically healing, righteous, nationalistic, song-and-dance form had led many a scholar (including me) to declare that that the *masala* form was too multifaceted and complex to parse holistically. And yet, Ong, in addition to the other orality-oriented scholars whom I would eventually read, singularly confirmed that those attributes which for so long had felt indeterminable (in the Heisenbergian sense of that term) were not only sensible as a narrative package, but downright *obligatory*.

For this reason I do not take up Ong's (1982) distinction between *primary orality*, which applies to peoples wholly untouched by writing, and *secondary orality*, which has "striking resemblances to the old . . . but is essentially a more deliberate and self-conscious orality, based permanently on the use of writing and print" (p. 136). Although Hindi popular film obviously emerges from a system based on the use of writing and print, I am reluctant to accept that its formula necessarily arose *self-consciously*—that is, by way of humans who were turned "outward" for reasons other than that "they had little occasion to turn inward," or who were group-minded only "self-consciously and programmatically" (p. 136). Ultimately the wisdom of my jettisoning these distinctions rests with the reader, but as I think the next chapter sufficiently bears out, existing distinctions between primary and secondary orality may be too wooden for our contemporary landscape.

My motives are the same in not invoking Ong's concept of *residual orality*, which intimates a slow, sloughing off of orality due to extended engagement with chirography. Such a teleological model, as Joyce Coleman (1996) notes, always implies "the *extinction* of one mode in favor of the other; *evolution*, not coexistence or covariation" (p. 17). What the oral and literate epistemes of visual narrative bring to the fore is the incongruity and non-necessity of trying to "explain away any apparent overlap of traits" (p. 8). It might behoove us to recognize, as one of Ong's exponents, Paul Lippert (2000), does, that "literate culture never entirely replaces oral culture; rather, it grows out of it and is added onto it" (p. 281). In fact, Lippert acknowledges this in order to make a chilling political point: that the oral culture is eventually subjugated by the literate culture, that "literate elites develop economic, political, and religious institutions based on the written word to rule over the residually oral masses" (p. 281). Under no condition would I argue against the complex, and even hegemonic, nature of literate-oral relations; but this project's discovery of a vigorous and durable oral episteme leads me to believe that the issue is even more politically and ideologically intricate than presupposed—a thread that I pick up, if only sketchily, in the final chapter.

The proceeding chapter, Chapter 2, "Excavating the Oral Episteme of Visual Narrative," does just what its title promises: it excavates those norms that derive from an orally inflected way of knowing as those norms are manifest in *popular* Hindi popular films from the 1950s to the 1990s. (A caveat: despite this historical bracketing of the films, for the sake of rhetorical ease, I often use the present tense [e.g., "Bollywood is . . . "; "a film must be . . . "]. I can only ask for the reader's indulgence.) These oral characteristics are teased out on the basis of the scholarly works of various players (in various fields), including, most prominently, Jack Goody and Ian Watt (in anthropology and literary studies, respectively), Eric Havelock (classics), Marshall McLuhan (media studies), Isidore Okpewho (African studies), and Ong (literary studies). Even these authors' scholarship is highly synthetic, built as it is on the work of earlier contributors, such as French anthropologist Marcel Jousse, and Milman Parry and Albert Lord, who uncovered the oral underpinnings of Homeric epic. To avoid allegations of my stage-managing, amplifying, or seductively fabricating the oral inflection of Hindi popular film, I have elected not to provide my own, potentially subjective readings of the species. Instead, I rely almost exclusively on the critiques and analytical contentions that *other* scholars have made about *masala* film during the time period. In other words, the critical unpacking of the films' oral inflection is demonstrated by way of scholars with no personal theoretical investment in, or intention of, forwarding an oral episteme of visual narrative. But the parallels between their readings and what Ong et al. have to say are so remarkable, not to mention plentiful, that they can only underscore the impossibility of categorically dismissing a link between orality and Hindi popular film. Admittedly, I sometimes take descriptions that are being used in a specific context and pull them out of that original context. However, I do so only if and when a description evinces a clear and unqualified relationship to the oral episteme. Even the illustrative examples that I provide as context and color, are, for the sake of impartiality, largely pulled from outside sources. Only occasionally I do insert my own.

For readers who have never engaged with a *masala* film from this time period, I offer as an appendix (Appendix A) a close reading through the oral-epistemic lens of a single hit film—*Baazigar* (Trickster, 1993). In this way, the uninitiated can experience the interplay of the oral attributes, which are detailed in Chapter 2 in only a comparatively abstract and schematized manner. My hope is that, with the aid of this appendix, readers will apprehend how, contrary to the academic belief that certain films are capable of traversing cultural boundaries because they are *independent* of language (Moretti, 2001),[4] those films are in fact significantly grounded *in* language, just not the kind of language that scholars typically identify when it comes to storytelling properties and form.

An excavation of the oral system of knowledge additionally provides the resources for charting what the *written word* has engendered

---

4. This statement was made with respect to action-adventure films, although in a manner that corresponds precisely to this discussion of Hindi popular films.

narratologically. What, for instance, are the "unnatural" discursive practices that literacy has stimulated, as measured by their nonpresence in
the oral schema? Might a particular film prove perplexing to certain—
often class-correlated—categories of spectators because of its literately
motivated formalized system or its literate modes of organizing knowledge? Chapter 3, "Mapping the Literate Episteme of Visual Narrative,"
explores this terrain, and tries unequivocally to get to the heart of those
questions. Following in the footsteps of Chapter 2, it addresses the species
of film known as "art-cinema narration" as a route to disinterring the decidedly *literate* characteristics of visual narrative. Although I use the
terms *art cinema*, *art film*, and *art-cinema narration* interchangeably in this
project (as I also do *masala film*, *Bollywood film*, and *Hindi popular film*), the
term art-cinema narration refers more exclusively to an international
array of films that emerged during the 1950s, 1960s and 1970s—films directed by the likes of Michelangelo Antonioni, Ingmar Bergman, Jean-
Luc Godard, and Satyajit Ray. My excavation relies particularly on David
Bordwell's insightful and scrupulous cataloguing of the species' narrational modes (indeed, the term *art-cinema narration* is his). Absence becomes as much a taxonomical marker as presence in this chapter; for,
when funneled through the prism of orality, *nothing* in art-cinema narration epistemically holds—or, in more pragmatic parlance, the entire species proves to be fundamentally grounded in a literate way of knowing.

To sufficiently ward off accusations of my engaging in a symptomatic reading, I call on scholars from the humanities and the social sciences who have previously engaged with notions of the literate, as well
as, in this case, the literary. I draw particularly from Luria's pioneering
work on mental development, and the human cognitive process as a historical process that is environmentally determined. True, in the foreword
to Luria's *Cognitive Development*, Michael Cole (1976) evinces skepticism
at the efficacy of applying developmental theories cross-culturally. "[W]hat
Luria interprets as the acquisition of new modes of thought," Cole is
more inclined to construe as "changes in the application of previously
available modes to the particular problems and contexts of discourse
represented by the experimental setting" (p. xv). The marked echoing in
the realm of art-cinema narration of Luria's modes, however, suggests
some cross-cultural appositeness. From the oral-literate as opposed to
social psychological viewpoint, in other words (somewhat ironical, perhaps, given that Luria was a social psychologist), one is able to posit an
infrastructural web through which culture is noetically and psycho-
dynamically refracted. Moreover, by inadvertently foregrounding the
possibility of an orality-literacy continuum for visual narrative, this
chapter ultimately "'englobes' high culture within a larger system of
popular, non-elitist, and national ways of thinking, feeling, and perceiv-
ing" (Simms, 1992, p. 59).

We are of course in pursuit of a relatively *invisible* context of representation (at least as compared with identification by sex, race, or class). This necessitates a more rigorous commitment to verifiable data, corroboration, and credible proof. To some degree, that is why, in the excavation of the oral and literate epistemes, I have narrowed my field to those two discrete strands of cinema, art-cinema narration and the *masala* film. Nevertheless, the epistemes reverberate more broadly, and so I have tried where possible to draw supplementary attention via footnotes to other national and generic cinemas (e.g., Hollywood, Hong Kong), to discrete films outside the bounds of my particular focus, and sometimes even to nonfilmic narrative. Because I see these notes as valuable extensions of the theory's relevance historically and transnationally, I have opted to include them as footnotes within the text proper, rather than to relegate them to endnotes.

Chapter 4, "Between the Oral and Literate Epistemes," explores some of the territory between the oral and literate epistemes of visual narrative. In order to productively highlight the nonpolarity of the paradigm, this chapter casts a lens on several strains of Indian cinema that exhibit clear *differentials* of oral-to-literate inflection. Here, the middle-class cinema of the 1970s to 1990s is examined, as well as the frequently government-sponsored *middle cinema* of that same period. As a parallel counter or corrective to homogenizing all Bombay cinema, this chapter also briefly considers Bollywood's post-2000 cinema, reflecting and speculating on how an incipient substratum of the Indian nation's popular films is currently uprooting itself from some of the high oral inflection of earlier decades.

Chapter 5, "The Future of the Orality–Literacy Paradigm, Cinematically Speaking," looks beyond the oral and literate epistemes as outlined in the preceding chapters to muse over impending prospects for the paradigm. Not only does this chapter alert readers to routes of inquiry that future film and media ecology scholars might pursue (such as ones having to do with reader-response theory, the nature of genre, and the politics of representation); as well, it contemplates how our current media environment may be ushering in a new kind of episteme, one contoured by our novel interactions with computer technologies that have already given rise to digital cinema, virtual reality, cyberspatial hypertext, and the like.

The reader can probably already discern the challenges of this project. Some of these no doubt stem from the project's unwillingness—or, more honestly, its incapacity—to divorce story from spectator. *Cinematically Speaking* presumes that a symbiotic relationship exists between the two, and that what each is (or can be) is fatefully determined by the other. That very flow and interconnectivity calls attention to a certain ineluctable theoretical slipperiness, however: for, how can we say for certain where story ends and spectator begins? And is there not an inherent danger in conflating, say, orally inflected texts with orally inflected individuals? Furthermore, how are we to account for literately inflected individuals who hold orally inflected texts dear? In fact, how can we even determine what makes one person sufficiently literate and another person not?

I could keep going: Where do affective responses factor in? And is it wise to ignore the entire cinematic apparatus, since films are always tied to a system of commerce? Indeed, how can one determine where orality's reign ends and capitalism's begins? Finally, what of the sensitive political ramifications of calling one species of visual narrative "orally inflected" and another "literately inflected"? Does that not invariably motivate a dangerous sort of caste-ism when it comes to issues of narrative content and form?

These are all sound and even appropriately troubling questions, and I can only hope that they will receive adequate contemplation in the future. (*Cinematically Speaking* may inaugurate a new film theory, but it in no way presents a *fait accompli*.) But to avoid disinterring these morphological underpinnings seems just as politically tenuous to me. Too often in our contemporary culture—and this is certainly true vis-à-vis the current trend in Bollywood scholarship—the subaltern viewer as a legitimate viewer gets lost. Although mine is a work of film theory and not of social action, there is some social urgency here, given that hierarchy is indisputably involved. After all, no nonliterate person can read this book, as I've already mentioned—just as he or she cannot apply for tenure, or fill out a W-2 form, or read a journal article on the subaltern's plight. That researching oral epistemologies in contemporary media already privileges the literate—in that "scholarship itself is traditionally a writing-based endeavor" (Gozzi & Haynes, 1991, p. 218)—speaks to the *lived* paradox of the relativistic approach. At the same time, I am sensitive to and hope that readers will avoid automatically labeling orally inflected cinema as "lesser than" or, even worse, "illiterate."

At this point, the reader may be suffering from the false illusion that nobody has ever applied orality conceptually to film before. This is certainly not the case. True, no one has as of yet proposed an orality-literacy paradigm for visual narrative, and I would suggest this is in part because, in order to map a literate schema, an oral one is needed first. Scholars in the past have been more inclined, when addressing orality, to point to speech-related features operating *in* a film. Additionally, media specialists, following Ong, have tended to foreground *listening* via modern technologies (e.g., radio, television, telephone). That is, they have isolated the voice in lieu of probing for structural commonalities—indeed, for a system of knowledge—that might link a contemporary text more broadly to, say, African oral epic or the *Ramayana*. Consequently, attributes that may have been limited to the voice at one time, but which have since migrated into modern-day storytelling and cinematic technique—for example, into editing, sound, composition, acting, and so forth—have gone unnoticed.

Still, Mishra, Jeffrey, and Shoesmith (1989) contributed extremely important work on orality's sway on dialogue and the oral utterance (and as manifest in the Bollywood films of mega-superstar Amitabh Bachchan, no less). Jesús Martín-Barbero (1995) drew connections between orality and the Latin American *telenovela*, although he too conceptualized its presence on the basis of the spoken/aural. Several decades earlier, John Fiske and John Hartley (1978) drew compelling connections between television's participatory nature and bardic culture; and Lippert (1996), whose work I already invoked, has written on how science-fiction film "exhibits features that are the same as those of mythologies of oral cultures" (p. 266).

Orality also has received major attention in the area of African film studies. Scholars like Tomaselli, Shepperson, and Eke (1995) and Manthia Diawara (1996) have worked to locate an African cinematic language by examining how critical (i.e., Third Cinema) filmmakers have consciously used orality to reflect African society and community or, in some cases, to rediscover them. Tomasseli et al. are not remiss in drawing attention to the distinctiveness of the *mentalité* of non-elite African viewers, "who still experience their lives in oral, timely, particular and very local ways, and [thus] experience the exhibition of film in much the same kind of ways" (p. 30). But even these authors discuss orality more as a narrative strategy or motif, as a film's subject matter rather than as an unconscious—or, at the least, innominate—force that can fundamentally mold a diegesis into a modern-day form of oral narrative.[5] Nonetheless, works like these have served as a pioneering minority in the film studies discipline, and I reference them frequently in the elaboration of the oral episteme.

Closest to grappling with orality as a matrix is perhaps Mikel J. Koven (2006), who, in articulating his theory on "vernacular cinema" by way of Italian *giallo* horror cinema, has made significant room for oral psychodynamics. (Indeed, our analogous interests in film and orality grew independently of each other, but, upon our discovery of those interests, engendered a quick alliance.) Sadly, most members of cinema

---

5. Manthia Diawara (1996), for instance, compares the role of the director directly to the traditional African *griot* (oral bard), particularly in terms of how the director might be reproducing "traditional modes of being" (p. 210). In other words, Diawara studies directorial *techniques* consciously influenced by oral tradition, such as how the incorporation of song and dance accentuates "a return to authenticity" (p. 211) or how, by making orality a film's subject, a question "Who owns discourse?" might be thematically posed in order to critique "the hermetic and conservative structure of tradition in oral literature" (p. 215).

studies are *not* conversant with the field of orality. Cinema studies and departments of communications (which are more open to ideas percolating in media ecology) seem to live a kind of parallel existence. More than once at the annual Society for Cinema and Media Studies conference, upon my explaining that my work is in orality and film, I have been greeted by a quizzical stare invariably followed by the question "Did you say *mor*ality?"

Even less common are scholarly assessments or theoretical models concerning how *alphabetic literacy* has impacted visual narrative. The only concrete reference that comes readily to mind is McLuhan's (1964) contention in *Understanding Media* that "movies assume a high level of literacy in their users and prove baffling to the nonliterate" (p. 285). McLuhan is of course speaking here of literacy in the sense of a *visual* literacy, which reckons with—at least in terms of where he takes his argument—depth perception and "the camera eye" (p. 285). For example, he alleges that nonliterates "don't get perspective or distancing effects of light and shade" and "do not know how to fix their eyes . . . a few feet in front of the movie screen" (p. 287). The present project, in contrast, has nothing to do with visualization, or optics, or camera eyes, all of which tend parametrically to constrict discussion by focusing too exclusively on competencies of vision. In fact, I make no attempt to privilege the *visual* in visual narrative, despite the fact that many scholars consider visuality the form's most salient feature and, hence, one that warrants special dispensation. But, alas, doing so would extricate visuality from the "totality of relations" (Foucault, 1972, p. 191) that comprises an oral or literate episteme.

Most interesting perhaps is the manner in which the orality-literacy paradigm intersects with several extant theories concerning *written* narrative, such as Roland Barthes' (1975) discrimination between writerly (*scriptible*) and readerly (*lisible*) texts. (I make significant use of Barthes' work in Chapter 3.) Umberto Eco's (1979) differentiation between "closed texts," which propel a reader along a predetermined path, and "open texts," which offer "a work *to be completed*" (p. 62), is also worthy of note, as is Anthony Easthope's (1991) cataloguing of the textual characteristics of canonical and pulp literature—which he maps onto the distinction between the pleasure and reality principles. Although *Cinematically Speaking* certainly benefits from, and willingly draws on, these diagnostic and psychoanalytical readings, its ultimate aim is, once again, to articulate a kind of material etiology not only for how, but also for *why* the readerly is readerly; for *why* it is that writerly texts, whether penned or projected, demand that a percipient know how to write.

Permit me to end this introduction on a personal note, one that illumines this last point about "knowing how to write" most poignantly.

Although every scholarly work ultimately rests on the foundations of previous scholarship, sometimes accidents of circumstance can play an integral part in the evolution of a project. For example, it was my mother's chance mention of Ong's *Orality and Literacy*, as I indicated in the acknowledgments, that led to the film theory elaborated in these pages. But Ong's book might not have registered for me with the same ethnographic import and authenticity that it did had it not been for my grandmother, Jaswant Kaur Nayar.

My grandmother was born and raised in a village in the Gujrat district of the Punjab at a time when girls did not regularly attend school. As a result, she never learned to read or write. Although she continuously urged her grandchildren to engage in the tasks of the literate ("*Parho, parho*" was her frequent injunction, "Read, read"), she herself did not. She owned only one book, which consisted of a single word, "Rama," repeated over and over, for several dozen pages. I remember as a child how she would run her finger along its printed lines, reciting out loud those indecipherable letters which only pictographically she could identify as the name of God.

My grandmother spoke in proverbs and prayed audibly to Hanuman, the Hindu monkey-god, when he appeared on the movie screen; and when she counted money, it was according to the distinctive shapes and colors of the coins and bills. She was flexible, almost impatient with truth and so-called factual history and, like the contours of her life, her discussions were narrow, concrete, and frequently repeated: entreaties that we eat, stories about Partition, comments about the heat, or a panegyric to her sons. She was savvy, sage, and definitely crafty, but she also was not literate. Most of my life—indeed, only up until my exposure to *Orality and Literacy*—I attributed these habits and idiosyncrasies to her "village mentality" or to that "traditional wisdom" about which people speak so reverently, almost sentimentally. Without having witnessed her particular way of interpreting, explaining, and experiencing the world, without having had intimate, long-term contact with the consciousness of a nonliterate person, I doubt that I would have taken Ong's book as anything more than an abstract theoretical exercise—as a "social-science fiction," as one contemporary scholar recently termed Ong's work (Price, 2006, p. 9). In many respects, it is to my grandmother that I owe this project. And so, I can only urge the reader onward as she would have herself: "*Parho, parho.*"

2

Excavating the Oral Characteristics of Visual Narrative:

Hindi Popular Cinema, 1950–2000

So let me see whether I can say my story in the language they understand . . .

—Bombay film director Prakash Jha

A CONTEXT FOR BOLLYWOOD

In some sense it is inaccurate to speak of a single Hindi film formula, or to talk of *masala* film as if it were a homogeneous genre.[1] As Tejaswini Ganti (2004) counsels, "not all Hindi films are *masala* films" (p. 139). There also is wide disagreement, if not an inability for academics to settle, on a single, clear-cut definition of the *masala* film. Ganti points to those films that "contain a potpourri of elements—music, romance, action, comedy, and drama" (p. 139). Rajinder Kumar Dudrah (2006) high-

---

1. As this is not a work on Bollywood per se, I refrain from providing an extended historical or cultural preamble on the industry. For readers who are interested, the academic attention given to the subject has expanded exponentially in recent years. Prior to the early 1990s, there were very few materials to which one could turn to engage with the topic seriously. Now, Bollywood finds itself academically center stage and addressed from a wide array of disciplinary vantage points, including encyclopedic (Rajadhyaksha & Willemen, 1999), sociological (Dudrah, 2006; Pfleiderer & Lutze, 1985), anthropological (Dickey, 1993; Ganti, 2004), historical (Gokulsing & Dissanayake, 1998; Thoraval, 2000); through a transnational "diasporic" lens (Kaur & Sinha, 2005; Kavoori & Punathambekar, 2008); as film genre studies (Dwyer, 2006; Gopalan, 2002; Vitali, 2008); cultural studies (Nandy,

lights the "all-action films" that are "loaded with glamour" (p. 178) and
Patricia Uberoi (2001) the films' less savory ingredients of "sex, sadism,
and violence" (p. 310). Lalitha Gopalan (2002), meanwhile, cautiously
advises readers that it is the *critics* who have dubbed films *"masala"* by
virtue of the films' spectacularity and excessiveness, and the "medley"
nature of their narrative strands (p. 18). Most wide (and even *masala-*
esque) in scope is Yves Thoraval's (2000) characterization of the species
as being one where

> all genres merge into a kind of "total spectacle." Then, completely
> transformed, in order to express the deeper preoccupations and ethos
> of "Indian" drama, comic interludes, musical sequences, religion, ad-
> venture, fights, sociopolitical considerations—all get mixed up to-
> gether in commercial (pan-Indian mainstream) cinema, often charac-
> terised by the epithet *masala* (spicy) and which [*sic*] has become the
> trademark of the "made in Bombay" films. (p. 118)

If anything, this typifies the struggle for many Hindi-film scholars, who
want to address the formulaic and anticipated features of Bollywood,
but without having to capitulate to the existence of an inflexible genre.
Then again, as Rosie Thomas (1985) comments, a popular film gets
called *masala* because it "blends the masalas in proper portions" (p. 124).
In other words, genuine skill and dexterity go into the creation of a *suc-*
cessful spice-mix film.

There is additional room for maneuver given that the films are often
quite categorizable by genre: as romance, action, devotional, mythological, historical, and even children's films. (Note the absence of a musical
genre, as virtually every film produced in Bollywood—at least until recently—is by nature a musical, containing anywhere from 4 to 12 song-
and-dance numbers.) There even are class discriminations when it
comes to film content and quality. Movies are generally graded as A, B,
or C, with "each category having its own class-defined market, and
hence its own aesthetic assumptions" (Desphande, 2005, p. 193).[2]

1998), film theory and postcoloniality (Mishra, 2002), film theory and politics (Kazmi, 1999;
Prasad, 1998b; Vasudevan, 2000); with respect to iconography and aesthetics (Dwyer &
Patel, 2002), and to the nation and nationalism (Chakravarty, 1996; Dwyer & Pinney, 2001;
Virdi, 2003). Other scholars whose work deserves citation (and reading) are the essays of
Sudhir Kakar and Rosie Thomas, as well as the *India International Quarterly 8.1* issue of
1981, which in some sense initiated the serious study of the industry. There also are many
books available that address discrete films and directors, sometimes in a less academically
rigorous, although no less vital, way.

2. See Volga (2000) for a particularly scathing condemnation of the B- and C-class
films that "cater to the countless poor, the lower middle class, women and dalits from rural
areas" (p. WS-19). Volga claims middle-class intellectuals are altogether ignorant of these
films, which level sadistic indignity at oppressed groups, and can only "systematically destroy their [audience's] aesthetic sense and any shred of human values" (p. WS-19).

Changes in social and political climate also can impact the content and existential sentiment expressed in the movies. For example, the Nehruvian optimism and post-independent nation-building films of the 1950s gave way to disaffection with the state, heralding the arrival in the 1970s of the "angry young man" films. In the 1990s and 2000s, these morphed into the post-economic liberalization romance films and "family entertainers," which display a more materialistic vision and diasporic address. A single craze's persistence does not preclude other genres from achieving box-office success, however. For instance, concurrent with the new millennium's saccharine entertainers have been gritty gangster films that depict an unequivocally violent underworld. Perhaps, then, it's wise to think of the genres as *collectively* speaking to a Hindi film-viewing sensibility.

Even those academics who outright contest the historical existence of a formula find themselves ceding to "a range of elements that get repeatedly strung together and reshuffled," including "mythical solutions to restore an utopian world" (Virdi, 2003, pp. 8–9). Moreover, industry insiders, such as Javed Akhtar, co-writer of *Sholay*, admit to the "Indian masses somehow want[ing] a story that will engulf generations and eras, a larger period of time and incidents, big influences on a larger spectrum" (cited in Ganti, 2004, p. 173). Perhaps this mythic quality is what led Richard Corliss (2002), film critic for *Time*, to refer to the movies as "restor-[ing] melodrama to its Greek tragedy and Italian-opera roots" (p. 3).

Only it is *not* a restoration, I argue, in the same way that Bollywood *is not*, analogically speaking, "like myth." Rather, Hindi popular films reflect the continuation of a storytelling practice that goes back farther than Italian opera, farther even than ancient Greek tragedy. Indeed, this chapter contends—and empirically demonstrates—that the *masala* formula is in many respects coterminous with epics like the *Mahabharata* and the *Iliad*, and with African oral epic and other bardic tales. To be sure, *masala* films consciously borrow from India's mythology, appropriating, among other things, its particular formalized modes of expression. But is it not also possible that the film formula is as drawn to how the ancient Indian epics get told *epistemically*, as it is to their cultural content, aesethetic principles, or nostalgic value?

The stylized figures of Sanskrit theater; the visual spectacle of Parsi theater; the iconicity of calendar art; even the "structure of spectation embodied in the tradition of *darsana*"[3] (Prasad, 1998, p. 74): All these are, likewise, part of the reserves from which Hindi film pulls—and, once more, may be doing so for reasons *beyond* artistic sensibility or cultural acquaintance. My intent is not to deny the significance of aesthetic

---

3. *Darsana* refers to the act and practice of seeing—and indeed of being seen *by*—the divine image. I discuss this concept at more length later on.

choice and national flavor to Bollywood filmmaking, nor to downplay
the effects of corporate interest in financial yields;[4] but we might ask
ourselves why these modes and styles of expression were privileged,
whereas others equally Indian were not. Furthermore, why *hasn't* realist
fiction been "a dominant form of narration in India," as Jyotika Virdi
(2003, p. 41) acknowledges? And why does Hindi popular cinema continue to display a "predilection for sagas and elaborate plot lines motivated by chance events and coincidences," and only "minimally etch[ed]
character psychology or the interior workings of the mind" (p. 41)? Finally, why is it that, almost without fail, conflicts arising from a protagonist's circumstances cause him to stray temporarily, only for him "to return to [his] original point in the course of narrative resolution" (p. 41)? I
quote Virdi here at length because, notwithstanding her skepticism concerning the existence of a Hindi film formula, she fully admits to this underlying web of Hindi film attributes. Not only will orality help to illu-
minate the etiology of these attributes; it will underscore that there is a
narrative *logic* to what, on the surface, may appear only as pastiche or an
excessiveness motivated only by fantasy escapism.

I have segued into speaking about the industry rather homoge-
neously, in spite of acknowledging upfront that such a position is not
really tenable. Doing so is especially perilous in the current climate. A
growing national economy, a rapidly burgeoning consumer class, and an
often more profitable audience base of Indians abroad have led in the
past decade to some major changes in the industry's output—something
I address briefly in Chapter 4.[5] For that reason, I have elected to bracket
the films with which I deal in this chapter to those produced between
1950 and 2000.

As K.A. Abbas tells us, it was around the time of World War II that
the working classes began heavily to patronize movie theaters, with
trends in production thus shifting toward lighter fare (Chakravarty,
1996, p. 42). K. Moti Gokulsing and Wimal Dissanayake (1998) maintain
that it was precisely during this period that the successful Hindi film
formula—consisting of "song, dance, spectacle, rhetoric, and fantasy"
(p. 15)—was forged. Aruna Vasudev (1986) confirms this, when she
points diagnostically to a middle-class restiveness with Bombay's fare in
the 1940s, one that left "the field free for a working-class mass public.
The watchword became extravagance—in sets, style, fantasy, music,
dance, emotion. Psychological relief was sought in escapism. Everything

---

4. Priya Jaikumar (2003) maintains that *masala* films were "a consequence of producers and directors trying to ensure that every film had a fighting chance to reap good prof-
its"—which meant "incorporating something in the film for everyone" (p. 26).

5. Even into the 21st century, appealing to the masses remains "the only guarantee to
that elusive success at the box office," and so remains "of utmost importance to the moguls
in the film industry" (Virdi, 2003, p. 213).

was exaggerated. The cinema became larger than life" (p. 13).[6] Interestingly, a similar, although more critically condemned, rupture marked the 1980s—a period that Anupama Chopra (2002) refers to as the "Dark Ages of Bollywood," when "the industry [was] haemorrhaging under the twin onslaughts of video and colour television . . . [and] the audience, mostly young men, seemed to prefer action and loud, gaudy melodramas" (p. 25).

Such masses of young men who prefer "gaudy melodramas"—and who typically fill a theatre's cheaper "front stalls" (ticket seats, like films, are graded in India)—have been largely underrepresented in academic scholarship. Outside of Sara Dickey's (1993) important anthropological contribution on film-viewing practices, *Cinema and the Urban Poor in South India*, most studies' indigenous informants have been either middle class or upwardly mobile, and usually betray a strong urban bias (see Mankekar, 1999; Uberoi, 2001). Although the present project admittedly does not engage with informants, and so is in no position to criticize scholars who actually carry out fieldwork, it does wish to draw attention to the critical relationship between subaltern audiences and the *masala* film formula.

True, who the public *is* is not always easy to gauge, in part because "box office hits are calculated as national aggregates" (Virdi, 2003, p. 8). But imagine for a moment that *you* were the average citizen, a potential spectator with no capacity to read or write: a bicycle rickshaw-*walla* perhaps, a village peddler. (If this seems like a cheap appeal to pity, keep in mind that, right when the film formula was coming into its own, the nation's literacy rate was a mere 18% [Ganti, 2004, p. 25].[7]) Such a nonliterate state of mind would mean you were incapable of writing down information in order to store it, as you were incapable of engaging with your past via genealogical charts or history books. Whatever you carried, you carried in your thoughts, in your memory; and the only way for anything to be deposited there was by word of mouth. How could such an exclusively oral engagement with the world not mold your methods of engaging with story or your particular tastes?

---

6. These descriptors apply to much of Bollywood's output today. In fact, the Hindi film industry still refers to its audiences in terms of the "binaries of 'classes and masses' and 'cities and interiors'" (Ganti, 2004, p. 63).

7. That by the new millennium the literacy rate had risen to 64.38% is surely a testament to India's ongoing commitment to education. At the same time, such figures can be deceptive, as functional literacy in India is defined solely by a person's capacity to write his or her name. Furthermore, even though literacy rates have risen substantially since Independence (1947), the actual number of nonliterates has *increased* because of population growth (Sekhon, 2000, p. 107). The 2001 literacy rate of 65%, for example, meant that, at the turn of the millennium, there were approximately 400 million nonliterate people—a number larger than India's entire population after Independence, and more than the populations of the United States and Canada combined.

At the same time, imagine an industry which, being rooted in profit, wished to cast as wide a net as possible in terms of appeal. This would be a difficult thing to do in a nation of multiple linguistic groups. In that sense, a reliance on the features of orally transmitted narrative might function as the most opportune way to reach across the myriad vernaculars of the potential viewing population. Reaching the public via the epistemically oral—whose characteristics are to a degree universally shared—would assure the highest number of viewers, regardless of whether a viewer's native tongue was Punjabi, Bengali, or Malayalam.

So, when social psychologist Ashis Nandy (1995) avers that "the basic principles of [India's] commercial cinema derive from the needs of ['low brow viewers'] caught in the hinges of social change who are trying to understand their predicament in terms of cultural categories known to them" (p. 205), does it not seem plausible, almost natural in fact, that one of those categories might be orality? Similarly, when elsewhere he notes that the right metaphor for Indian popular films is "the urban slum"—because the films offer a "slum's point of view of Indian politics and society and, for that matter, the world" (Nandy, 1998, p. 2)— might that be because this worldview is contoured by a particularly oral way of knowing, one that would have rendered the films intelligible and accessible to the envisaged slum-dweller?

It would be a mistake to presume that oral inflection necessarily travels hand in hand with poor quality, whether as a deficiency of aesthetic concern or weak production values. After all, some of the most *lauded* A-grade films in Bollywood evince strong links to orality. Suffice it to say that exigencies of pocket probably make good commercial bedfellows with orally inflected exigencies of mind. Indeed, one might argue that this partnership is precisely what led to the *masala* films' migratory potentials. Though Bollywood films have long been popular with Indian expatriates, sometimes their overseas audiences have not been Indian at all. For much of the latter half of the 20th century, in fact, Bombay delivered "the most popular cinema throughout much of the developing world" (Thomas, 1995, p. 180). Northern Nigerians, for instance, have had a long-term relationship with Hindi popular film—and sometimes this was without the benefit of *linguistic* comprehension, given that, in earlier decades, the movies were often viewed without dubbing or subtitles (Larkin, 1997a, 1997b, 2005). In Egypt, the films are quite simply recognized as being part of Arab culture (Power & Mazumdar, 2000); and they continue to appeal to Romany Gypsies in eastern Europe (who have documented low levels of literacy; see Kenrick & Clark, 1999), as they do to Swahili-speaking schoolgirls in Zanzibar (Power & Mazumdar, 2000) and "Greek mothers and Morrocan nomads" (M. Desai, 2007). In fact, Thoraval (2000), the author of *Cinemas of India*, became interested in the species when, during his travels, he kept coming across Bollywood screenings in "places as diverse as Iran, the Maghreb, Indonesia, Salalah in Oman, or Mukalla in South Yemen . . . or Kassala in Sudan, Asmara in Eritrea, Uzbekistan, Cambodia or Syria" (p. ix).

Numerous factors indubitably account for the *masala* films' success overseas: their comparative inexpensiveness in the marketplace, for one; and their provision of a more kindred set of cultural mores than those propagated by Hollywood (their "alterity" from British and American film, as Brian Larkin, 2005, describes, p. 297). But surely it is possible that orality, too, could have aided or eased the movies' cultural crossover. How else to explain the connection those Nigerian audiences felt to stories being told in an untranslated foreign language—or Afghani audiences who, despite having no facility with Hindi, likewise acknowledged having little trouble understanding the movies (Farrell, 2001)?

Consider, for instance, that the Hausa in northern Nigeria candidly expressed that, on the basis of the films, Indian culture was "'just like' Hausa culture: in its depiction of relations between genders; in the negotiation between a reified 'traditional' culture and an equally reified 'westernisation'; and, in the mise en scène and iconography of everyday life" (Larkin, 2005, p. 296). On the surface, this may appear to support the more conventional scholarly reading that these stories were reflecting the Hausa people's own comparable experience as a traditional society undergoing modernization. But such an opinion needs to be weighed in light of other statements that the Hausa made, ones that complicate any impulsive hoisting of a "society-at-odds-with-itself" point of view. (This is not something Larkin does, mind you; his analysis is much more nuanced than that.) What I am referring to here is Larkin's admission that, what he took to be the films' "overt sentimentality," the Hausa experienced as legitimate and real. Where he saw trite melodrama, they saw authentic representation. The Hausa didn't experience the films "in terms of fantasy," in Larkin's own words, "but as something that emerge[d] out of the historical experience of common people. . . . [P]eople see Indian film as *representing real, everyday problems* and *not in the terms of kitsch fantasy* with which they are greeted in the West" (p. 297).

"Representing [the] real" is a description quite in contrast to the critics' characterizations of the *masala* genre, which I offered at this chapter's outset, and which emphasized the species' spectacularity and the minimally etched psychology of its characters. Clearly, the Hausa percipients were engaging phenomenologically and existentially with the material in an entirely different way. One might even argue they were watching altogether different movies. So, how to explain such a dissonance in viewpoints? I advocate that the answer lies less in trying to distinguish Hindi popular cinema from realist cinema than in trying to de-

termine what, for some viewers, might have made Hindi popular cinema *real*. And the way to do that, no doubt predictably now, is via parsing the formula for its decidedly oral features. Let us begin by considering the structural make-up of the *masala* film.

NARRATIVE COHERENCE, SPICE-MIX STYLE

It would be imprudent to discount the sway of acculturation on Bollywood film viewing. As Ganti (2004) warns in her guidebook to the industry, "to some who have never seen a Hindi popular film, a tough
street-wise hoodlum fighting violently in one scene and singing a love
song in another may appear jarring and nonsensical" (p. 140). Nevertheless, acculturation does not of necessity dictate comprehension. Viewers
may be bemused or caught off guard at the sight of a criminal breaking
into song, but that does not preclude them from being able to *follow* the
story. *Masala* plotlines are rarely difficult to follow, anchored as they are
in exhibition, in narrative structures that are loose, stringy, digressive,
and episodic, but almost always intelligibly so. Indeed, the films have
long been excoriated by critics for being simple-minded and naïve (in
Rajadhyaksha, 1987, p. 21). Even the dramaturgical system of the social
films of the 1940s and 1950s, as Ravi Vasudevan (1995) tells us, displayed
a "relationship between narrative, performance sequence and action
spectacle loosely structured in the fashion of a cinema of attractions"
(p. 307). Here, Vasudevan means a cinema whose tendencies are exhibitionistic, discontinuous, and indifferent to both realism and linear narrative logic. (Although the term *cinema of attractions* was coined by Tom
Gunning, 1986, to describe early American cinema, it has often been
used as a descriptor of the Bollywood narrative style.)

In a similar vein, Vijay Mishra (1992) argues that Bombay cinema's
"narrative structures respond more to a sensationist theory of audience
response than to the demands of structural cohesiveness" (p. 112). In
other words, the *masala* film is a medium of provocation, eliciting impulses and feelings, often contradictory, in lieu of deferring to an organizing principle. Structurally it relies on shock value and pastiche rather
than on seamless linearity and paring.

Mishra considers this deeply de-centered form to be an extension of
a deeply de-centered society—"a culture of deferral and flux bonded to
ahistorical principles drawn from metaphysics rather than lived experience" (p. 112). The consequence of this existential positioning culturally,
he says, "is that Indian genres lack the organic consistency and inner
structural harmony . . . normally associated with Western generic types.
This is not a statement of value, simply one of *difference*" (p. 118).

I am not equipped to argue with Mishra's claim that all Indian genres lack organic consistency; nor could I prove or disprove whether this

derives from an epistemological state of being honed by philosophy. However, I am also unable to disregard the fact that, in oral cultures, narrative expression tends toward the additive rather than the subordinative, and perhaps this too has some bearing on the Bombay film's lack of structural cohesiveness. Let me explain—or, rather, let me let Ong explain.

Oral structures look to pragmatics; that is, they are structured in ways convenient to the speaker. Structures produced by chirographic cultures, on the other hand, are more geared toward syntactics, toward the actual organization of discourse itself: "Written discourse develops more elaborate and fixed grammar than oral discourse does because to provide meaning it is more dependent simply upon linguistic structure, since it lacks the normal full existential contexts which surround oral discourse" (Ong, 1982, pp. 37–38). In other words, discourse shaped by the existence of writing and print encourages a flow of narration that is *foreign* to oral discourse. Syntactically shaping and tightening a sentence (or an entire composition) so that it contains subordinate elements— which thus yield or draw attention to the *principal idea* of the sentence (or composition) and eliminate its digressive quality—is a skill that comes only with chirography. The oral mind does not have the luxury of time or of paper to subordinate elements inventively or to tighten the episodic looseness of spoken language. (For those who have ever endeavored to tell a story out loud, recall one's continuous reliance on the transitional "And then . . .," "And then . . ." as a means of keeping the narrative glued together.) To some degree, the literate person's syntactical organizing of discourse is but the process of "editing out" the naturally oral formulation from prose—of eliminating its coordinative untidiness. In fact, in early prose fiction, such as that of the Tudor period, one can still see a tendency toward "a loosely strung-out episodic style" (Ong, 1965, p. 150).

What this implies is that orally transmitted narratives cannot be structurally cohesive in the way that alphabetic readers have come to anticipate. This is because the pyramidally structured plot—the "strict plot," as Ong refers to it—is something that emerges specifically through writing. Such a plot design, which is commonly referred to as Freytag's Pyramid, is one where "an ascending action builds tension, rising to a climactic point, which consists often of a recognition or other incident bringing about a *peripeteia* or reversal of action, and which is followed by a denouement or untying" (Ong, 1982, p. 142). Anyone who has seen a classical Hollywood film will no doubt recognize that linear arrangement. Only an increased conscious control over the creative process, enforced by the writer's isolation from his or her audience and the slowness of the writing process, can result in a story line developing "tighter and tighter climactic structures in the place of the old oral episodic plot" (p. 148).

The tight control and minimal deviation common to Freytag's Pyramid are, of course, altogether absent in oral epics. Orally transmitted narratives are instead built on, through, and around thematic recurrences, chronological breaks, and other such episodic techniques. In fact, the ancient Greeks, aware that episodic structure "was the only way and the totally natural way of imagining and handling lengthy narrative" (Ong 1982, p. 144), referred to their own epic songs as "rhapsody" (*rhapsōidia*), a term that means literally "a stitching together" (Ong, 1965, p. 149).

Although this episodic form may have its origins in the bard's necessarily pragmatic approach to his material, his *listener*'s ability mentally to accommodate the material cannot go unstressed. The additive, sequential, episodic form is indubitably more comfortable, easier to follow, and less complicated to digest—not to mention, closer to the human experience. Indeed, a narrative progression that does not rely on tight climactic structure lends itself more easily to excursions and diversions that satisfy the varied—one might even say *masala*—expectations of an audience. After all, this tendency can be seen in African oral epics, where individual scenes or episodes that do not materially advance the plot—especially ones involving horror or humor—are often "developed for their own independent appeal" (Okpewho, 1979, pp. 209–210).

Hindi popular film is likewise rife with stand-alone sketches and deviations (often of a slapstick or violent nature), which are amplified for full effect. In the first half of *Sholay*, for instance, a 15-minute sequence is devoted to the comical in-prison escapades of the film's co-protagonists. In *Hum Aapke Hain Kaun . . . ? (Who Am I to You*, 1994), a vaudevillian mishap is included for the sheer pleasure of a vaudevillian mishap and serves no narrative causal function. Even the song-and-dance numbers that pepper every film could be said to derive as much from an orally inflected willingness to digress as from a culturally beloved aesthetic component.[8]

The overly slack and digressive nature of some Hindi films also can be—and often is—attributed to industry profiteering and a culturally elaborated requirement on the part of audiences that at least half-a-dozen musical numbers be interspersed throughout the narrative. As Shyam Benegal, a noted non-mainstream Indian film director, put it, "the compulsion to picturize songs and dances in every film tend[s] to circumscribe the subject matter of the films themselves. Often this form [is] a hindrance to cinematic self-expression" (cited in Datta, 2002, p. 35).

Certainly it is much easier for producers to "slap together" an episodic fiction hinged by songs than to conceive a tightly woven story.

---

8. Sometimes the songs are narratively hinged to the text proper. In these cases, if one misses a song, as director Raj Kapoor warned, one has "missed an important link between one point of the narration and the next" (cited in Dudrah, 2006, p. 49).

However, the *complete absence* of complex plotting and tight narrative structure, in tandem with an indigenous generic economy of storytelling that has emerged as a kind of rule or expectation (yes, even in a 3-hour film), suggests that the reasons for that absence—indeed for audiences' *acceptance* of that absence—go much deeper than some Machiavellian opportunism on the part of movie moguls.

Scholars of Hindi popular cinema seem inadvertently to confirm this. Gokulsing and Dissanayake (1998), for one, note that the typical storyline of an Indian popular film "does not progress in a linear fashion but meanders, with detours and stories within stories," in a "circular form of narration [that] is commonly found in classical and folk literature" (p. 29). The classical and folk literature to which the authors allude is no doubt a reference, at least in part, to the *Mahabharata*, which was itself orally transmitted and only later written down, and, ergo, preserves many of the traits of oral narrative. In fact, the authors' characterization of the Bollywood storyline bears striking resemblance to Cedric Whitman's description of the *Iliad* as being "built like a Chinese puzzle, boxes within boxes" (Ong, 1982, p. 27).

Slightly less merciful in his portrayal of Hindi popular cinema is Ashish Rajadhyaksha (1987), who sees the species as operating "by means of accumulation of stimulus-response scenes, of loosely strung together bits of business each of which constitutes a bet on box office returns: fights, cabarets, suggested nudity, a stereotyped 'star' identity" (p. 58). To a certain extent, this view echoes Mishra's, although Rajadhyaksha sees the form as emanating more specifically from the industry's willful production of an "exploitation cinema." Setting exploitation aside (as here it is intended as a marker of capitalism), couldn't such "strung together bits" pertain just as well to the peripatetic adventures of Gilgamesh, or to the Pandava brothers' exploits in the *Mahabharata*?

Perhaps it is Vasudevan (1995) who grazes cinema's orality most closely, albeit unawares, in his discussion of Hindi cinema's "disaggregative"—that is, its discontinuous and unintegrated—address.[9] Conventional Indian films may lack Hollywood's contemporary linear narrative logic, but Vasudevan sees them as bearing a palpable resemblance to *early* Euro-American cinema. Here, Vasudevan is referring to the narrational style of those silent films that Gunning conceptualized as a "cinema of attractions," and which, in Vasudevan's words, only disappeared as "the [Euro-American] audience, earlier understood to be composed of workers and immigrants, was 'civilized' into appreciating the bourgeois virtues of a concentrated, logical, character-based narrative development" (p. 319). In light of the conceptual studies of oral tradition, the ease with

---

9. Further concordance can be found in M. Madhava Prasad's (1998a) reference to Hindi popular film's "fragmented, episodic structure" (p. 43).

which one might replace his use of the term *bourgeois* with that of *literate* cannot be disregarded.

For those who remain skeptical still, let us consider one of the chief building blocks of episodic structure: the flashback. In simplest terms, the flashback is a device that permits an inclusion of information or back story that would either be impossible or too complicated to incorporate directly into a master narrative. A flashback allows for recall, for clarification, for the feeding to the audience of data necessary to elicit empathy or a sense of justification for an action to be executed later on; and, naturally, it does so without adherence to sequential storytelling. In the *Odyssey*, for instance, sage and wily Odysseus regales a banquet hall of Phaeacians with the tale of his crew's sea-bound adventures, thus transporting the reader directly to "his voyage fraught with hardship [. . . while] homeward bound from Troy" (Book IX: lines 43–44). The ensuing 4 "books"—one-sixth of the *Odyssey*'s 24—are devoted exclusively to this flashback. Consider as well the numerous stories within stories (and even, again, within stories) in the *Mahabharata*, such as that of the king Nala being recounted by a sage to the Pandava princes, who are themselves being recounted by a sage to one of those princes' own great-grandsons (C. Narasimhan, 1965).

Such a configurative movement between "present-past-present is rather typical of the Bombay film," grants Sumita Chakravarty (1996), "and serves to bring all the main characters together in the end" (p. 49). In fact, it is difficult to conjure up a single hit film that does *not* make use of this device at some point during the course of its narrative, whether as a character's momentary surrender to nostalgic recollection, or as a 1-hour portrayal of a protagonist's adolescent descent into crime. In *Khal Nayak* (*The Villain*, 1993), for example, we straggle in and out of a coarse underworld tale, a Ram and Sita-type love story, and a mother-son melodrama, stalling on several occasions in order to voyage back in time. Through these flashbacks, we witness the experiences that led to a decent child's transformation into a heinous villain, as well as the traumatic aftermath that this metamorphosis had on the boy's upright family. In *Sholay*, we get a police chief's story-within-story recall of how he met the two thieves whom he plans to hire to execute his vengeance. This is followed by protracted flashbacks to the chief's once idyllic family life and to his family's tragic ruination at the hand of the film's nemesis, with a third flashback portraying the exuberance and compelling life-force of the police chief's daughter-in-law, now reduced to forlorn widowhood.

Previous critics, albeit with very different motivations, have pointed to the meaningful presence of this formal device. Koushik Banerjea (2005) describes the flashback structure of *Deewar* (*Wall*, 1975)—one of the biggest releases of the 1970s "angry young man" period—as being one "through which the whole of [the film] is coded" (p. 175). Here, he takes up a thread introduced by M. Madhva Prasad (1998a), who suggests that *Deewar's* flashback structure "imbues the tragedy of [its protagonist] with a secrecy, a subterranean quality" because it codes "the narrative as a mother's memory hidden from public view" (p. 148). In other words, the mother's *memory* of the tale frames the tale to come, and in this way, an "unofficial history" is evoked, one that offers the spectator "the pleasure of a secret liaison with the mother as a surrender to the political power of matriarchy" (p. 148). Prasad comes close to recognizing the oral inflection of such a storytelling device when he posits that such a structure "evokes the community of the 'pre-historic,' the solidarity of the mother's world against the world of the father, the Law" (p. 148). But these flashbacks are so pervasive in *masala* film that one would be remiss in limiting one's negotiation of their puissance to ideological or psychoanalytical readings of isolated films. The extreme resilience of the device, the fact that it has become so utterly conventionalized, suggests a level of complicity on the part of the audience that transcends (which is not to say precludes) the working out of masochistic fantasies. Perhaps the resilience of the flashback is more compellingly explained by the viewer who does not expect or even desire a strict linear progression of events. He or she favors the structures familiar to oral storytelling and has subliminally aided in cementing a particular kind of logic into a national cinematic code.

OF WEIGHTY WORDS AND OUTSIZED HEROES

Hindi popular cinema displays a major affinity for verbal superfluity and fulsome dialogic delivery: There will be fast, sharp, comical exchanges between characters; highly charged debates; lyrical romantic intercourse; and long drawn-out monologues, which are greatly prized and often delivered with the moral fervor of a zealous prophet. Virtually every frame of Hindi film celluloid is accompanied by some kind of audible consort, whether in the form of colloquy, soliloquy, banter, lyric or, if none of these, clamorous sound effects that augur the arrival of the human utterance. In the Bollywood universe, sound is generally aggrandized, exaggerated expression is favored, and the value of the visual is conditioned less by cinematography than by a collectively agreed-on ascendancy of the voice that inhabits the image.

According to Lothar Lutze (1985), the Hindi film's attraction to hyperbole may have its seeds in ancient Sanskrit poetics, where *atishyokti* (exaggeration) is considered the central figure of speech. Although this may be true, it is also important to note the encouragement of hyper-

bole—of *copia*, or the fluency, volubility, and abundancy of speech—
which is prevalent in oral cultures (Ong, 1967). (Indeed, the rules of traditional poetics may well have their origins in orality.)

Sound, and especially the "oral utterance, which comes from inside
living organisms," is dynamic to oral people (Ong, 1982, p. 32). This is
because nonchirographic societies depend exclusively on the use of *spoken* words and, hence, on human interaction for determining attitudes
and courses of action. As Jack Goody and Ian Watt (1968) explain,
"There can be no reference to 'dictionary definitions,' nor can words ac-
cumulate the successive layers of historically validated meanings which
they acquire in a literate culture. Instead, the meaning of each word is
ratified in a succession of concrete situations, accompanied by vocal in-
flections and physical gestures" (p. 29). Ong (1982) provides in his work
the concrete example of a traditional Arab souk, where the act of purchasing something is not limited to a quick or quiet economic transac-
tion, but is at heart a rhetorical exchange, "a series of verbal (and so-
matic) maneuvers, a polite duel, a contest of wits, an operation in oral
agonistic" (p. 68).

High-technology cultures, on the other hand, rely more on "non-
verbal, often largely visual input from the 'objective' world of things"
(Ong, 1982, p. 68). They no longer think of words as "primarily oral, as
events, and hence as necessarily powered" (p. 32). As a result, "verbomotor" cultures (as Marcel Jousse termed them in 1925 [p. 20]) may
strike literate cultures as "making all too much of speech itself, as over-
valuing and certainly overpracticing rhetoric" (p. 68). So, whereas a literate viewer may embrace the quiet restraint of a film by Satyajit Ray,
verbomotor cultures more likely will respond to the agonistic vibrancy
of Bombay cinema, with its acting style that is "louder, more theatrical
and more oriented toward mannerism" (Kazmi, 1999, p. 83).

This dynamism of the utterance is no less applicable to the Indian
viewer who is sitting in front of the goings-on on the screen. Often as a
masala story unfolds, "the audience cheers, mouths dialogue, and sings
with the songs" (Chopra, 2002, p. 8). A similar sort of engagement is to
be found in Egypt, where, in third-class theaters that commonly screen
Hindi films, the largely male audience "often knows the films by heart,
interacts vigorously with the action and even repeats or comments on it
during the projection" (Shafik, 2001, p. 39). But this conduct is not restricted to interactions with Bollywood fare. Consider Hamid Naficy's
(2003) description of Iranian audiences during his youth. As he makes
clear, "Audiences' oral interaction with the diegesis . . . heightened the
contentiousness of the viewing experience. People would not hesitate to
tell the actors on screen what they should do next: 'Oh, watch out, he is
behind you;' 'Yeah, punch him hard in the stomach, hit him, hit him'"

(pp. 189–190).[10] This of course contradicts Ong's (1967) claim that "An assembly of individuals using only their eyes to assimilate what is presented to them . . . does not form a group as it would in listening to a public speaker or in attending a sports spectacle accompanied by shouting and cheers" (p. 258). But when one factors in the cinema halls of historically developing nations, one has good reason to disagree. Clearly there are visual-media audiences that continue the tradition of instigating the types of vocalizations that make "individuals cohere with one another" (p. 258).

Conceivably, this mandatory deference to sound is why so many *masala* films begin in a manner best described as *in medias res*. That is, the films begin with an almost shocking abruptness (e.g., lightning flashing, someone running for help), as if we were being plunged into a story already in progress—into the *middle* of an exploit, a conversation, a friendship. It is of course the kind of suddenness with which the oral epic also typically commences, in part because that is the only natural way for an oral poet to approach a lengthy narrative (Ong, 1982). In the case of the Hindi film, however, the rationale is perhaps due more to the currency of, and to the visual's inherent need to be tied to, the *voice*. A beginning can only logically take place *with* action and sound—or, perhaps, more accurately, with action *as* sound. Silent lead-ups and slow establishing shots, as one finds in the openings of other species of film, are not to be found in the *masala* picture. One might even say that silence is generally leaden, not golden, in Bollywood, marking as it does an *absence* of story rather than any sort of meaningful transcendence.

Nowhere is the *masala* film's predilection for aural agonism more apparent than in its highly dramatized verbal oaths. Here, sons will pledge to avenge mothers, heroines to sacrifice themselves, and the truly valiant will demonstrate their mettle by vowing reprisal as they slide their palm down a foe's sharp scimitar. According to Ivan Illich and Barry Sanders (1988), "Oaths are among the forms of utterance most carefully guarded against change" (p. 34). This is because the swearing of oaths "makes the word visible—not on paper, but in the living body of the person concerned. It incarnates the veracity of what he is saying. In the context of orality, truth is inseparable from veracity. The oath reveals an epiphany of this unity of form and content that captures the essence of the oral mentality" (pp. 33–34). That the oath in the Bombay cinema is more than simply the effective use of a *visual* medium (how exciting can the unrav-

---

10. Compare vaudevillian variety theater with its direct address to the spectators and its "singing along [and] heckling," which were what fueled early American cinema, according to Gunning (1986, p. 65).

eling of a legal document be?)[11] is apparent in the manner of its delivery. It is a performance done in earnest, with much emotive quaking and broad gesturing. In fact, the moment is often distended, turned into a drawn-out monologue, with the camera remaining fixed on—or, better yet, rapidly encircling—the oath-giver, while penetrating music or atmospheric sound effects "respond" to the verbalized pledge.

Illich and Sanders further indicate that, well into the 18th century in Europe, oaths continued to take place in the open air, so that they might be "manifest to the gods, the spirits, or the dead" (p. 33). Often in Bollywood, the oaths are performed in a like manner, with the pact either spoken out loud as if to the gods or unabashedly delivered to one's own reflection in a mirror. In fact, "scenes where the protagonist looks into and speaks to his or her own image in the mirror are well-worn devices" (Virdi, 2003, p. 95), which Virdi attributes to their capacity to connote a duality of the self, a "split between the 'real' self and the 'image' of the self, or between the different selves inhabiting the same body" (p. 95). However, given the primacy of *speech* in the oral arena, rendering the word visible, either as a route to incarnating the veracity of one's word, or even as a way to make "the inner voice" physically manifest, also might underpin this perceived solipsistic behavior.

Thus, when the police chief in *Sholay*, or Shah Rukh Khan in *Pardes* (*Beyond India*, 1997), wants vengeance, he expresses such in the form of a highly dramatized vow for vengeance, one full of bravura and overstated spite. A vendetta is no less an imminent action than a *verbal articulation* of that imminent action. There is of course a certain irony to aurality's pre-eminence here, given that the medium in which it occurs is primarily assessed by critics in visual terms. Or, perhaps it is more that, in not locating orality's sway on visual narrative, we have downplayed the significance of aurality, and certainly of how the aural gets *subsumed* into the visual.

The aural accessorizing of the typical oath-giving (e.g., with the sound of wind, or of temple bells) reflects more profoundly the oath's existence as truth-incarnate. (Koushik Banerjea, 2005, inventively calls attention to the soundtrack's capacity to achieve a "talismanic potency," p. 171.) In films like *Baazigar* and *Ghulam* (*Slave*, 1998)—the latter a Bollywood adaptation of *On the Waterfront* (1954)—setting literally becomes animated with the oath-giver's rhetorical (and, hence, existential) investment. In this way, the Bollywood oath acquires an almost iconographic sacredness, an apartness from the rest of the film that underscores the

---

11. Havelock (1963) recounts something similar (as I came only later to discover) with respect to the early polis communities of Greece: "You cannot flourish a document to command a crowd: it is symptomatic that as late as Aristophanes the use of the document for this purpose is regarded as funny and inept" (p. 127).

oath's authority and meaning. The moment becomes a ceremonial one in which the significance of, and an exclusive trust in, the *spoken* word is validated and reinforced.

But the heightened performance of such scenes, statements, and exhortations serves another purpose, too: It renders interactions memorable, that is, easily susceptible to recollection. Thanks in part to the intensity of delivery, words and lines and sometimes entire scenes are capable of being enlisted to the mind. They are memorized and recited by audiences. As one interviewee commented regarding *Sholay*, "many near illiterate people who had seen the film could repeat verbatim large chunks of the dialogue" (Dissanayake & Sahai, 1992, p. 128). This is something to which Mishra, Jeffrey, and Shoesmith (1989) draw critical attention, perceptively identifying that, in the conventional Hindi cinema, the ideal dialogic scenario "is one in which a lengthy debate takes place between two people: mother and son, brother and brother, father and son, hero and villain" (p. 59). According to the authors, this is because, given "the power of the dialogue and the culture's valorization of the 'oral,'" it is only through a verbally developed dramatic encounter that an actor-hero-star can generate a powerful enough momentum for him to be inscribed into the consciousness of the Indian audience (p. 60). Such augmented confrontations thus permit "a kind of *smrti* discourse, a 'memory-text,'" which spectators are able to recall and thereby participate in (p. 60). In this way, the dialogic situation endures in the minds of viewers; it is kept from vanishing, as the oral utterance unavoidably does. Might this valorization of the oral and conjoint participation by way of a memory-text explain the multiple visits that 70% of theater goers interviewed by Preminda Jacob (1997) acknowledged making to particularly relished films? It might also account for why the Nigerian spectators with whom Larkin (1997a) watched *Mother India* (1957) had all seen the film "at least fifteen times" (p. 1).[12]

Feasibly this valorization explains, too, why oral address in the Hindi film is inclined toward repetition and redundancy. It is not uncommon for characters in a Bollywood film to repeat phrases or choice lines of dialogue, even periodically to synopsize or recap narrative events. True, this may be a contrivance on the part of producers to facilely lengthen a script; but such a device additionally provides the oral spectator a valuable tool. For, when there is nothing outside the mind onto which one can backloop, as is the case with oral discourse, "the mind must move more slowly, keeping close to the focus of attention much of what it has already dealt with. Redundancy, repetition, the just-said, keeps both speaker and hearer surely on track" (Ong, 1982, p. 40).

---

12. Similarly, Chopra (2002) speaks of spectators who saw *Dilwale Dulhania Le Jayenge* (*The Brave-Hearted Will Take the Bride*, 1995) "15, 20, even 30 times" (p. 8).

What this consequently lays bare is the reason for Bombay cinema's persistent use of clichés and platitudes, of formulary expressions that typically strike those who have been inculcated into a literate way of knowing as mindless or stale. For, proverbs and set phrases are the formulary essentials of oral processes of thought. In oral societies, traditional expressions cannot afford to be cavalierly dismantled. As Ong explains, "it has been hard work getting them together over the generations, and there is nowhere outside the mind to store them. So soldiers are brave and princesses beautiful and oaks sturdy forever. . . . Once a formulary expression has crystallized, it had best be kept intact" (p. 39). And thus, in the blockbuster *Hum Aapke*, when there is discussion regarding familial ethics, it is housed not in personal admittances or intimate confessions, but in *publicly shared* truths or memories. Likewise, at the end of *Baazigar*, the protagonist's disdain for his nemesis is articulated in the argot of proverbs: "You have only seen the crown on his head," the protagonist warns his fiancée (who also happens to be the daughter of his nemesis). "Look under the thief's sleeve and you will find blood." Indeed, it is rare to find a *masala* film that has *not*, by its denouement, skidded into language that is noticeably aphoristic, into proverbs and other rhetorical vessels that ease preservation and recollection. In a sense, this reflects the oral parameters of *wisdom*—as a knowledge that is not only experientially acquired, but transmitted down the line in efficient packets.

The films' set expressions are perhaps most readily detectable in the song numbers that interpolate or extend the diegesis proper. Formulary epithetic expressions, such as a vagabond's self-comparison to a *badal awara* (wandering cloud), or a lover's description of his *dil deewana* (love-crazed heart), have crystallized and become wholly standardized in their use. Often one will hear panegyrized a *sapnon ki rani* (queen of my dreams) or a *raja hindustani* (Indian king). These are phrases that are as familiar today as they were 50 years ago. As such, they carry with them a host of references, perhaps stimulating a spectator's own filmic "memories." We might liken them even to "the acoustic jingles" that Eric Havelock (1963) identifies in Homeric epic, and that "characteristically creep into the formulas of religious ceremony, revealing their character as familiar and popular definitions but ones for which, however familiar, there [is] the felt need of constant recall" (p. 74).

But the noetic value of formulary utterances that inflate soldiers into brave soldiers or princesses into beautiful princesses transcends the solely dialogic or lyric. Also impacted are the very *personalities* that inhabit the narrative. This is because "colorless personalities cannot survive oral mnemonics"; hence the omnipresence of "'heavy' [or 'flat'] characters, persons of extra *weight*, whose deeds are monumental, memorable and commonly public" (Ong, 1982, p. 70). The characters must themselves be brave soldiers or beautiful princesses, in other words—personages of "enlarged status and inflated importance," as Havelock describes apropos their presence in Homeric fantasy: "In the context of military confrontation they become generals, commanders of great masses of men; in their civil aspect they become kings and queens and princes and princesses, grandiose versions of members of that public for whose benefit the oral epic is being composed" (p. 97). Think of the *Mahabharata*'s five Pandava brothers, or of Beowulf and his (literally) monstrous nemesis. Everyone must play his or her part—only more so. This is "not for romantic reasons or reflectively didactic reasons but for much more basic reasons: to organize experience in some sort of permanently memorable form" (Ong, 1982, p. 70). Some scholars of course maintain that Homeric epic's ceremonial style has been molded to suit a restricted elite, an aristocratic audience desirous of seeing itself reflected;[13] but as Havelock (1963) stringently declares, it makes more sense to think of the heroic tradition in Homer's poetry "as though it were a technical convenience" (p. 119).

Needless to say, this tendency toward outsize characters is highly palpable in the Bollywood universe. The only difference is that, here, kings and queens are contemporarily inflated into top industrialists and beautiful models, into patriotic soldiers and musical stage stars, with their nemeses transmuted into avaricious business partners or overly Westernized vamps. Even when playing the likes of a protagonist coolie or an ignoble taxi driver (who will *enfin* win a millionaire "princess"), or a brawny hero-gangster (about to avenge his long-suffering mother before acquiescing to the law), such characters are always larger than life, epic in size, if not downright superhuman. For this reason, they often are likened by critics to India's mythological figures, the Ramas and Sitas, the Radhas and Krishnas.[14] Dudrah (2006), for instance, observes how, in song sequences, characters "directly provide a route back to the mythic discourses" and, because of that identification, they themselves become mythic figures (p. 48). But this underplays the extent of their deification, for these characters are also at every turn *the movie stars that they are*. Distinctions between an actor and his or her character are largely collapsed, with stars less playing characters than "sets of expectations, created by the audience" (Mishra, 1992, p. 141). It is no wonder,

---

13. Mishra makes this same claim regarding the *Ramayana* and *Mahabharata*: that both were employed by a ruling class eager to legitimize its own existence. Certainly it could be argued that the Bombay film industry does something similar, that is, it legitimizes itself by re-inscribing *its* values onto those epics (Dissanayake & Sahai, 1992).

14. That oral folk epics in India have been influenced by Sanskritization (i.e., "the desire to achieve a higher status by imitating the Sanskrit epics" [Kothari, paraphrased by Hiltebeitel, 1999, p. 19]) probably shares parallels with the popular Hindi film's patent leanings toward fair-skinned stars and allusively high-caste heroes and heroines.

then, as Dickey (2001) opines, that "[s]tars are the most crucial factor in the financial success of most Indian films, a primacy they have maintained since the 1950s" (p. 220). In effect, when on screen, they are doubly amplified: They play roles that are oversized and they are simultaneously conflated *with* those roles.[15] The degree to which this collapse of star and role can manifest is perhaps best reflected in the career of Amitabh Bachchan, the "Biggest Film Star in the World" (according to the Film Society of Lincoln Center) and *the* celluloid representative of the Indian underclass during the 1970s and 1980s.[16]

Additionally, actors can often be found moving from one film to the next *within* character, that is, reprising their heavy (or flat) role as the good father or the political archenemy, as the devoted servant or the "paragon of maternal affection" (Kakar, 1981, p. 15). In this way, a single player, whether star or sidekick, can replicate a role in literally hundreds of films. In fact, it is not uncommon for the same bevy of leads to appear in a contiguous series of films that narratively have nothing to do with each other. As Shah Rukh Khan once said concerning his frequent avatar-like pairing with actress Kajol, "We've been seen so much that now the director no longer has to work hard to show that we are in love. In *Kabhi Khushi*, we come on screen and we are in love. The audience accepts the pair" (cited in Ganti, 2004, p. 91).[17]

Sometimes the characters move from one film to the next carrying with them totemic objects and props (e.g., a violin for a musically inclined hero, a particular outfit identified with a heroine), as if these are mementoes too cherished to be abandoned. Other times, the characters take their (often generic) names along with them. As Desphande (2005) reveals, major stars of the past half-century, like Raj Kapoor, Dev Anand, Dilip Kumar, and Dharmendra, "all spent a lifetime playing characters who got introduced, a trifle ludicrously, as 'Mr. Amar,' or 'Mr. Anand,' or 'Mr. Raj.' Even Amitabh Bachchan, as the angry young man, was normally just Vijay" (p. 194).[18] Although conventionally identified as the

---

15. This same conflation (and presentation of character as social type) is evident in the film posters that advertise the films (see Dwyer & Patel, 2002).

16. When Bachchan suffered a serious accident while shooting a fight scene for *Coolie* (1983), a freeze frame was included in that fight scene "with an explanatory caption pointing out Bachchan's life-threatening injury" (Banerjea, 2005, p. 169). Certainly, this spotlights the profound blurring that can take place between star and performance.

17. This same propensity for an actor to travel between films archetypally, even stereotypically, can be found in the Turkish popular comedies of Kemal Sunal. Sunal essentially plays a man of the people, retaining that identity from film to film—films that are (by no accident, I think) critically denounced for appealing to "the lowest common denominator of public taste" (Öncü, 2000, pp. 304–306).

18. Desphande (2005) distinguishes these specifications of name from the more recent tendency (in the romance films) to specify heroes as "Malhotra and Khanna . . . Oberoi and Grewal," that is, as Punjabis who are high-caste and moneyed (p. 194).

producers' way of ensuring the films' appeal across India's disparate regions, such bland nonspecificity also certifies the star as an enlarged, collective Everyman. Amitabh Bachchan is *always* going to be Amitabh Bachchan, regardless of his label. It may be that a star's "disappearance" into a singularly unique role is undesirable, possibly even anathema, to the orally inflected percipient. Better is the experience of a recognizable role that gets endlessly *re*-played.

True to the characteristics of orally transmitted narratives, these characters are of a type that "never surprises the reader [or viewer, in our case] but, rather, delights by fulfilling expectations copiously" (Ong, 1982, p. 151). Identities in this epistemic realm *must* be worn on the sleeve. So, although the outsize dimensions of the *masala* film's hero may be "to arouse quick sympathies and antipathies, and thus encourage identification that helps us to savour our fantasies more keenly" (Kakar, 1981, p. 13), they also may necessarily serve a function apropos the organization of knowledge in a highly orally inflected universe.[19]

This requisite fulsomeness of rhetoric and character also helps to explain the more general visual volubility or non-realist excessiveness of the Hindi popular film.[20] Few would deny the contemporary Bombay film's provision of a fantasy world of abundance and sensuous materialism. As Ganti (2004) phrases it, "Popular Indian cinema is very open and comfortable with the artifice that is at the heart of [its] feature filmmaking" (p. 141). Sometimes the 70-mm screen can feel like nothing less than a foyer that leads into gilded domestic interiors, arena-sized offices, trendy nightclubs, not to mention to opulent engagement parties and ostentatious dance recitals. Almost without fail, there will be sports cars to drive vicariously, land deals to make, and some manner of wealth to be

19. In recent years, this surplus in (and of) representation has engendered a series of innovative queer readings of Bollywood. As Dudrah (2006) explains, the films' excess of representation and centrality of caricature make them "a rich cultural resource where meanings of 'queer' and 'camp' can be readily created and contested"; this is because the heteronormative content is itself "queered" by excess, which thus marginalizes "questions of authenticity (of straightness for example), since both queer and straight are equally caricatured" (p. 137). To be sure, there is intentional parodying of gender roles in the films, as well as a fairly regular presence of non-heteronormative persons, such as eunuchs and courtesans, lesbians and gays (even if they are only *visually* coded as such). But it might be worth determining if *orally inflected* queer viewers read the films through the same ideological or queer-signed lens that literate scholars do. (In a similar vein, we need wonder if we have sometimes critically overemphasized the psychoanalytic perspective in our readings of orally inflected popular cinema, such as with respect to issues of muscularity and bodily representation.)

20. In *Mystifying Movies*, Noël Carroll (1988) models what he calls "erotetic" narration, that is, narration that evinces a basic narrative connectiveness or intelligibility (such as one finds in American mass movies). Although Carroll insists that spectatorial engagement is a *pictorially* based phenomenon, I see definite parallels between his erotetic narration and orally inflected narrative—such as that both have a propensity for being "larger than life" (p. 181).

conspicuously savored. Although the climax and resolution of a story may rest ultimately with moral righteousness or filial duty, invariably we will get there through The Moneyed, through The Haves (or Will-Gets).

In his analysis of Hollywood musicals, Richard Dyer (1985) proposes that cinematic utopian abundance speaks to the material and communal scarcity of its audience. This, he surmises, is why entertainment on some level works: "it responds to real needs *created by society*," while at the same time "delimiting what constitutes the legitimate needs of people in this society" (p. 228). For Dyer, financial profit is the entertainment industry's "sole (conscious) aim of providing pleasure" (p. 222). But as Havelock (1987) makes apparent, the relationship between abundance and entertainment extends far beyond a capitalist quest for revenue; for, Homeric epics, too, "glory in conspicuous consumption" (p. 98). True, the major reason for this is because—much as Dyer posits for cinematic utopia—descriptions of excess "reinforce the spell over the memory of the listeners. A culture in reality based on meager economic resources and a simple lifestyle will respond to their fascination with a kind of vicarious greed" (p. 98). But the oral singer's penchant for striking imagery is not due alone to the aesthetic pleasurablity of such images. Such images also serve "as storage and recall devices—the ocular equivalents of verbal formulas" (Havelock, cited in Ong, 1967, p. 25). In other words, a palace belonging to ancient Kaurava royalty (or a sprawling marble mansion inhabited by a contemporary industrialist) is more permanently memorable than, say, a laborer's meager, innocuous hut. But if in the Bollywood scenario a laborer *should* live in a hut (or in the rural outback, or in the slums), that too will be rendered as "a kind of visual commonplace" in order to facilitate audience recall (Ong, 1967, p. 53); as a collectively agreed-on and simplified indicator of what constitutes a "hut" (or "the slums," or the quality of "slum-ness"). If the Bollywood world is "constructed and stylized rather than 'real' and 'authentic,'" as Rachel Dwyer and Divia Patel (2002, p. 52) maintain, it is likely for this reason. Places, much like people, must be familiarly patterned and larger than life—or what literately inflected folk might call *stereotypes*.

The relationship between visual spectacularity and the reinforcement of a spell certainly helps to elucidate the prevalence of *frontality* in the Bollywood film. Art historian Geeta Kapur argues (with respect to Indian popular arts in general) that this style of representation models itself after devotional engagement with a religious icon. A subject on the canvas or screen, in being addressed full-frontally, is privileged as a sign, and effectively becomes *iconicized* (Dwyer & Patel, 2002). Hence, the tendency in this sort of representation toward "flat, diagrammatic and simply profiled figures; a figure-ground pattern with only notational perspective; repetition of motifs in terms of 'ritual play'; and a decorative mis-en-scene" (Kapur, cited in Prasad, 1998a, p. 18). Doubtlessly, there can be an artistic component to this representational style, one that is, refreshingly, not identified or strictly aligned with exclusively Western aesthetic principles. But could this mode of representation also be a further manifestation of the flatness and commonplaces that we have been discussing apropos their integrality to oral epic? Frontality can operate as a style *divorced* from orality, to be sure (see Chapter 3); but in the case of the *masala* film, more likely that style gained prominence for noetic reasons expressly connected to orality.

Vasudevan has addressed frontality's application to Hindi popular cinema directly, shrewdly alerting readers to how it renders cinema "culturally intelligible because it incorporates a familiar visual address" (cited in Prasad, 1998a, p. 20). In this way, he involuntarily tips his hat toward an oral etiology. Given that etiology, we might postulate that the frontal privilege given to the face is no more because the face serves as the nexus of emotional expressions (as exhibited in the eyes, facial muscles, etc.) than because the face is an adjunct to the *mouth*, whose primacy comes from its being the residence of *speech*.

True, in thinking about frontality in Bollywood, one must make space for a production system that capitulates to "an assemblage of prefabricated parts" (Prasad, 1998a, p. 43) and that thereby authorizes stereotypical glosses on character identities, since these are the most convenient means by which to appeal to a pan-Indian audience. But viewers clearly privilege the nonrealism that such settings and flat representations evoke, and this recommends something deeper as an impetus. Besides, this frontality is not exclusively a visual phenomenon. The same notational strain is found in the aural elements of the *masala* species: in the flat nature of the dialogue, for instance—or what Prasad (1998a) calls the films' "*already interpreted* speech, whose meanings are readily visible on the surface" (p. 71). It is present, too, in the films' recurrent aural cues, such as a melancholy leitmotif that signals the imminence of a song, or a high-pitched ricocheting sound effect that emphatically alerts a viewer "this means danger"—or "the hero is caught"—or "he is the villain."

One might even propose that the high circulation *between* films of material clichés is a form or extension of frontality. Here, I refer not only to those clichés that are nationalistically weighty ("the flag, patriotic songs . . . the map of India" [Virdi, 2003, p. 112]), but to others that time, tradition, and filmic recurrence have imbued with equally affective import: the emblematic act of applying a *tikka* (religious mark) to the forehead or *sindoor* (mark of a married woman) to the part in a woman's hair; the plaintive timbre of the *sarangi* (a string instrument); a child offering *namaaz* (Muslim prayers); a wife's foot extending over a husband's doorstep after marriage; a knife drawing blood; a red sports car; a violin; a mandolin; a trumpet. Although I refer to these as "clichés" because of their categorically *pre*known nature, I do not employ the term as a criticism or aesthetic affront. My intention, rather, is to acknowledge that these filmic moments are visual crystallizations of verbal formulary expressions. If there is artistry to them, it lies in how imaginatively they get reshuffled. Literately inflected individuals are sometimes wont to read them as instances of pure fetishization, but excavating their oral origins perhaps warns us to be more ginger in applying psychoanalytic readings to what may be functioning more accurately as "stock visual phrases" that are mutually owned.

But let us return once again to Hindi popular cinema's aversion to silence and stillness. As earlier mentioned, Bollywood is not prone to long, wordless sequences or to lingering, quiescent shots from which one is expected in contemplative solitude to extract meaning. This is a cinema that privileges communication by way of immediate and comparatively exaggerated sensation. It is a medium interested not in interior consciousness but in outward display and external exploits, in tales of action that, much like African oral epics, have "little room for the passive, lifeless, and immobile" (Okpewho, 1979, p. 229). And so, we find legitimate reason for Bollywood cinema's affection for pleonasm, for its exaggerated, theatrical acting style—and, yes, even for the hypertrophied brutality of its kung-fu fistfights.

SO MUCH VIOLENCE! . . .

In the 1980s, Mira Reyn Binford (1988) described the violence in the Hindi commercial films as "cold-blooded, ritualistic, and staged entertainingly" (p. 87). According to several scholars (Banerjea, 2005; Prasad, 1998a), that decade's violence emerged primarily as a response to the sociopolitical climate of the 1970s, which was one of rising unemployment and inflation, and "an overarching sense of government mismanagement" (Banerjea, 2005, p. 167). For this reason, as Prasad (1998a) asserts, "the middle class became amenable to the seductions of a new identity based on disidentification with the 'socialist' programme in the national project" (p. 138). One of the ways they "disidentified" was by retreating from the commercial film industry's theatrical venues. As a consequence, a new breed of protagonists took center stage. These new Bollywood heroes were largely "figures of resistance who appeared to speak for the working classes and other marginalized groups" (p. 138)—and they brought with them an "aesthetic of mobilization," a populist aesthetic grounded in a heightened attraction to violence and a greater representation of criminality (p. 155). Although inarguably these "angry young men" reflected and displaced the disaffection of their underclass audience,[21] could there have been an additional motivation for the films' amplification of violence? After all, in *masala* films well into the new millennium, jaws continue to be kicked in—savagely; blood can still flow— too copiously; and there remains nothing exceptional in seeing a man's bruised, mangled body hurled into a glass pane (a wall-size mirror, a fragile dining table), with the shards driving ever so pointedly (and sound effectively) through his chest. Sometimes even the romance and social films will include an assortment of whippings, beatings, and (although less often these days) half-obscured almost-rapes. The results are very stagy perhaps, and the violence no more a part of the *masala* film than the musical numbers and comedy routines (indeed, sometimes the fights are rendered half-comically); but the violence *is* often irrefutably extreme.

This is certainly the case of *Baazigar*, whose final sequence—a protracted 12-minute showdown—is built out of kicks, punches, stabs, chokes, visible snaps of limbs, two impalings, and the sadistic splendor of five persons meeting up with glass (with the blood running a viscous scarlet throughout). Many of the sequence's shots are distended by slow motion and all are accompanied by sounds (cracks, punches, screams, music), which are acoustically enhanced for maximum effect. And this is *before* the final showdown, during which the film's wounded protagonist, after fending off more thugs, will receive seven more kicks to his torso and some 10 resounding punches to his face; he will be choked once, thrown against a wall twice, brutally impaled—and still he will live long enough to crawl into his mother's lap and die in oratorical splendor.

According to Fareed Kazmi (1999), critics too frequently dismiss the violence in Hindi popular cinema as senseless, when it is in fact "not only integral to, but one of the most important elements in the discourse of conventional films" (p. 80). This is especially the case, he says, when the violence is in its most grisly hand-to-hand forms. Presumably stun guns, iron bars and other such instruments of seemingly misanthropic torture allow viewers "to witness a spectacle, to gloat over and enjoy every second of that spectacle. . . . The fight is structured in such a way that the audience has a ringside view, to witness a spectacle of epic proportions" (p. 80).

But why the need for violence in such epic proportions? Kazmi makes the wholesale claim that such barbarous pageantry "privileges the physical over the mental, brawn over brain, the body over the mind,

---

21. Intriguingly, the "angry young man" subgenre also emerged in Egypt in the 1970s. Operating on the basis of a "quasi-mythical attraction," its socially stereotyped star persona was likewise a "nihilist young urban underdog" (Shafik, 2001, p. 42).

the non-rational over the rational, the primitive over the cultured" (pp. 80–81). In a way, he is right, although I think we can explicate the reasons in a manner slightly more paradigmatic and a little less arbitrary. The key lies in disinterring why *oral epic* incorporates violence in such epic proportions.

One of the characteristics that distinguishes the bardic form from other "literatures" is its enthusiastic and (frequently overly) spirited portrayal of physical violence. As Isidore Okpewho (1979) candidly describes with respect to African oral epics, "From dark humor to tragicomedy it is only a short step to full-scale horror, and in a song of terror the bard does not hesitate to make the most of that element without the least intent to amuse anyone" (p. 208). Compare, for instance, the aforementioned description of *Baazigar's* ending with this ripe and gruesome excerpt from the *Iliad*:

> Idomeneus stabbed Erymas in the mouth with the pitiless bronze, so that the brazen spearhead smashed its way clean through below the brain in an upward stroke, the white bones splintered, and the teeth were shaken out with the stroke and both eyes filled up with blood, and gaping he blew a spray of blood through the nostril and through his mouth, and death in a dark mist closed in about him. (Book XVI: lines 345–350, cited in Okpewho, 1979, p. 209)

Or consider the following excerpt from the *Odyssey*:

> [The nurse] found Odysseus in the thick of slaughtered corpses, splattered with bloody filth like a lion that's devoured some ox of the field and lopes home, covered with blood, his chest streaked, both jaws glistening, dripping red—a sight to strike terror. So Odysseus looked now, splattered with gore, his thighs, his fighting hands, and she, when she saw the corpses, all the pooling blood, was about to lift a cry of triumph—here was a great exploit. (Book XXII: lines 426–433)

And one last excerpt, this one from the *Mahabharata*:

> Drawing his keen-edged sword, and trembling with rage, [Bhima] placed his foot upon the throat of Dushasana and, ripping open the breast of his enemy, drank his warm lifeblood little by little. Then, looking at him with wrathful eyes, he said, "I consider the taste of this blood superior to that of my mother's milk." (Book LXVIII, cited in C. Narasimhan, 1965, p. 163)

Clearly one can see, based on this exaltation of the physical, that an oral culture's inclination toward the agonistic is not restricted to verbal performance alone.

To be sure, an oral art form's overamplification of violence may reflect the physical hardships and struggles endured by its society. However, as Ong (1982) vigorously maintains, the amplification also exists because writing *does not*; that is, without writing, there is nothing to foster abstraction, nothing to "disengage knowledge from the arena where human beings struggle with one another" (p. 44). If orality must keep knowledge grounded in the extant human world, then it is best, even essential, to situate that knowledge within the context of a *struggle*: "When all verbal communication must be by direct word of mouth, involved in the give-and-take dynamics of sound, interpersonal relations are kept high—both attractions and, even more, antagonisms" (pp. 44–45). As a result, name-calling, tongue-lashings, and descriptions of physical violence—all of which permeate oral discourse—are taken to the agonistic extreme, sometimes stylized, even celebrated. The fact that *masala* films with higher levels of combative display find greater popularity with audiences comprising India's interior (i.e., its rural areas and uneducated provinces) may have its roots in this aspect of orality.

But there is more. For, in India's conventional cinema, we find such agonistic traits additionally converted into a *technical* kind of violence. That is, Bollywood has found a way through its camerawork and editing to *visualize* verbomotor speech: through fast motion sequences and amplified camera movement, such as in a heavy (but never ironic) use of multiple zooms-in on a heroine's horrified look, or the rapid encircling of a leading man in trouble. Although painfully overwrought perhaps to literately inflected individuals (which is not to say those individuals can't electively enjoy the films), emphatic cinematography of this kind provides cues that are easy to read. One might even argue that they are modern-day extensions of the oral epic's reliance on clichés.

But there is an important antipode to this enthusiasm for exoterically heightening interpersonal relations. Despite that the oral world wields a stun gun in one hand, with its other hand it comes bearing "fulsome praise" (Ong, 1982, p. 45), a veritable glorification of socially prescribed good relations. Certainly this applies to *masala* films, in which praise-poems exalting long-suffering mothers, honorable fathers, love interests, devoted sisters-in-law, and bosom buddies are regularly declaimed or sung. Such effusive paeans are easily and unself-consciously stitched into tales that may elsewhere resemble a *Rambo* flick. In *Sholay*, for instance, two fugitives from justice head down a rural road on motorcycle, boisterously declaring in song, "This friendship will never be destroyed/We'd sooner die than let that occur"; and in *Khal Nayak*, a saintly mother, who is devoted to her neglectful terrorist son, is lugubriously eulogized by a third party in song:

> *Oh, Maa, tujhe salaam/Oh, Maa, tujhe salaam*
> *Apne bacche tujhko pyaaray*
> *Ravan ho ya Ram/Ravan ho ya Ram*
> Oh, Mother, I salute you/Oh, Mother, I salute you

Your children, they are dear to you
Whether they are villain or hero / Whether villain or hero[22]

Much like their antagonistic counterparts, these attractions are converted
into a more amplified "struggle" in the films, sculpted into agonistic displays that are righteous, or magnanimous, or altogether maudlin—and
always, once more, completely sans irony. It would not be remarkable,
for instance, to see that same beefy underworld son being fed by his
mother or weeping copiously in her embrace, or to participate in some
very charged rituals of male bonding, or to witness a hero defer to his el-
ders with a kind of grandstanding noblesse oblige. In fact, in *Khal Nayak*,
the villain's "Ma," who is cast as the receptacle of all goodness and the
mute bearer of all ills, is exalted not only within that sentimental song,
but also verbally by her son as he takes part in a hyperbolic fistfight.
Could this be because, for the individual who is faced psychologically
outward, both tributes *and* hostilities must also be directed outward—
"and chiefly to what [that individual] is most intimately aware of in that
aurally or vocally conceived world, that is, to his fellow man" (Ong,
1967, p. 134)? Thus, one also finds verbomotor speech technically augmented into ripe, glorifying musical motifs, and "attractionist" camerawork such as the protracted slow-motion shot of a romantic hero removing his racing helmets and shaking off the sweat. Homages like these
may strike literate minds as "insincere, flatulent, and comically pretentious," but in oral cultures such praise "goes with the highly polarized,
agonistic, oral world of good and evil, virtue and vice, villains and heroes" (Ong, 1982, p. 45). No wonder, then, that in the Bollywood universe, that which is deemed honorable, pure, noble, or chaste must be as
gloriously overstated in terms of its ethical and spiritual allure as evil
must be in its repellence.

Such kinetic amplification-cum-polarization unavoidably breeds another of Hindi popular cinema's enduring characteristics: melodrama. In
some respects, melodrama is the *sine qua non* of the *masala* movie. As
Anjum Rajabali, a Bollywood screenwriter, explains with respect to how
Hollywood films differ from Hindi films:

When you Indianise a subject, you [need to] add emotions. Lots of
them. Feelings like love, hate, sacrifice, of revenge, pangs of separation.
. . . Our mythology, our poetry, our literature is full of situations where
lovers pine for each other. Take the *Mahabharat* and you'll see what I
mean. (cited in Ganti, 2004, p. 183)[23]

---

22. Song is of course an intriguing aspect of the oral that unfortunately goes unad-
dressed in this study. My hope is that scholars who specialize in Hindi film music will take
up this thread.

23. This is no less the case with early Hollywood film (see Gunning, 1986; Singer,

And so, when in *Dilwale Dulhania Le Jayenge* (*The Brave-hearted Will Take the Bride*, 1995), the heroine's father discovers that his daughter is eloping with her suitor, Raj, the father "slaps Raj, not once but eight times" (Chopra, 2002, p. 82). Or consider *Baazigar*, where the protagonist prepares for death by dragging himself into his mother's lap, imploring her, "Envelop me in your arms. I've been yearning for your love since childhood." By the time he draws his last breath several anguished minutes later (declaring "Now I can sleep peacefully"), he will have intoned the word "Ma" 22 times. Such emotional exchanges are ripe, to say the least, but when one takes an oral economy into account, one sees that this flatulence may extend from an epistemic requirement. Characters need to project (and to be projected) in comparatively black-and-white—and, by turn, good-and-evil—ways. We might even say that orality breeds an *antipsychological* aspect to narrative presentation, at least in the modern sense of that word. But, again, there is an oral rationale for such an iconographic Manichean projection—one that persuasively underscores why melodrama has been the "characteristic form of narrative and dramaturgy in societies undergoing the transition to modernity" (Dissanayake, cited in Vasudevan, 1995, p. 308). This is not to say melodramatic display is restricted to the oral domain (see Brooks, 1985); but more often than not, at least in the case of Hindi popular film, it performatively operates in—and *as*—a language that is governed by oral principles.[24] Hence, when Rosie Thomas (1995) comments that in "reading broadly across the body of Hindi cinema, two archetypal figures emerge: the Mother and the Villain," and that "in them the opposing values of good and evil are most centrally condensed" (p. 166), orality likely bears some responsibility for this. But, as next we shall see, such archetypes do not only polarize good and evil. Much as Albert Lord discovered in his 1950s study of oral performances by Slavic bards, they also function as

---

2001). In fact, a 1919 issue of *Photoplay* likened the early sensationalist films to modern dime novels because of the forms' mutual antipsychological aspect. The film serials, like the novels, emphasized not only high melodrama, but also "violent action, highly formulaic and disjointed narratives [and] lack of psychological depth" (Singer, 2001, p. 13). Ben Singer attributes that broad-based phenomenon of sensationalism to the new proletariat viewers' "predispos[ition] toward startling and violent spectacle" (p. 96). Perhaps the films' "hyperstimulus" was born more of the medium's reliance on orally inflected attributes. Such attributes would have both transcended linguistic discrepancies and cultural differences between migrant viewing populations and demanded much less spectatorial foreknowledge in order for the stories to be understood. This film/dime novel correlation intriguingly points to the fact that *written narrative*, despite requiring a capacity for alphabetic literacy, can still manifest a notable connection to, or contouring by, orality.

24. The same might be said for melodrama's mechanisms and functioning in Mexican *telenovelas*, which are, as Ana M. Lopez (1995) observes, "notorious for their weepiness, extraordinarily Manichean vision of the world, and lack of specific historical referents," as well as for their display of an excessive baroqueness of mise-en-scène (pp. 261–262).

part of the flotilla of themes and formulae out of which all stories are variously constructed (Ong, 1982).

. . . AND STILL "THE SAME OLD SONG"

One of the most frequent and vocal laments of Bollywood film critics during the 1980s and 1990s was that the industry was vulgarly wed to worn storytelling—was aesthetically crippled, in fact, by a proclivity for recycling stories and themes that displayed only the most superficial gloss of innovation. In the words of noncommercial film director Mani Kaul, "The commercial cinema peddle[d] a set of myths, but the myths [didn't] change; they [were] endlessly repeated" (*India International*, 1981, p. 163). Fairly safely we can construe from Kaul's statement that the average spectator already possessed familiarity with whatever story was about to unfold on a screen. In fact, according to Nandy (1981), the Indian spectator was *expected* to know a movie's key elements "by heart and to experience in the films a feeling of *déjà vu*" (p. 90):

> If the storyline chooses to depict the hero as an apparent mixture of good and evil he must eventually be shown to be essentially good, whose badness is thereby reduced to the status of a temporary aberration. If the hero is a dacoit, the heroine must find in him a heart of gold and the story line ultimately should reveal that he was forced into robbery by the "ideal," wholly bad, evil-doers who finally are defeated by the hero when he rediscovers his true self. (pp. 89–90)

This is not only the case with moral transformations, but with the key themes and situations that virtually every *masala* film from the period tackles. For instance, one can fairly safely predict A Romance (a young couple meeting and falling in love); A Romantic Crisis (spurred by a villain, or the unwanted interest of another, or the disapproval of parental figures). There will be The Pleasures of Modernity (nightclubs, girls, whiskey, freedom), which will be followed by The Perils of Modernity (nightclubs, girls, whiskey, freedom); and some Colorful Ceremony or Celebration (marriage, engagement, festive holiday). A Sacro-Symbolic Traditional Act (such as the honorable donning of one's "fighting" turban) will lead to The Victims Avenged (typically through the villain's annihilation). On the heels of this will come The Sacrifice (wherein achievement of personal good by the hero will be eschewed for the good of the group), and the resulting All's Well Because It Ends Well (which is to say traditionally *right*) Denouement.

Instinctively one's impulse may be to blame producers who, in their attempts to capitalize on past hits, *still* simply rejuggle successful elements and plot lines. But audience responses recommend that the incentive for repetition lies somewhere deeper. Remember, after all, that more often than not in Hindi popular cinema, "experiments are not tolerated [by audiences] and are punished by non-attendance with all its financial consequences" (Lutze, 1985, p. 13). Scholarly speculations as to why these elements have jelled into ritual, if not rule, have ranged from the perceived need of viewers to see the traditional self perennially safeguarded against the alien (and alienating) imposition of modernization, to the more opaque contention that an aesthetic imperative that *forces* a conscious rendering of the world into simple, coherent, and mythical patterns has crystallized (Nandy, 1981; Thomas, cited in Gokulsing & Dissanayake, 1998; Valicha, 1988). When examined in light of orality, however, what additionally surfaces is that such endless retellings may be satisfying an exigent and bona fide noetic *need* on the part of oral populations.

As I have already suggested, conceptualized knowledge that is not continuously repeated aloud in oral societies invariably vanishes. As a result, oral societies must "invest great energy in saying over and over again what has been learned arduously over the ages" (Ong, 1982, p. 41). The upshot of this is that any kind of thought experimentation is necessarily inhibited. Because of the pragmatic need to repeat and "store" the past, the mind must focus on keeping what is already there *there still*. Understandably this forces a disposition toward a conservative mindset. Rather than promoting speculation or originality, the mind seeks instead to accommodate the novel by reshuffling the old and already existent. Originality consists here not in introducing entirely new materials, "but in fitting the traditional materials effectively into each individual, unique situation and/or audience" (p. 60). Any events or tensions that are generated by the contemporary political or social scene, as Alf Hiltebeitel (1999) adduces, must be "creatively grafted onto the core of the oral epic's older themes and formulae" (p. 26). In this way, the unique is seldom touted for its uniqueness, but instead is "presented as fitting the traditions of the ancestors" (Ong, 1982, p. 42).

Perhaps, then, it is not solely a culturally or aesthetically driven sensibility that craves Nandy's *déjà vu* or Kaul's endlessly repeated myths. Rather, these are the natural fruits of a conformist mentality, which is itself the direct consequence of an oral economy. And Bollywood producers, in their allegiance to profit and high ticket sales, serve as unwitting accomplices to that economy. One might even say that, although his motives lie elsewhere, the film producer is not entirely unlike the epic singer, for the producer too "works unavoidably with a deep sense of tradition, which preserves the essential meaning of stories"; and the producer too "possesses an armory consisting of formulas or metrically malleable phrases (together with near-formulas or 'formulaic' expressions), and of themes or situations. . . . Formula and theme are the stuff which [he] rhapsodizes or 'stitches' into his oral epic fabric, never worded exactly the same on any two occasions" (Ong, 1965, p. 149). In this sense, there may be an overriding cognitive reason for the *masala* film's *non*particularist vision, which Prasad (1998a) attributes chiefly to the industry's "heterogeneous form of serial manufacture" (p. 32).

Even *Dilwale Dulhania*—a 1995 film whose portrayal of nonresident Indians (NRIs) is said to have stirred the Indian overseas population from its spectatorial slumber—followed this basically oral model. In the words of Anupama Chopra (2002), the film opted against new characters in favor of "tweak[ing] every stereotype": "From clichés, Aditya [the director] refashioned a contemporary blockbuster. He told a story that had been told many times before, but made it new" (p. 58). Perhaps the best testament to this mode of reshuffling old materials can be found on *Dil*'s (*Heart*, 1990) imdb.com web page. As one user-critic commented there, *Dil* was to be congratulated for being "A cliché beautifully done."

Could it be that the corpus of hit *masala* films between 1950 and 2000 was, at heart, a handful of tales undergoing endless revision? The tales were perpetually updated and refined, of course, in order to accommodate the latest innovations (fashions, technologies, social codes), or to reflect prevailing subjugations (political, economic, even familial); but they were also necessarily stitched (or spliced, in their case) into a work of preservation. Each film reflected its times, but it did so from within the confines of all "out of which all stories are variously built" (Ong, 1982, p. 60).

And so, the *masala* films from this period have no recourse but to exist in a kind of ahistorical limbo, given that the present must be integrated into—or, rather, compressed—with the Great Past (as distinct from the Little Pasts of cinematic flashbacks). This is a facet of storytelling that some analysts have interpreted as reflecting a particularly Hindu notion of reincarnation. In light of the constraints put on the oral mindset, however, it seems more likely that it reflects a synthesizing of history or ages (or of generations, if you will) into a single tale. For, unlike chirographic cultures, which think of the past in historical terms—as "an itemized terrain, peppered with verifiable and disputed 'facts' or bits of information"—for oral cultures the past is "the domain of the ancestors, a resonant source for renewing awareness of present existence, which itself is not an itemized terrain either" (Ong, 1982, p. 98).

The synchronic nature of *masala* film storytelling has certainly been detected by scholars. Nandy (1981) uses the twin term *antihistorical* to describe the Bombay film, although without being cognizant of that trait's fundamental relationship to orally based narrative. He does adroitly observe, however, that in these movies there is "an ineluctable continuity between the past, the present and the future and each of these temporalities gets telescoped into the other" (p. 91).[25] Why this is the case is perhaps best articulated by Oswald Spengler, who notes that *writing* is what liberates man's consciousness from "the tyranny of the present" (cited in Goody & Watt, 1968, p. 53). Without writing, time must perforce be telescoped, for that is the only means by which to carry the past into the future. The oral Tiv of Nigeria, for instance, were found in the 1960s to be quite comfortable "adjusting their past geneological records for the sake of regulating the changed social relations of their contemporary world" (Goody & Watt, 1968, pp. 33–34); and in ancient Greek poetry, contemporary decisions are traditionally "framed as though they [are] also the acts and words of the ancestors," in order to mitigate the strain on memory (Havelock, 1963, p. 121). Could this explain why, in *Khal Nayak*, the cosmopolitan pursuit of a terrorist (via cell phones, helicopters, and fast cars) ends with a simple, coherent return to the mythic patterns of human relations, especially as expressed through visual allusions to the epic *Ramayana*?[26] Similarly, in the final scenes of *Baazigar*, the contemporary city setting metamorphoses (some might say regresses) into ancient ruins where deep-rooted principles regarding family obligation and honor are played out.

To be sure, this emphasizes a point raised earlier regarding flashbacks and how they operate analogically as a visual representation of memory. As Desphande (2005) remarks, in the "angry young man" films of the 1970s, it is always memory which drives the

> hero to aggrandizement, revenge, vigilantism, crime, murder, or all of these. . . . If one were to ask what makes the angry young man angry, the answer will surely be memory: the memory of [Bachchan's] parents' murder in *Zanjeer* [*The Chain*, 1973]; of his being an illegitimate child in *Trishul* [*Trident*, 1978] and *Lawaaris* [*Orphan*, 1981]; of his childhood sweetheart in *Muqaddar ka Sikandar* [*The Emperor of Fate*, 1978]; of

---

25. Vivian Sobchack (1995) draws similar attention to the lack of any real historical interpretation in Hollywood historical epics like *The Ten Commandments* and *Cleopatra*. Such films, which she describes as "wantonly expansive, hyperbolic, even hysterical," favor instead "a fantasy of History" (pp. 281–284). She suspects this is the result of a particular temporal consciousness on the part of spectators, one that is phenomenologically shaped by the American citizenry's historical lack of founding myths. Nevertheless, Sobchack seems almost to be discussing oral pragmatics when she theorizes that, in popular consciousness, history emerges from a peculiar "*transcendence of accuracy and specificity*"; and instead of going for mimetic precision, stars generalize "historical specificity through their own *iconographic* presence. Stars are cast not as characters but *in* character—as 'types' . . . who signify universal and general characteristics" (p. 294).

26. According to Vinay Lal (1998), Manmohan Desai, who directed hit films like *Amar Akbar Anthony* (*Amar, Akbar, and Anthony*, 1977) and *Coolie*, claimed that "all his films were inspired by the *Mahabharata*, and on occasion everything in the Hindi film, from the archetypal figure of the mother to the anti-heroic hero, appears to belong to the deep recesses of the Indian past" (p. 232).

his own betrayal under trying circumstances in *Kaala Patthar* [*Black Rock*, 1979] and, most famously, of his being [literally] branded a thief's son in *Deewar*. (pp. 201–202)

Perhaps the flashbacks serve, then, not only as oral structuring devices, but as existential repositories for the past—that is, as vessels for visualizing the past for the present, which in a sense is what will carry the past into the future.

Bollywood's continuous self-referentiality buttresses this claim of temporal conflation and preservation. There are, after all, omnipresent allusions in Bollywood films to pre-existing films: borrowings, memorializings, outright filchings of lines of dialogue, of tunes and songs, of scenes, themes, iconic props, physical gestures, whole characters, sometimes entire narrative threads. Whatever is worth keeping from the past (because it is charming or puissant or comically irresistible) is, one might argue, continuously being re-incorporated into the present. With no place outside the mind to store knowledge, that knowledge must live in *this* moment in order to persist and maintain any relevancy.

To be sure, the reappearance in the *masala* film of familiar faces, jokes, and snippets of dialogue creates a powerful sense of the familiar, of a personal experience revisited, of intimacy even. This is a characteristic scholars have noted, as well, of the oral epic—that is, that repetition, regardless of the religious or recreational context in which it may have arisen, is "first and foremost a token of the joy of recollection" (Okpewho, 1979, p. 154). In fact, so fundamental is this joy of recollection to Bollywood that characters *within* the films typically know the movies: they quote them; they discuss them; the films are in effect part of *their* popular culture. In *Hum Aapke*, for example, when an extended family gathers postprandially to play a game (a sort of cross between "Dare" and musical chairs), one father poignantly sings a song from *Bobby* (1973), and another re-enacts Dharmendra's famous drinking scene from *Sholay*. *Hum Aapke* itself has been referenced, used, and abused in at least a dozen movies since its release, by way of reprised melodies, quoted lines, borrowed costumes, embezzled props heavy with sentimental weight, and even one farcical send up of a musical number.

All of this poses an interesting dilemma with respect to plagiarism. After all, don't such commemorative moments creatively, even criminally, tromp on proprietary rights? Again we might turn to Nandy (1981), who insists:

> the issue of plagiarism in such films has been wrongly posed. The story-writer and director of the Bombay film are not brazen thieves who do not care what others think of their theft or who foolishly hope to escape detection. They operate within a consensual system which rejects the idea that the elements of a story are a form of personal property or individual creation. (p. 91)

Most striking about this observation is the manner in which it reflects extant scholarship on orality. Havelock (1963) has shown that knowledge in the Homeric encyclopedia is inherently nonproprietary: One quotes in order to *keep*, not in order to maintain exactness; and one keeps quoting—restating, rehandling—but not for reasons of lack of skill. Only with typography and the fixity of print is the word turned into a commodity (Ong, 1982). In oral cultures, conversely, the shared nature of knowledge, the need for information to be constantly heard and publicly revised in order to survive, means that there can be no "romantic notions of 'originality' and 'creativity', which set apart an individual work from other works" (p. 133). A work is worthy in this scenario not because it is singular and original, but because it is *shared* and wholly *connected* to outside influences. Artistry and inventiveness arise in this circumstance from successfully manipulating *public* stories, themes, and patterns in new and innovative ways.[27]

THE COGNITIVE TIES THAT BIND

As noted earlier, the outcomes in 1950s–1990s Bombay formula films virtually are always the same: The bad guy will be duly (often gruesomely) exterminated; the good guy will come through with flying colors; and everybody on the side of the morally correct will somehow benefit, whether by obtaining a hand in marriage, a general beatific happiness, or wealth and honor. Those who follow the virtuous path (i.e., dharmic duty, sacrifice, protection of one's kin) are always rewarded, whereas those who do not (i.e., men who spurn the bonds of blood and, by extension, of nationalism) succumb to bad things. No film, in other words, ends with a character (or its audience) loitering in moral ambiguity or an ethical quandary. In the Bolly-world, there is no such thing as a residual moral dilemma, let alone an impasse. Spectators depart from

---

27. In no way is this to pardon Bollywood producers and screenwriters who readily and steadily rip off entire storylines from their own historical corpus, as well as from outside India (e.g., Hollywood, Hong Kong), often keeping the originals sizably intact (see Nayar, 1997, 2003). Obviously industry members feel relatively safe from the legal repercussions regarding property rights; but to suggest that this kind of plagiarism is born of some residually oral disposition would be a tremendous stretch. On the other hand, there does seem to be a more oral dimension to script-related preproduction practices in Bollywood. Producers regularly hold script "narration" sessions, during which crew and key cast are recounted orally the script. Although these sessions may have more "to do with the fact that the script is often incomplete prior to casting," they can take anywhere from 30 minutes to several hours to perform; indeed, "narrating a film is in itself considered a skill and certain directors and writers are renowned in the industry for their narrating prowess" (Ganti, 2004, pp. 68–69). One cannot help wonder if this speaks to a kind of approbation in the industry concerning the powers, and perhaps even, unwittingly, the structural modus operandi of oral storytelling.

the theater safe within the confines of a dependable utopian moral universe.

Many have theorized as to why this is: Dickey (1995), in her analysis of Tamil films, concludes that happy endings of this type are intended to "allay the anxieties of the poor viewers by implying that the problems and contradictions of their lives can be resolved without effort" (p. 136). Rajadhyaksha (1987) ties post-Independence cinema's resolution-ary nature to the establishment of the modern state, wherein films become "an escape route for the people's miserable existence while at the same time preventing them from taking a more radical view of their plight" (p. 56). To Vasudevan (1991), the entertainment industry provides a "systematic outlet, both from the rigours of the working day and of domestic life"; but in order to do so effectively, the industry also tenders a "return to the orbit of the normative and morally acceptable, and an annulment of the excesses which have been released in the narrative" (pp. 182–183). In other words, to Vasudevan, the moral reintegration process at the conclusion of a film exists precisely because it *permits* all the previous temporary excesses and transgressions of the moral world.

Psychoanalyst Sudhir Kakar (1981) posits that Bollywood movies function as "contemporary myths which, through the vehicle of fantasy and the process of identification, temporarily heal for the audience the principal stresses arising out of Indian family relationships" (p. 20). They are like children's fairy tales, he says, which exist to remind viewers that struggle and adversity are inevitable:

> but if one faces life's hardships and its many, often unjust, impositions with courage and steadfastness, one will eventually emerge victorious. At the conclusion of both films and fairy tales, parents are generally happy and proud, the princess is won, and the villains are either ruefully contrite or their battered bodies satisfactorily litter the landscape. (p. 13)[28]

---

28. Similar claims have been leveled at Italian *peplums*, the sword-and-sandal films popular during the first half of the 20th century. Those mythical-historical spectacles, according to Michèle Lagny (1992), "catered to uneducated audiences" and possessed a fairy tale structure; a straightforward oppositional nature (viz., good vs. bad); "violently contrasting images" (viz., black vs. white); a slapdash inauthenticity; and a general simplicity of theme. As well—and by now the orally inflected nature of the genre should be well apparent—the films displayed a shoot-from-the-hip didacticism; occasional repetition to assist viewers in getting their bearings; a love of violence; a kinetic privileging; an archaeological and chronological implausibility aided by *"mise-en-spectacle,"* which highlighted in exaggerated proportions an episodic convoy of wrestling, singing, and dancing (pp. 163–170). Also worthy of note are the *terza visione* or third-run spaghetti westerns of the period, which presumably inherited "the comic-book functions" of earlier westerns (Wagstaff, 1992, p. 259). Critics have vilified these films for their cultural baseness and impoverished production values, leading Christopher Wagstaff to assert that the critics' own cultural val-

But could this need for a victorious emergence have some other epistemically motivated justification? Perhaps there exists a conjoint explanation tied less explicitly to Freud or Marx—one capable even of subsuming in some measure these two other interpretations. Once again, let us inspect the *masala* film through the prism of orality.

If we return to the notion that, to oral peoples, a worthy work is one that is shared and outwardly oriented, then it follows that the experiential process of hearing (or viewing) a narrative is a *collectively* experienced act. That is to say, it is an event that occurs *with* others—even if only in spirit alone. This is because the "individual's reaction is not expressed as simply individual or 'subjective' but rather as encased in the communal reaction, the communal 'soul'" (Ong, 1982, p. 46). (One might even assert that the agonistic diplays of spectators who fill the Indian theaters' cheaper stalls reflect the inherent communal-ness of the film-going activity.)

But this communal soul is not simply a product of wish fulfillment. It is born of noetic necessity. This is because, in oral societies, judgment bears on the individual from the outside, not from within; as a result, evaluation of the self is "modulated into group evaluation ('we') and then handled in terms of expected reactions from others" (Ong, 1982, p. 55). What this ineluctably fosters are "personality structures that in certain ways are more communal and externalized, and less introspective than those among literates. Oral communication unites people in groups" (p. 69).

Certainly this helps illumine the highly intergenerational nature of Bollywood stories, which typically hinge on the struggles of sons at variance with fathers or in conflict with mothers, or (although less so) of parents at odds with defiant daughters. Such relationships may indeed function, as critics avow, as a metaphor for the individual's relationship to the state, or as a very real representation of an axis of anxiety regarding transfers of power (Virdi, 2003). But in taking into account the exigencies of oral transmission, we find a concomitant reason for the pervasiveness of this story component—not to mention, for why it plays out in such an oratorically dilated and didactic way (i.e., with the younger generation exhibiting an initial rebellion, and the older generation succeeding in due course at reinforcing traditional virtue and morals). Such a modus operandi is in effect a vigorous participation in, and manifestation of, the *dialectical method*, which is "an essential social process in which the initiates pass on their knowledge directly to the young" (Goody & Watt, 1968, p. 50). Not to link that outward-bound generation

---

ues have prevented them from adequately explaining the *terza visione* formula (p. 259). Fortunately, Mikel J. Koven (2006), in his work on Italian *giallo* (pulp) movies and the saliency of orality to their "vernacular," is already attempting to redress this gap.

materially with the incoming generation would beget a story with a distressing *lack* of story, in the sense that there would be no *self* being transmitted meaningfully into the future. For, the self in these circumstances is not the single individual alone; the individual functions, rather, as an express contact with (and carrier of) "the group's patterns of thought, feeling and action" (p. 59). It would be quite correct, accordingly, to theorize that individuals under these conditions have *less* free play; they are bound to a community in a face-to-face and integrally intergenerational manner, and consequently their only option "is between the cultural tradition—or solitude" (p. 59).

Thus the *masala* film, not unlike oral minstrelsy, addresses itself to a "group-sense of history. . . . [T]he future is added as a further extension of the present, not to prophesy change but to affirm continuity" (Havelock, 1963, p. 105). Of course, literately inflected individuals may be more inclined to interpret such a depiction of group relations as a kind of fetishization; or, alternatively, given their remove from the psychic need for a setting that preserves group identity, they may view the relations as a "symptom of romantic nostalgia" (p. 118). In fact, nostalgia is often the explanatory direction that film critics take in trying to unpack Hindi popular film's fondness for foregrounding group celebrations, whether these be domestic ceremonies, lively festivals, or religious rites. After all, virtually no Bollywood film comes without an extensive "picturizing" of lavish weddings or springtime *holi* celebrations, of engagement parties and birthday parties. Nor are the films bereft of more solemn rituals and social events, such as an involuntary participation in nuptials, or solemn lighting of a funeral pyre, or a visit to a temple (or mosque, gurdwara, or church). Although these settings definitely serve as convenient milieus for the elicitation of pathos, and also for songs (and sometimes tacit ideological agendas), they also importantly reinforce the arena of preservation. They root traditions compactly in the present—which is, once more, in the oral conception of things, the only way for traditions to endure. What better to underpin and act as an amalgamator for community? Participating in ceremonies and rituals are an express *doing* of culture, which is essential in a world where knowledge cannot survive outside the voice. In this way, the lives (and deaths) of characters in the *masala* film play out in ways not unlike those of their counterparts in oral epic, who are likewise "linked in endless series by formal and ceremonious marriages and equally ceremonious funerals in which the obsequies to the dead repeat and re-enforce the tribal imperatives which the survivors must preserve" (Havelock, 1963, p. 172).

Perhaps it comes as no surprise, then, that one of the fundamental characteristics of oral narrative is its ultimate dedication to the preservation of the ordered society, which is adjudged "the highest good and the goal toward which the hero's physical and intellectual development is bent" (Scholes & Kellogg, 1966, p. 36). Oral epic is inclined as matter of course toward *the protection and conservation of the existing social structure*—as so, too, is Bollywood. Thus, we find Nargis, in *Mother India*, shooting her wayward son rather than allowing him to run roughshod over the ethics of their community. In *Sholay*, it is Gabbar Singh who is extinguished, with the village returned to the good management of the police chief. And in *Hum Aapke*, where no villains exist, two families—once united by a marriage that has since terminated due to a death—are bound together once more by another marriage within the same family. All ends happily because, in effect, all ends *just as it started*.[29]

True, sometimes in the *masala* films it is the *protagonist* who is the unrepentant transgressor, a vigilante-hero who wreaks remorseless havoc on the social order. In such cases, he too—he *especially*—must conform to the social order or face expulsion, occasionally in the form of death. Hence, in *Deewar*, Vijay, given his criminal antics, has no recourse but to "d[ie] in his mother's arms"; indeed, this is as close as he can get "to some form of reconciliation with legitimate citizenship" (Banerjea, 2005, p. 175). An alternative scenario in the movies, as Virdi (2003) explains, is for an "essentially good son to turn bad by succumbing to the underworld, only to return to the point of origin, suitably chastened" (p. 38). Do your social dharma, in other words, and you can return to the fold. But this should not be mistaken as a materialization of an expressly Eastern religious philosophy or Hindu worldview. The tales of *griots*, or traditional African raconteurs, are just as "concerned with disorder and the restoration of traditional order," with the storytellers necessarily advocating a return to the old order at the end (Diawara, 1989, p. 201). In fact, in Kuranko oral narrative from Sierra Leone, ambiguous situations are capable of being brought up within the confines of the narrative precisely because they will be safely resolved within the acceptable norms of the community (Jackson, cited in Larkin, 1997b).

Such a "reconstitution into a communal subjectivity may come across as paradoxical to Western film scholars and audiences," acknowledge Tomaselli, Shepperson, and Eke (1995, p. 26). But, as the authors stress in an illuminating essay on how Western, and especially psychoanalytic, film theory has failed to understand African art film and its representations of cultures heavily inflected ontologically by orality, this kind of reconstitution is hardly puzzling to the audiences of developing nations. Such audiences "find their identities within communal rela-

---

29. According to Patricia Uberoi (2001), *Hum Aapke* surrenders to a fetishized capitalistic cosmopolitanism and, as a result, "the old antinomies of south Asian melodrama" (such as of good vs. bad, poor vs. rich, East vs. West) no longer hold (p. 333). Nonetheless, when considered in light of the reticulate norms of oral storytelling, the film still displays a profound relationship to the "old," via its melodramatic form, plenitude, and exoteric antipsychological stance.

tions. As forms of life, deliberately expressed in the plural, oral traditions rely on the contact between generations for the elaboration of individual subjectivities" (p. 26).

Resolution in the orally inflected narrative is thus truly a resolving, a
kind of social *suturing*—to appropriate (for very different purposes) the
Lacanian term. Because face-to-face interaction between peoples is the
prerequisite of communication in oral societies, because discourse is incapable of being detached from its speakers and held outside the mind,
what results is a *mentalité* that privileges integration and reform and that
is less inclined toward resistance and rebellion.[30] (In fact, according to
Marshall McLuhan [1962], only with literacy and print do we historically get "the eager assertion of individual rights," p. 220.) Dickey (1995)
indirectly validates the connection between orality and conformity
when she addresses how the poor, urban Tamilian cinemagoers whom
she interviewed never suggested that the class system itself was im-
moral or ought to be eradicated. Instead, they hoped only "to improve
their position within the hierarchy, or to eradicate negative stereotypes
of the poor" (p. 144).

Conceivably, for similar reasons, we find a collectively agreed-on pa-
pering over in the Hindi popular film of caste, regional, and religious tensions, and a persistent concatenation of feudalism and capitalism. For
without these, we might not be able to return to that "orbit of the normative and morally acceptable" that Vasudevan (1991) describes, or to "the
achievement of something like a joint family" (p. 183), as he elsewhere remarks in an inadvertent echo of Scholes and Kellogg. In societies devoid
of writing and hence of documents, what kinsmen are and how they
should behave must be tirelessly drilled into the successive generations,
for that is where "the content of the educational apparatus of the group is
to be found"—namely, in the "living memories of successive living people who are young and then old and then die" (Havelock, 1963, p. 42).

In this way, maintaining the status quo is less an escape or existential
evasion than an existential *obligation*. Chopra (2002) draws attention to
this when, in discussing the resolution of *Dilwale Dulhania*, she addresses
how the film, despite its acknowledging gender inequity, ultimately ca-

---

30. See David Thorburn (1987) on "consensus narrative." Such narrative, he theorizes,

operates at the very center of the life of its culture and is in consequence almost
always deeply conservative in its formal structures and in its content. Its assign-
ment—so to say—is to articulate the culture's central mythologies, in a widely
accessible language, an inheritance of shared stories, plots, character types, cultural symbols, and narrative conventions. Such language is popular because it is
legible to the common understanding of a majority of the culture. (p. 168)

Consensus narrative is also inherently communal, he observes. I leave it to the reader to
decide whether consensus narrative owes something to orality.

pitulates to preserving the status quo: "The road to happiness lies in preserving the structure of ownership and power, not rebelling against it" (p. 82). Chopra argues that the film, like most romance films of its period, can only be described as an "'epic' in the most cursory sense": Although it offers characters who are larger than life and who live idealized lives, the film avoids "that profound sense of tragedy and the shattering spectacle of individuals being overwhelmed by time and circumstances," which she claims are integral to the epic (p. 87). In primary epic, however—that is, in *oral* epic[31]—tragedy and any sense of being overwhelmed are *always* carefully framed by, and sealed within, a reconstitution into the status quo. In that sense, *Dilwale Dulhania* is much more like epic than only in a superficial way.

Perhaps there is even a coarse logic to the way romance often takes up the first half of a Bollywood narrative, before finally that narrative is steered toward a joint family/socially sutured type of resolution. Romance, after all, as Eva Illouz explains, "reenacts symbolically the rituals of opposition to the social order through the inversion of social hierarchies and affirms the supremacy of the individual" (cited in Virdi, 2003, p. 200). Hence, as Virdi helpfully extrapolates, "romance is *the* trope for transgression, and the romantic couple's bond stands for the transforming of the status quo" (p. 200). Conservation of the social order unavoidably wins out in the end, but the higher the emotional force threatening the order—whether these be lovers, or turncoat army soldiers, or urban slum vigilantes—the more intense the narrative experience will be. It may thereby be in the subaltern viewers' interests—indeed, is maybe their ironical wont—to ultimately squelch the very hero who is fighting on their behalf.

There is of course a concomitant logic to the mythical feel that suffuses the final scenes of most Hindi popular films, one that goes beyond the necessary telescoping of the present with the past. For, mythologized space invokes the realm of the ancestors and thereby renders said space *sacred*. The past is not only being carried into the present; so too is the present asseverating its bonds with the past—and not only with one's forebears but also one's *gods*. No wonder, then, that the physical and ethical battles that play out in concluding sequences often do so in forests and jungles or the desert of Rajasthan; in view of the flames of a wedding's sacred fire or inside some collectively consecrated locale such as Fatehpur Sikri. From the oral vantage point, this extraction from any clear measurable present acts as a connection to, rather than an avoid-

---

31. The distinction here is to *secondary epic*, which comes into existence as a result of a writer styling his or her creative enterprise after primary (i.e., legitimately oral) epic. Virgil's *Aeneid* is the classic example. Unfortunately, misapprehensions about what characterizes primary epic continue to persist in contemporary scholarship, due to a general lack of awareness of the pressures that oral formulations put on storytelling content and form.

ance of, the real. This, in effect, is the oral community's mimesis, given that, for such a community, the real is an *ontological* locale, one in which the spectator affectively verifies that "these things 'were before' also with our ancestors, and became what they are now because of our ancestors" (Havelock, 1963, p. 105).

Thomas (1995) contests the notion that the Bollywood film ending has any connection to the existence of a conservative audience, insisting that "the ideal moral universe is not necessarily believed by anyone: it is a construct of the filmmakers, with the connivance of their audience, and it is as much a product of the history of Indian cinema and the genre conventions it has evolved as of other discourses in Indian society" (p. 164). It would of course be imprudent to claim that there are not other, inherited influences and antecedents that have helped mold the Hindi film narrative. The films, not unlike folk epic, have been, and continue to be, the repository for other cultural and historical influences (be they aesthetic or pragmatic), as well as for conventions of genre. But Thomas' perspective belies the constancy of the Indian audience's expectations—one might even say its demands—regarding narrative resolution.[32] In fact, it is precisely this intransigence on the part of the viewing public that compels one to ask: Why *this* construction? Whence the attraction to "a narrative which ritually neutralizes the discomfiting features of social change" (Vasudevan, 1995, p. 309)?[33] And how to explain this same tendency in Egyptian popular cinema, where one also finds a universe that is, as Viola Shafik (2001) writes, not only constructed "according to a largely conservative moral system which is ruled by clear binary oppositions—good and evil, virtuous and vicious"—but that exists because of the industry's "permanent readiness to compromise in line with the oft-cited motto *'al-gumbar 'ayiz kidda'* (a colloquial phrase meaning 'the audience wants it that way')" (p. 44)? The answer (no doubt foreseen) may lie with an *oral* compulsion, self-interest, and need to incorporate—to assimilate and adjust—the new into the old, the now into the past, so that the past may exist as the always and continuing present.

NOETIC NATIONALISM (AND INTERNATIONALISM)

Given the discussion thus far, the reader has probably already discerned that the cognitive apparatuses required for the viewing of a *masala* film

---

32. I differ as well with Thomas' position on the ideal moral universe. That universe may indeed be interpreted by percipients as fantastic, in the sense that one is not expected to act analogously (i.e., to take on another's code of conduct); and yes, a spectator may not even fully subscribe to the particular traditional stance of, say, gender relations as depicted in the films. However, the notion of *dharma*, or social duty, which drives and permeates every film ending, is absolutely believed in and endorsed.

33. Vasudevan is summarizing Nandy here.

are largely operational. That is, the films call for little of the sort of thinking (either during or after a screening) that one might call self-reflective, analytical, or categorizationally abstract. This is of course in keeping with the characteristics and requirements of oral narrative, which, as Havelock (1991) felicitously reminds us apropos ancient Greek epic, "had to tell a tale in which the actors were persons doing things or suffering them, with a notable absence of abstract statement. One could reflect, but always as a human being, never as a philosopher, an intellectual, a theorist" (p. 24).

Oral individuals have in fact been found to dismiss, and even disdain, thinking that is too far removed from the lived, experienced world. In his 1930s fieldwork with nonliterate Uzbek and Kirghiz peasants, A.R. Luria (1976) discovered that thinking that was overly abstract or too conceptual was rejected entirely or considered irrelevant. And why not? To the oral mindset, such thinking serves no practical purpose or function. How then could it possibly be a signifier of intelligence? That Indian viewers sometimes refer to Western films as "cold" (Thomas, 1995) or "dry" (Anjum Rajabali, cited in Ganti, 2004) may have its genesis in this phenomenon. Reason in the oral world is rarely extricated from nature. Self-analysis, on the other hand, "requires a certain demolition of situational thinking. It calls for the isolation of the self, around which the entire lived world swirls for each individual person, removal of the center of every situation from that situation enough to allow the center, the self, to be examined and described" (Ong, 1982, p. 54). To the oral mindset, that kind of distance signals a divorce from, rather than a greater comprehension of, the world. One might even say that, without the additive, agonistic, copious, conservative, and homeostatic qualities that characterize oral narrative (and *masala* films), a story *just isn't* a story. If nothing more, this should remind us that "literate" visions when cast on a screen are no more real or fixed than orally derived visions. Following this, one might assert that the ahistorical nature of the Bombay film is no less (or more) valid than a preoccupation with historicity, which is an outgrowth of literacy and, even more, of print. After all, if it is only with print that characters expressing community concerns are supplanted by individuals preoccupied with purely personal matters (Havelock, 1982, p. 267), how then to measure authenticity?

No doubt we need likewise to interrogate anew the recurrent themes in these Bollywood films. Kinship, for instance, is indisputably an important component of Indian society, and it is therefore only fitting that it be everywhere apparent in Hindi popular cinema. However, as Tomaselli et al. (1995) insinuate, characteristics we typically ascribe to tradition might well (also) be reflecting the orality of a social or cultural group. The prominence of kinship, the way the theme is shaped and heralded, may speak as much to the oral needs of an audience as to that audience's expectations in seeing social or familial norms reflected.

Orality does not only influence or govern depictions of one's ties to the ancestors or to ancient traditions, however. It may hold equal sway over one's connection to modern concepts like nationalism. Critics are continuously emphasizing, analyzing, and all-out decrying the covert (and often not-so-covert) state agenda that plays out in the Hindi popular film. Accusations of paternalism and of forcibly propagated instruction in national conduct frequently make their way into print. Then again, according to Sumita Chakravarty (1996), a national cinema has an ideological imperative "to establish the claim upon the individual's allegiance by a secular source of authority, the state, [and thus] to supersede the traditional sources of authority residing in religious and parental figures" (p. 132). As anyone who has studied Bollywood films must grant, however, the films do so by paradoxically funneling nationalist allegiance and loyalty *through* traditional sources of authority. Thus, the modern state (i.e., the government, the army, the courts) may be portrayed as effete, corrupt, even parasitic on the community (Prakash, 1983), but this portrayal always occurs from *within* the arena of the sacred state, that is, from within the (ironically patriarchal) social and moral order known as "Mother India"—and *She* must always in the end be preserved and protected, upheld and worshiped.[34] For this reason, many Hindi films manage to conclude with a pro-India, all-India, indeed jingoistic-India sentiment. Invariably, this projects a siphoned image of the true state, one falsely drained of the deep clefts of caste, class, region, and religion that may divide spectators in life. But the image also, as recompense, is highly self-congratulatory.

Based on the exigent need of the oral psyche to see the community preserved and the traditional order restored, this embrace of national unity, this willing incorporation into a body politic, is only logical.[35] Without the kind of introspection that grows from literacy, without literacy's cognitively isolationist position, which is what promotes analysis and abstraction—which in fact *induces* history—noetically, there can be *no other world than this one*, and *no other group than ours*. That the *masala* film remains disinterested, even dismissive of the outside world—that is, of the world of foreigners and transnational arenas that do not directly impact (face-to-face) its oral, collective sense of self—seems to underscore this point.

---

34. Similarly, in the *Iliad*, morality is "secular no less than sacred. The usages prescribed by religion are at the same time the usages of the political apparatus. . . . The one passes imperceptibly into the other" (Havelock, 1963, p. 75).

35. Bollywood films that transgress the social restoration of the traditional order do exist, but virtually every film that has obtained hit or superhit status in the past few decades squelches subversion by a story's end, thus restoring the orally inflected community of the modern era—that is to say, the nation-state.

And yet, it is precisely this chauvinistic disinterest in the rest of the world that leads to these Indian films ultimately *transcending* India. Somewhat helplessly, the nation in these circumstances functions as *an allegorical extension of an orally inflected worldview*—which is why a film as "patriotic" as *Mother India* can resonate so deeply for a Hausa villager in Nigeria, or for spectators in Egypt, or in Ghana or China.

This of course explicates (and also productively complicates) Fredric Jameson's (1986) "theory of the cognitive aesthetics of third-world literature" (p. 88), which film scholars sometimes cite for its relevance to Bollywood cinema. Jameson's claim is that texts of developing nations "necessarily project a political dimension in the form of national allegory: the story of the private individual destiny is always an allegory of the embattled situation of the public third world culture and society" (p. 65). I would recommend that, in some cases, this political dimension may be more the byproduct of the noetic requirements of the oral mindset—which, as I discuss later, *cannot* be rightly applied to all Indian cinema, just as it cannot be confined solely to "third-world" texts. (Consider in the non-Indian context *Rambo* or the James Bond films, for instance.)

We need simultaneously to redress accusations that the *masala* film form reflects little more than "'a pure dream, empty and vain,' alienated from the 'concrete history of concrete material individuals materially producing their existence'" (Mishra, 2002, p. 17).[36] Indeed, when readings like these are pitted against Ong's (1967) comment that nonliterate peoples "do not commonly withdraw into themselves to create a little dream-world where everything can be ideally ordered" (p. 134), the potential inaptness of such charges emerges. Although Ong is here critiquing the literate person's mania for systematizing and categorizing, the statement reverberates in another way critical to this discussion— namely, in adverting to how one world may be *no less* a dream than the other. Literately inflected individuals may recoil at such a statement, surefire in the knowledge that the realist vision is superior (more accurate, more authentic, certainly more progressive). But, alas, this may speak to their literate bias no less than it does to their well-intentioned rectitude.

None of this eclipses the fact that the Hindi popular film is an indigenous and culturally unique product, one that has undergone aesthetic and ideological transformations that neither can, nor ought to, be glibly explained away by orality. But at the same time, film specialists need to be open to the possibility that certain aspects of Indian popular cinema, which they themselves have termed "native," may have deeper, or at least variform, roots. Indeed, once one has been conceptually introduced to orality, it is almost impossible to read an analyst's description

---

36. Mishra was borrowing here from Louis Althusser.

of the Hindi film as being one where "narrative is loose and fragmented, realism irrelevant, psychological characteristics disregarded, elaborate dialogues prized, music essential, and both the emotional involvement of the audience and the pleasures of sheer spectacle privileged throughout" (Thomas, 1995, p. 162) and *not* reflect on the psychodynamics of orality. Certainly cultural distinction and oral inflection are sufficiently mutually inclusive, such that the former can be mapped *through* the latter without fear of reductively flattening the *masala* genre. I imagine few readers today would maintain that the *Mahabharata* is the same as African oral epic, or that the journey Gilgamesh makes to the underworld is indistinguishable from Odysseus' serial island-hopping. Despite the universal features that orality foists on these narratives; despite the strains and pressures of oral performance that delimit how their stories can be told, each bears the imprimatur of its sociocultural origins and preoccupations—and also, to be certain, the creative spin of its bards. Such tales, to recast a concept popular in the contemporary social sciences, are truly *glocal*.

We need only turn to particular strands of national cinemas outside India to extend this glocality into the 21st century. In footnotes throughout this chapter, I have alluded already to Turkey's comedies and Mexico's *telenovelas*; to Egyptian popular cinema and Italian peplums; to early American cinema and recent Hollywood blockbusters (see, also, Appendix B, where I analyze the film *Titanic* on the basis of its oral idiom). Still, nowhere is this epistemic likeness (as difference) more patent than in Hong Kong cinema's "distinct aesthetic" (p. 2), which David Bordwell (2000) unpacks in *Planet Hong Kong*. Although seemingly unacquainted with the movies' oral underpinnings, Bordwell describes that mass entertainment as noncontemplative, nonrealist, "Manichean," loosely plotted (and "kaleidoscopic" in its variety), kinesthetically arousing, flashback-using, and tradition-refining (as opposed to originality-seeking); further, Hong Kong cinema favors formulas and clichés, is brutal in its violence, is plagiaristic, and possesses a tendency to "swerve into a happy ending" (pp. 2–20).[37] I cannot imagine a more succinct, comprehensive (and completely indeliberate) corroboration of orality's transnational currency.

---

37. The possibility of a Bollywood–Hong Kong "connection" has been intuited by S.V. Srinivas (2005), who mentions that particular Hong Kong films strike him "as being recognizable, indeed very 'Indian,'" and elicit in him "a strange sense of familiarity" (p. 289). Srinivas notes that Stephen Chow's films have been received indifferently in India (thus drawing unwitting salutary attention to the fact that orality *cannot* explain everything); however, his characterization of Chow's *Kung Fu Hustle* (2004) as a film that privileges parody, spectacle, exaggeration, a melodramatic structure, and the tendency for a spectatorial "in-the-know" (p. 289) definitely resonates in terms of the oral attributes laid out in this chapter.

Finally, as a route to my emphasizing orality's capacity to circulate without surrendering cultural and regional distinction, I ask the reader to consider one last illustration. The following is a description of a dramatic production:

> You went to see a *new [film]* but it was *at the same time an old [film]* full of the *familiar clichés* rearranged in *new settings*, with much *aphorism and proverb* and *prescriptive example* of how to behave, and *warning examples* of how not to behave; with *continual recapitulation* of bits of tribal and civic history, of *ancestral memories* for which the artist serves as the unconscious *vehicle of repetition* and record. The *situations were always typical*, not invented; they *repeated endlessly* the precedents and judgments, the learning and wisdom, which the . . . culture had accumulated and hoarded. (emphases added)

For those who have read this chapter closely, this description probably rings familiar. One might suspect that the author was describing a *masala* film. But replace the contents of the quotation's square brackets with the original word, "*play*"; fill in the elliptical gap between "the . . . [and] culture" with the word "*Hellenistic*," and what you have is Havelock's (1963) description of an Athenian stageplay from sixth century B.C.

The point of this comparison is not to expose some backward or premodern sensibility apropos the *masala* film. Rather, it is to underscore oral inflection's migratory potentials, both synchronically and diachronically, as well as its nondiscriminatory nature. Orally inflected narrative's existence is no more linked to India than it is to Greece, or Latin America, or North America, or to the modern Middle East or the Late Middle Ages. Orally inflected storytelling is ancient and also startlingly new. . . . Which is something that *cannot* be said for the next species of narration that this project explores.

3

Mapping the Literate Characteristics of Visual Narrative:

Art-Cinema Narration, 1945–1980

> Within the mind, the camera can do anything.
> —Robert Bresson (cited in Schrader, 1988, p. 65)

A CONTEXT FOR ART-CINEMA NARRATION

Just as misleading as contending that Bombay has historically produced nothing but *masala* films would be to discuss art cinema as a homogeneous genre. Geoffrey Nowell-Smith (1996) suggests that art cinema's heterogeneity, especially during its heyday in the 1960s and 1970s, "makes a mockery of the attempts that have occasionally been made to treat it as a distinct genre analogous to those that flourished in Hollywood and other mainstream commercial cinemas" (p. 570). And yet, no matter how diverse their styles, art-cinema directors shared a common philosophical impetus, which derived from early 20th-century modernism. As an artistic movement, modernism challenged tradition, "particularly the tradition of art as comforter—the locus of satisfaction and harmony, the guide to transcendent visions of nature, or the place of ideological reconciliations" (Kolker, 1983, p. 123). Thus, during modernism's heyday, Virginia Woolf rebelliously reconceived the novel via a poetic plaiting of action and memory, and Picasso cut up and rewrote perspectival space on canvas. Following such literary and plastic-arts muses, film directors began in the 1950s "to challenge attitudes about the work and place of art, to attack the conventions and complacency, to reorder the relationship of the work and the spectator" (Preface). Although their medium was different, their desires were the same: to counter the illusionist practices of art and "the seamless verisimilitude of realism," and to invest in a comparatively radical self-reflexivity (Hayward, 2000, p. 234).

David Bordwell (1985) specifies even further that art-cinema narration's aesthetic strategies were born largely of its having taken "its cue from *literary* modernism" (p. 206), of its having allied itself with written works "roughly from James, Proust, Joyce, and Kafka through Faulkner, Camus, and the Theater of the Absurd to Cortázar and Stoppard" (p. 310). Such a compendium surely speaks to modernism's lack of monolithicity and to its subsequent ability, when extended into the film arena, to house as eclectic an assortment of directors as "those belonging to the French new wave, the New German Cinema, Bergman, Antonioni, Fellini, Kurosawa, Ray (Satyajit not Nicholas) and the like" (Cook, 1985, p. 106). The *Cahiers du cinéma* would also rank Bresson, Dreyer, Mizoguchi, and Ozu as part of the art-film pantheon. The wide array of nations represented—in this paragraph alone appear France, Germany, Sweden, Italy, Japan, India, and Denmark—has sometimes led to the species' auxiliary label, "international film."

The collective wisdom, however, is that the miscellany of modernist films *did* share a common ancestor: the Italian neorealist film. Neorealism, as elaborated in Cesare Zavattini's (1953) famous manifesto, was a concerted attempt by directors starting in the 1940s to work against the cinema's contemporaneous inclination to "tell fables" (p. 143). The task for the neorealist artist was to make audiences "reflect (and, if you like, be moved and indignant too) on what they and others are doing, on the real things, exactly as they are" (p. 144). It sought, in other words, to "*excavate* reality" rather than to kowtow to myth (p. 143).[1] As Aumont, Bergala, Marie, and Vernet (1992) summarize, the school of neorealism was characterized by

> location shooting in natural settings (as opposed to the artifice of studio production); the use of nonprofessional actors (as opposed to the "theatrical" conventions of professional actors' performances); . . . a concern for simple characters (as opposed to the carefully woven classical plots and their extraordinary heroes); and a reduction of the action per se (in contrast to the spectacular events staged in the conventional commercial film). Finally, the neorealist cinema was to have been low budget. (p. 110)[2]

---

1. Significantly, Italian audiences of the period did not spend much time watching neorealist films, which they considered more news than narrative (Sorlin, 1996). The popular genre of the time was instead the *peplum* (see chapter 2, n. 28).

2. Aumont et al. were here summarizing the words of neorealism's most ardent academic proponent, André Bazin.

So, although neorealism predated film modernism, it also in a sense *facilitated* it (Kolker, 1983). One might, thus, in Foucauldian terms, isolate neorealism as the site of a significant epistemic break.[3] Its concentration on a "ground-zero" style of filmmaking that privileged verisimilitude above all else paved the way—unbeknownst to its aesthetic architects—for future radical plays with cinema: the dream perversity of Luis Buñuel's later films, Jean-Luc Godard's iconoclastic struggle *against* cinematic verisimilitude. The breadth of form that neorealism paradoxically provoked is perhaps most conveniently foregrounded by Christian Metz (1974a):

> One could say that Alain Resnais and Jean-Luc Godard represent the two great poles of modern film: meticulously indirect realism as opposed to a generally abandoned realism; . . . in the first instance, the triumph of *"mimesis"* and of the reconstruction of the model, and, in the second instance, a luxuriating avatar of *"poeisis,"* to restate some Barthesian concepts. (p. 201)

According to Robert Kolker (1983), the emergence of the species was due not to the influence of neorealism alone, but also because "the old, established forms of cinema were simply no longer terribly interesting" (p. 129). What modernist cinema sought to prevent was the traditional cinema's too-easy slippage "through the structures of presentation into an emotional world of character and action" (p. 159). "We don't live life according to 'genres,'" as Karel Reisz and Gavin Millar pronounced (cited in Neupert, 2002, p. 80). But if life *were* independent from genre, if it were ergo to be *personally* (as opposed to corporately) materialized, then it only could be expected that discrete films would end up reflecting a marked heterogeneity.

For those directors who were part of the French New Wave (most of whom had worked initially as critics for *Cahiers*), the words of filmmaker Alexandre Astruc no doubt best encapsulated the new aesthetic philosophy: "Direction is no longer a means of illustrating or presenting a scene, but a true act of writing. The filmmaker/author writes with his camera as a writer writes with his pen" (cited in Kolker, 1983, p. 171). Astruc had, in coining the term *la caméra-stylo* (camera-as-pen), with its emphasis on a cinema of *écriture* (writing-style), foreseen harnessing an imaginative and expressive rendering of thought as an alternative to surrendering to spectacle and the visually anecdotal (Neupert, 2002). That his words, written in 1948, would become a major impetus for those emerging French artists was surely in part because of the words' alluring recognition of the authorial presence. As Kolker (1983) explains, directors like François Truffaut, Godard, and the like wanted to inscribe

---

3. Deleuze (1986b) proposes just such a break, declaring that neorealism precipitated the rupture from the movement-image to the time-image.

"their personality and perception of the world directly into images and sounds, into narratives told by them with film, *in* film" (p. 172).

This desire was made public in Truffaut's essay "*Une certaine tendance du cinéma français*" ("On a Certain Tendency in the French Cinema"), in a 1954 issue of *Cahiers*. There, Truffaut questioned the outmoded psychological realism so common to bourgeois literary adaptations of the period, which he claimed downplayed the potential for film to create a language, or *écriture*, of its own (Higgins, 1996). (In this sense, the clarion call was as much directed *to* literature as it was materializing *from* it.) Like the sophisticated novelists and readers who had earlier expressed dissatisfaction with Balzac's realism and a suspension of disbelief grown increasingly mundane, these directors were similarly unified only insofar as they pursued "the self-conscious and paradoxical search for the new" and were demonstrably "oppositional, confrontational, sometimes unpleasant, always stubbornly *contestataire*" (pp. 13–14).

And yet, in some respects, the films were *not* that different from those that they were allegedly contesting, as more than one critic has pointed out. Kolker (1983), for instance, observes that modernist filmmakers like Federico Fellini were handling the same material as Hollywood melodrama and in equally manipulative ways. Subjects like "the struggles of good and evil, innocence and corruption, the place and worth of the self in a cruel world" were merely "presented in a more abstract, apparently more sophisticated form. But only apparently. The forms of melodrama and their demands for unmediated emotional response [were] largely the same regardless of the particular subject" (p. 86).

Indeed, Anthony Easthope (1991) argues that "ideological content differs little in contemporary examples of high literature and popular modern genres" (p. 86). For example, *Heart of Darkness*, which "trembl[es] on the edge of modernism," shares the very same themes, imperialist drives, and dominantly masculinist cultural point of view as its canonically lesser cousin *Tarzan of the Apes* (p. 86). So if the former is not ideologically autonomous, where then does the difference lie, and how can we specify it in sufficiently material terms? Perhaps, much as Easthope believed, the key to unlocking these "contrasting modes or categories of discourse [lies in] asking not, 'What do they mean?' (hermeneutics) but rather 'How do they work?' (poetics)" (p. 80).[4]

---

4. Ultimately, Easthope (1991) maps the contrasts between these two textual forms onto the reality and pleasure principles. Nevertheless, his commitment to the texts having a "*common origin* in textuality" (p. 90) clearly overlaps with the present project's theoretical assertions. This is especially the case given the textual characteristics he teases out of both works—characteristics that conspicuously mirror those of this project. *Tarzan of the Apes*, for example, is distinguished by its concrete, simple, denotative nature; its literalness and immediacy of meaning; its explicit univocal character and visual (iconic) and unironic play.

Not only do I think that we can legitimately explicate how modernist film discourse worked, we can find the answer in the filmmakers' own published avowals and manifestoes—although, granted, not as the filmmakers intended those materials to be read. Here I am speaking of the emphasis those publications placed metaphorically on *writing*. True, the association emerged largely out of the filmmakers' desire to equal the novelist and in this way to render their medium equal in stature to that of the book; but lodged in that aspiration was also a recognition of the "creative range and freedom of the novelist" (Higgins, 1996, p. 10), which included placing novelistic-type demands on the spectator engaging with the text. As Alain Resnais said of his film *Hiroshima mon amour* (1959), "I wanted to bring into being the equivalent of a new form of reading, so that the spectator would have as much freedom of imagination as the reader of a novel" (cited in Higgins, 1996, p. 10). Marguerite Duras, who penned the screenplay for that film, even commented that Resnais worked like a novelist: what he showed in images was being continuously surpassed by what he *wasn't* showing, in order "to signify art as a self-conscious absence, even as loss of the world" (cited in Higgins, 1996, p. 24).

Obviously novelistic traits were *not* exclusive to the printed word. This of course muddies the diagnostic waters, at least for those persons trying to assert traditional disciplinary boundaries with respect to storytelling forms. Perhaps more efficacious is to isolate what literacy requires in order for it to achieve valuation: *readers*. Who were the readers of art-cinema narration? What characterized the audiences that participated in this new aleatoric cinematic impulse? How were these films working on them, and how are we to account for a spectatorial body *eager* for "an extraordinary reorientation of imaginative intent and response," for a cinema that relished (or wallowed, as the case may be) in a "refusal to communicate meaning and feeling instantly" (Kolker, 1983, pp. 124–125)? As Kolker grants, the demands modernist cinema made on audiences "could only cause resistance and even resentment among the majority of people too busy or simply unwilling to meet these demands. A new artistic elitism threatened—a separation of the work of art from a broad and engaged audience" (p. 125).

Robert Bresson insisted that one needed merely to *accustom* the public "to divining the whole of which they are given only a part. Make people diviners. Make them desire it" (cited in Kolker, 1983, p. 219). But could he have been wrong? Scholarly research points with frequency, after all, to how art-cinema narration appealed in its heyday to "young, educated audiences," as Nowell-Smith (1996) writes in *The Oxford History of World Cinema* (p. 567); to "college-educated, middle-class cinéphiles," as Bordwell (1985, p. 230) phrases it; to that "better-educated section of the American population," as Janet Staiger (1992, p. 186) cautiously admits based on what social science data from the period illustrate. Staiger elaborates even further on this population, calling attention to its being "better educated than the average American" and "more likely to fit some general representation (or self-image) of being 'highbrow'" (p. 187). Conceivably, then, it was not a case of *un*interested parties being simply too preoccupied or emotionally averse to putting in the extra effort that "divining the whole" requires.

True, one might argue that educated audiences, by virtue of their education, were being exposed to the modernist novel and, hence, were predisposed to the formal experimentation and epistemological inquiry of films like Ingmar Bergman's *Persona* (1966) or Yasujiro Ozu's *Tokyo Story* (1953). (This is precisely the position that Bordwell, 1985, takes in calling attention to the art-house patrons' "looking for films consonant with contemporary ideas of modernism in art and literature," p. 230.) On the other hand, one might ask why these patrons took to the modernist novel in the first place, whereas other audiences did not and remained committed instead to a comparatively "effortless" form of print storytelling. Could it be that the conditions necessary for engagement with literary modernism were built out of more than mere exposure—or, rather, that a pre-existing *capacity* for engagement (which includes the social pressures and institutional practices that are tied to such engagement) was what led to the development of something like the art house? After all, "The 'literacy' which a writer can exploit," as Havelock (1963) tells us, "depends on whether the educational system creates readers for him" (p. 293).

Bordwell (1985) so much as concedes in *Narration in the Fiction Film* that the type of text produced by the art-cinema industry "required machinery to interpret it" (p. 231) and that, in order to be comprehended, it actually necessitated a "higher-level interpretation" (p. 212). Regrettably, he does not explore this avenue further, though this is only because his real intention is to tease out the species' defining traits, a project that necessitates his operating from the position of an "ideal reader." Interestingly, in his book *Film in the Aura of Art*, Dudley Andrew (1984b) makes (and just as quickly abandons) a similar thesis—namely, that films that function in the realm of art demand "a type of critical activity not required of more standard cinema" (p. 13).[5]

This chapter plans to pick up that thesis and to prove that the higher-level critical activity that art cinema demands owes much to the legacy of *alphabetic literacy*. In fact, it will demonstrate that literacy's tie to art-cinema narration is so fundamental that reading and writing cannot rightly be extricated from any etymological discussion of film. Undoubtedly, this gives double meaning to Truffaut's assertion that "The

---

5. The same sentiment is echoed, but also not quite adequately taken up, by Clement Greenberg (1957) in his well-known essay "Avant-Garde and Kitsch."

idea that we should try to reflect the society we live in is false—we will reflect it in any case, intentionally or not" (cited in Higgins, 1996, p. 150).

Substantiating this chapter's premise would not be easy were it not for the orally inflected characteristics that were quarried from Hindi popular cinema in Chapter 2. What that previous comprehensive study provides is a schema for an *oral episteme of visual narrative*, one that lends itself more readily to a taxonomical proposition (see Table 3.1). By using the oral episteme as a map, we can trace what precisely the *written word* has engendered narratologically. For, no species of film departs more radically from orally inflected norms—is in some sense anathema to them—than art-cinema narration. Art cinema may reflect tremendous heterogeneity, but what follows empirically demonstrates just how it is possible that "so many different kinds of films could be gathered into this species" (Staiger, 1992, p. 178). Moreover, when examined through the conceptual lens of literacy, the species proves much *less* heterogeneous than has been previously supposed—no matter whether one is speaking of the elliptical, self-referential fantasy of a film like Fellini's *8½*, or the non-bourgeois two-dimensionality of Godard's *Weekend* (Henderson, 1970–1971), or the poetic realism of Jean Renoir's *The Rules of the Game* (Bazin, 1967).[6]

Even if only intended as a means of institutionalizing a film form *contra* Hollywood, art-cinema narration's norms are so patently divorced from the oral episteme that we can, in advance of forthcoming proof and explication, theorize that an orally inflected percipient would likely be disinclined to engage with the species. (That art-cinema narration derives its inspiration, if not its stories, directly from literature—which *masala* film *rarely* does—is in itself telling.)

We might even call art-cinema narration a *cinema of detachment*, that is, a cinema that has detached itself as a way of knowing from oral modes of story construction and performance. Indeed, the level of interpretation that art-cinema narration demands of its spectators appears tied to an advanced stage of literacy known as *high literacy*. The hierar-

---

6. Provocatively (although not accidentally, I argue), a similar sentiment is expressed by Sumita Chakravarty (1996) about Indian art film:

> A single umbrella term like the "new" or the "parallel" cinema is simply not sufficient or accurate to designate the diversity of approaches and techniques, aims and intentions that informs the works that are included under its rubric. . . . [I]f Mrinal Sen and Ritwik Ghatak, along with [Satyajit] Ray, are included in the new cinema [India's art cinema], we not only have a problem with chronology but with the sheer impossibility of constructing a framework within which the significant differences that mark the work of these filmmakers—differences in style, tone, and texture, in sensibility and inspiration, in politics and ideology— may be accommodated. (p. 237). See Chapter 4, where I address India's New Cinema directly.

TABLE 3.1. THE ORAL EPISTEME OF VISUAL NARRATIVE AS EVIDENCED
IN HINDI POPULAR FILMS, 1950–2000

Structure and Form
- Episodic narrative form, including flashbacks and digressions
- Repetition, recycling, formula privileging
- Spectacle (flat surface—a "cinema of attractions")
- Narrative closure (no ambivalent or open endings)

Visual, Verbal, and Aural Tone
- Agonistically toned (e.g., inflated violence, melodrama)
- Heavy, amplified characters and settings
- Frontality
- Syntagmatic kinesthesia
- Plenitude, redundancy (e.g., visual, material, and dialogical excess)
- Use of rhetorical devices (e.g., clichés, proverbs)
- Noninterpretive, unambiguous meaning (e.g., privileging of oaths, totemism in lieu of symbolism)

Worldview and Orientation
- Manichean worldview
- Nonpsychological orientation
- Nonhistorical (synchronic, synthetic, experiential telescoping)
- Unself-conscious (e.g., presence of parody but not irony)
- Fulfillment of audience expectations
- Participatory
- No anxiety of influence (imitative, no concept of plagiarism)
- Focus on social suturing, preservation of the status quo
- Collective social orientation ("we" inflected)

chical shadings of the word *high* may distress some readers, but the term is common to the field of the cognitive science of learning and instruction and is intended to distinguish literacy's higher-order goals from the more elemental ability to read and write. In short, these higher-order goals include the ability to yield multiple solutions; to make nuanced judgments; to apply multiple criteria and deal with uncertainty—all in a manner that is nonalgorithmic and complex (in that the process cannot always be specified or rendered "visible"); as well as to self-regulate the thinking process and impose meaning (Resnick, 1987). The recent social scientific yield in the area of literacy and cognition intriguingly corroborates one of Ong's (1982) contentions, which is that the thought of those who have developed high literacy possesses "different contours from those of orally sustained thought" (p. 96).[7] In other words, that "higher-

7. See Benjamin Bloom's (1956) educational objectives taxonomy, which offers a means for educators to conceptualize a categorization of learned levels of abstraction. Its

level interpretation" of which Bordwell and others have spoken is tied to a mindset that education not only actively stimulates, but all-out *permits*.

One of the favorable derivatives of this chapter is the way it does away with—or, at the least, inhibits—the false premise that the educated are educated because of some intrinsically superior talent of observation, attentiveness, or critical perspicacity. Furthermore, mapping a literate episteme for visual narrative gainfully confounds the conceptually oversimplified notion of, what Easthope (1991) wittily phrases as, "high culture good, popular culture bad" (p. 79). Although other factors indubitably collide with an individual's noetic capacity for textual engagement, filmic or otherwise, evidence of literacy's sway on narrative may help dispel, in Stuart Hall's formulation, the ridiculous notion that people are the "cultural dopes" critics often decry them to be (cited in Easthope, 1991, p. 79).

NARRATIVE COHERENCE: A PREAMBLE ON PLOTS AND POTHOLES

Bordwell provides an efficient and, more crucially, a neutral scaffold for assessing the high-literate inflection of art-cinema narration. As I mentioned earlier, he catalogues with meticulous grace in *Narration in the Fiction Film* the species' particular norms of style and *syuzhet* (plot). Most interesting, perhaps, is the manner in which he executes his analytic probing; for, he does so through absence as well as presence—that is, by discussing the norms' virtual nonappearance in classical Hollywood cinema. Characteristics of art-cinema narration that he in this way adduces include a general lack of causality, an emphasis on verisimilitude and heightened subjectivity, and a persistent level of unreliability, compounded by relativistic notions of truth. At the same time, Bordwell (1985) counsels that this modernist brand of realism is "no more 'real' than that of the classical film; it is simply a different canon of realistic motivation, a new *vraisemblance*, justifying particular compositional options and effects" (p. 206).

If these characteristics are departures from classical Hollywood cinema, then one of the obvious implications of this for us is that classical Hollywood cinema still functions on the basis of norms that do not radi

---

stages are (a) knowledge; (b) comprehension; (c) application; (d) analysis; (e) synthesis; and (f) evaluation. Other looser conceptual distinctions can be found in the low-road and high-road transfer schemata introduced by Salomon and Perkins (1989) and skill theory's likening of learning to a succession of tiers: "reflex, abstract, representational, and abstract" (Parziale & Fischer, 1998. p. 100). Although these routes, systems, and pyramids do not always necessarily set out to demonstrate or even investigate the relationship between higher-order goals and *literacy* (taken here to be a socially and educationally shaped process that can, in turn, shape an individual's cognition), the connection between abstraction and learning will become patent in the ensuing pages.

cally depart from or diminish oral inflection. Nevertheless, there are at the same time several literately inflected norms that the Hollywood industry has altogether institutionalized, and this may explain why its more orally inclined nature (at least when compared to art film) has gone unobserved until now. No such norm is probably more conspicuous than Hollywood's almost doctrinal fidelity to the tight, linear storyline. That classical Hollywood narrative privileges pyramidal plot and clear goal-orientation is almost truistic. A viewer can fairly safely anticipate, as Bordwell puts it, some "expository material at the outset, a state of affairs disturbed by a complication, and some character ready to function as a goal-oriented protagonist" (p. 35). Thus, we get Neo in *The Matrix* (1999), who, despite his futuristic environs, traverses the same structural territory that Dorothy does in *The Wizard of Oz* (1939). For some viewers, such strict linearity may feel *too* familiar (i.e., worn, predictable, formalistically superannuated, even clichéd). This is likely because the tight storyline has had a presence, even if an erratic one, in Western culture for some 2,500 years. The ancient Greek move away from a "cultural 'book'" that required storage in oral memory (Havelock, 1963, p. vii) can be found in the taut catharsis-oriented plots of the Hellenic playwrights. A self-contained stage drama with a definitive beginning, middle, and end, such as Sophocles' *Oedipus Rex*, could only have emerged out of its author's ability to consciously manipulate his narrative materials *on the page*.

Although chirography may have permitted the development of a storyline's ascending action and building tension, and its climactic recognition and denouement (Ong, 1982), it is important to recognize that a controlled, linear architectural design that foregrounds "cause-and-effect pairs" (Branigan, 1992, p. 217) can *still* function as part of a fundamentally oral schema. In fact, one researcher found that, as regards contemporary audiences, "comprehension and memory are best when the story conform[s] to the drive-to-a-goal pattern" (Bordwell, 1985, p. 35). In other words, a narrative can possess tighter structures climactically and *still* be contoured by melodrama, a high rhetorical delivery, a collective orientation, and so forth. Certainly, this was the case with much ancient Greek tragedy. Indeed, that a tight plot would not undermine an otherwise epistemically oral drama, and thus its overarching *noetic accessibility*, would have been essential in the ancient Greek context. Despite that a play like *Oedipus Rex* reflects the structure of Freytag's pyramid, much of the fifth-century audience at the time "was still largely at the point of transition from being an 'oral' society" (Green, 1994, p. 2); or at the stage of "semi-literacy," to borrow Havelock's (1963) term.[8]

---

8. Havelock writes at length on the complex transition in ancient Greek society from an oral ethos to a written ethos. See especially his *Preface to Plato* (1963) and *The Literate Evolution in Greece and Its Cultural Consequences* (1982).

Of course these plays were relatively short, at least when compared to oral epic or the epically sized Victorian novel. Ong (1982) suggests that it was print that gave *true* rise to those "tightly closed verbal art forms" (p. 133) to which today we have grown accustomed. Until the novels of Jane Austen, lengthy plots largely maintained an episodic quality. Only several centuries after the emergence of the novel as a typographically circulated form did storytelling reach its "exquisitely tidy" shape (p. 144).

If this plot style fell out of favor during the modernist period, that was most certainly because it had become identified with being "too 'easy' (i.e., too fully controlled by consciousness) for author and reader" (Ong, 1982, p. 151); or, in the idiom of Noël Carroll (1988), it had become too "legible," with a "flow of action [that] approaches an ideal of uncluttered clarity" (p. 181). This is not to suggest that deforming a story in order to render it more difficult is *any less* a form of conscious control; but the interest for film modernists was clearly in constructing something that *appeared* less consciously crafted and in developing a narrative organization that more realistically reflected the experiential and ontological tenuousness of human existence. Bresson, for instance, expressed an outright antipathy for plot and foregrounded the quotidian less out of concern for what constituted real life than as "an opposition to the contrived, dramatic events which pass for real life in the movies" (Schrader, 2001, p. 301).

Just as emancipation from the Homeric rule of epical construction could only have come with the exploitation of pen and parchment (Havelock, 1986), so too the modernist emancipation from the pyramidal plot could *only* have come about subsequent to the exploitation of the printing press. Print, in other words, had generated a wide-enough audience that was *prepared* for—or, at the least, was literately open to—a deformation of a modernist structural type. So, although members of the French New Wave shunned strict plot and tight causality in deference to a more aleatoric form of storytelling that they identified with *écriture*, ironically the organizing principle that they were pulling away from was itself categorically *literately* inflected.

It could be argued that these modernist directors, in favoring a more tenuous linking of events (Bordwell, 1985), *returned* to the episodic structure that was a defining feature of oral epic. (Richard Neupert, 1995, even parallels art film's paratactic ordering to that found in folksongs and myth). Of course this "return" was taken up not out of epistemic need (as is the case with oral communities), but purely for the sake of expressive effects. In the name of verisimilitude, directors elected for a loosened causality, which, as a narrative organization, projected in their estimation a universe rife with chance, digression, spontaneity, and happenstance. In the film *L'Avventura* (1960), for instance, it is only "by chance that Anna is not found"; and in *Bicycle Thieves* (1948), it is only "by chance that Antonio discovers, then again, loses his bicycle" (Bordwell, 1985, p. 206). Indeed, in art-cinema narration, entire films may consist of little more than a series of chance encounters "linked by a trip (*The Silence* [1963], *La Strada* [1954], *Alice in the Cities* [1974]) or aimless wanderings (*La Dolca Vita* [1960], *Cleo from 5 to 7* [1962], *Alfie* [1966])," which ultimately render stories "picaresque" or "processional" in form (p. 206). In this storytelling universe, protagonists are often "drifters," who, instead of "speed[ing] toward a target" as one anticipates in Hollywood narrative, slide through the universe, thus unavoidably projecting a *syuzhet* that is more "slice of life" (p. 207).[9]

Once again, such episodic structure is not employed for the orally pragmatic purposes of stitching narrative together. Rather, its creators are intent on producing deliberate narrative breaches and causal gaps. André Bazin (2001), for instance, writes with respect to Rossellini's *Paisan* (1946) that the film exhibits "enormous ellipses—or, rather, great holes. A complex train of action is reduced to three or four brief fragments, in themselves already elliptical enough in comparison with the reality they are unfolding" (p. 22). Lest this appear lacking in positive valuation, scholars like Philip Rosen "attest to Bazin's continuous interest in contingency as the principal measure of the humanity (and reality) of cinema" (Margulies, 2003, p. 3). And Bazin is not alone. As Neupert (1995) observes, critics like Pauline Kael and Frank Kermode repeatedly "praise fiction that preserves a sense of contingency, since chance and uncertainty permeate our experience in the real world" (p. 76).[10]

To the spectator reared on literacy, such narrative loosening scarcely qualifies as storytelling insurrection. But as I point out later, such gaps within a film are a perplexing, if not potentially threatening, departure from an orally inflected worldview. In order to explore this aspect of art film's lacunae satisfactorily, however, we need to cover some other territory first. And for the sake of doing so coherently—"tidily" even—let us begin by examining why the structural *experimentation* that these modernist directors were attempting would necessarily spring from a sensibility that was literately shaped.

---

9. Deleuze (1986a), in his attempt to define the constituent elements of the cinematic "time-image" (as distinct from the more sensory-motor-oriented "movement-image"), points to the time-image's predilection for "deliberately weak links," which loosen up or stretch dramatic action (p. 210). Stories whose cause and effect are calculatedly slackened invariably become structurally more akin to "the stroll, the *balade* [ramble, jaunt], and the continual round-trip journey" (cited in Bogue, 2003, p. 108).

10. Although scholars also draw attention to the Hindi-film genre's "predilection for . . . elaborate plot lines motivated by chance events and coincidences" (Virdi, 2003, p. 41), that species' flukes and fortuities do *not* stem from an authorial desire to reflect the contingencies of life, as the scholars themselves discern.

SOVEREIGNTY AND SUBJECTIVITY (AS SUBVERSION)

Scholarship in orality studies has already well established that it is only the *literate*-minded human being who looks toward experimentation in storytelling. This is not because he or she possesses some mysterious or inherently superior cognitive ability; rather, it is that individuals nurtured from within writing and print culture are the only ones who can *afford* to abandon the story of their communal "self." In oral communities, much as we saw in the last chapter, "conceptualized knowledge that is not repeated aloud soon vanishes," and so, great energy must be invested "in saying over and over again what has been learned arduously over the ages" (Ong, 1982, p. 41). Perhaps this is why Spengler contends that writing extricates man's consciousness from a tyranny of the present (cited in Goody & Watt, 1968, p. 53). For, if "literate society leaves more to its members," as Goody and Watt assert, if "it gives more free play to the individual," that is because it has the means by which to relinquish "a single, ready-made orientation to life" (p. 63). Only a mind no longer beholden to the arduous task of conserving knowledge can afford to turn itself to brand-new speculation (Ong, 1982).[11] And so, formula—which otherwise houses knowledge most economically, as Milman Parry discovered in his 1930s fieldwork with South Slavic bards (Foley, 2002)—can be foregone; and conservation of the social order—which is the natural byproduct of a form of communication that unites people in groups (Ong, 1982)—can for the first time be eschewed. Released of its "memory storage" work (Goody, 1977, p. 37), the mind can now set its sights on novel circumspection, on the autonomously imaginative, on developing a "fresh" perspective or an "original" point of view.[12]

Thus, we see that the traits most often lauded about art film—such as its "independence of vision," or its "personalization of creation" (Bordwell, 1985, p. 231)[13]—are quite intimately tied to the species' *sovereignty* from oral exigencies. "Bold invention," as Havelock (1963) reminds us, "is the prerogative of writers, in a book culture" (p. 46). Oral

---

11. The Muses, whom artists today may still call on for inspiration, even if only metaphorically, are in fact the daughters of *Mnemosune*, the Greek word for memory. But *Mnemosune* implies more than memory alone: "It includes or implies the notion of recall and of record and of memorisation" (Havelock, 1963, p. 100). In other words, those Muses are ironically "not the daughters of inspiration or invention. . . . Their central role is not to create but to preserve" (p. 100).

12. Might this not explicate (and also spotlight the built-in elitism of) that quality which H. Bloom (1994) isolates as seminal to making literary authors culturally authoritative and canonical—namely, *strangeness* or freshness?

13. The latter term is Bordwell's (1985); the former is a 1965 comment made by Arthur Knight about the European film product (Bordwell, 1985).

cultures, conversely, must attend to the expectations of a communal re-action, to the compulsory reflection of a communal "soul."

Being able safely to disengage from the group allows for something even more revolutionary than narrative non-assimilation: it allows for a wholesale *subversion* of the status quo. Without the requirement for a face-to-face discourse, which fosters and even necessitates empathetic identification (Ong, 1982), there is no longer the corresponding need to be "less inclined toward resistance and rebellion," or to "privilege integration and reform" (Nayar, 2001, p. 142). True, Benedict Anderson (1991) may point in *Imagined Communities* to the deep "fraternity" that print helped generate among citizens toward the nation-state, but that is quite distinct from what storytelling as a "self-proclaimed fiction" (Godzich, 1994, p. 99) sanctions.

Such narrative insurgency is perhaps nowhere more apparent than in the irresolution of so many art films' endings. It is almost a common-place that art-cinema narration privileges denouements that are in no way resolved, that instead intentionally leave the spectator sans narra-tive closure. So integral is the absence of closure to this species of film-making, in fact, that Neupert (1995) devotes an entire book to the sub-ject—appropriately titled *The End*. There, Neupert draws particular attention to the Italian neorealist films, which frequently lack conven-tional resolution. At the end of Rossellini's *Open City* (1945), for example, "The audience cannot say where Francesco is," just as it will never learn "what eventually happened to any of the characters still alive at the end of *Paisan*" (p. 76). We might add to these one of Bordwell's (1985) cases in point: how in De Sica's *Bicycle Thieves* "the future of Antonio and his son remains uncertain" (p. 206); or John Orr's (1993) elaboration on the openness of Antonioni's *L'Avventura*, and how its "'adventure' of the search for [Anna] is not an adventure at all, for by the end of the picture she has not yet been found, not known either to have escaped from the island and started a new life or been kidnapped, committed suicide or drowned" (p. 90). Consider, as well, Satyajit Ray's *Pather Panchali* (*Song of the Little Road*, 1955), which concludes with the slow retreat on a bul-lock cart of Apu and his parents, each family member absorbed in his or her own numb speechlessness. Such an ending, as Ben Nyce (1988) opines, is really more an "opening to the story of Apu's growth and re-generation" (p. 16).

Most famous of all as an open ending—indeed, it has obtained something of a canonical status in film textbooks—is the final shot of Truffaut's *400 Blows* (1959), whose freeze-frame of Antoine Doinel on the run does little to suture up story in a calculable way. Instead, the shot conveys only a *sense*—a *possibility*—that the troubled adolescent may be trapped "in a system from which there is no escape" (Fabe, 2004, p. 131). Thus the film ends neither happily nor unhappily, as Georges Sadoul declares: "It is an 'open end' with a question mark. . . . [T]his story flows along like life" (cited in Neupert, 1995, p. 89).

Neupert theorizes that viewers who are satisfied by such "incomplete" resolutions are in pursuit of a "deigetic 'purity'" inaccessible in formulaic filmmaking (p. 76). Open-ended films are, for them, like modern novels which—here he quotes Armine Kotin Mortimer—"grope with asking 'How can one pretend verisimilitude . . . without encoding a lack of finality? . . . How does one render an unfinished life in a finite form?'" (p. 76). There is unavoidable consequence to this "purity," however. At the end of a film, we find ourselves *right back at the beginning*, weighted down by all the same anxieties that the start of a narrative journey typically foments: Where are the characters going? Where will they end up? Will they manage? Will they make it? What's going to happen? One might even propose that—quite in contrast to orally inflected visual narrative, which often opens "in the middle of things"—the art film *concludes* in a fashion that is *in medias res*. The films, much as Bordwell (1985) yields, "make you leave the theatre thinking" (p. 209).

The expectation of a "postprandial" thinking may seem hardly subversive to spectators reared on literacy. More likely, they will find such thinking stimulating; even intellectually beneficent; at the least, reflective of the vagaries of life. But more significant here than the thinking that is being required is what precisely one is being asked to think *about*. For, to end with questions, as all these films categorically do, severely undercuts the orally inflected expectation of social restoration, of a return to and confirmation of the traditional order. As Havelock (1963) declares, the "Homeric state of mind" is of necessity a "general state of mind" (p. 135). Indeterminacy of the art film's type thus constitutes a structural, and even existential, violation of the orally inflected narrative, whose reinforcement of the status quo is vital because it assures self-perpetuity.

That no successful Hindi popular film comes close to shirking narrative closure surely bolsters this point. Epistemically oral stories *must* be discrete, noncontinuing, "tied-up" affairs, regardless of where they may be taken in the future in the form of sequels.[14] Only when a collectivity is permitted to leave the "we"-inflected nature of storytelling *without cause for social jeopardy* can an open ending appear provocative or fulfilling. Group consciousness, in this way, yields to self-consciousness—not because nonliterate persons lack acute self-awareness but because, by

---

14. Neupert (1995) makes an important distinction between open-ended film *series* (such as Truffaut's Doinel series or Ray's Apu trilogy) and closed-text *sequels* (like *The Thin Man* series or James Bond films): A sequel "often exploits a work's success, prolonging its story," but it completes its hypotextual story, which is not the case with an open-ended film (p. 79).

virtue of the exigencies of their way of knowing, they cannot afford such an uncertain, incomplete, or ambiguously suspended state.

As addressed in Chapter 2, narrative expression of the self in oral communities is outwardly oriented: agonistic in delivery, nested in speech. The self in these circumstances is experienced in and through connection with others—even if this means having to talk out loud to oneself onscreen. (To some degree, this explains why tighter climactic structures that are exoterically moving toward a target can work in oral venues: In effect, these structures simulate verbomotor speech.) The literately inflected individual, on the other hand, is released from the necessity of group definition, and so, too, from all the extrospective expressions of self that such definition dictates. As a result, characters can begin to act for reasons that are *not* outwardly oriented, that are *no longer* motivated by other persons or external circumstance. They become free, in a sense, to dwell on their existence as independent entities. No longer bound by the need to visualize knowledge in a manner that will most effectively preserve experience, they can even reorganize that knowledge in ways that are decidedly more abstract (Havelock, 1963, p. 189).

Once again, this is not because oral peoples are not *self*-conscious (i.e., self-aware). Consciousness of the self is "coextensive with humanity" (Ong, 1982, p. 178). But writing, permitting as it does an exceptional divorce from the group, fosters an increased and even articulable introspectivity. The self-searching art-film character is, in a sense, a *reading* character, one whose motivations have been shaped, even if only unconsciously, by the book. But why would reading foster interiority? In short, it is because the human sensorium, which prior to literacy functions largely on the basis of acoustics (the voice for speaking, the ear for hearing), now confines itself primarily to *sight* (Ong, 1967). The modern student, unlike his Homeric counterpart, "pours his energy into book reading through the use of his eyes instead of his ears" (Havelock, 1963, pp. 44–45). Because reading can make "meaning available for much more prolonged and intensive scrutiny," it actually "encourages private thought [. . . and] enables the individual to objectify his own experience" (Goody & Watt, 1968, p. 62). With the socializing effects inherent in the human voice minimized, a more profound individualism thus emerges (Ong, 1967, p. 72). Writing and print, in effect, "created the isolated thinker . . . and downgraded the network of personal loyalties which oral cultures favor as matrices of communication and as principles of social unity" (p. 54). Without needing any longer to exhibit primary allegiance to the voice, an entire *film* can now abandon the voice's cinematically mediated properties (e.g., sound effects, kinetic camera movements that signal emotion, etc.). Given this, we need ask if modern cinema came less to function the way consciousness does (i.e., with image and sound operating discontinuously, as in the Deleuzian proposition) than to reflect a decidedly *literate* type of consciousness that only a *literately* inflected viewer might be able to interpret.

The development over time of the novel actually reflects this shifting consciousness, in the way that the narrator's observation and command post eventually become "set up inside, in man's innermost self, and consequently events themselves are more and more shifted to the interior of the narrating ego" (Kahler, 1973, p. 168). Perhaps it is best I defer more fully here to Kahler, who with inimitable grace elaborates print's long-term unfolding:

> The direction of the interacting development of consciousness and reality is . . . a progressive *internalization* of events, an increasing displacement of outer space by what Rilke has called inner space, a stretching of consciousness. This in turn brings with it an incorporation, an internalization, of more and more of the objective world— which means taking in a wider range of the world, and plumbing it more deeply. In penetrating into unexplored strata of reality, consciousness transforms that reality. In a much higher and more complex sense the process resembles what happens in a child who tries to master wider and wider circles of his external world. By his efforts to organize that world he becomes aware of his own inner world as a coherent self. (p. 5)[15]

Although Kahler's observations may strike the reader as too speculative, they find social scientific backing in Luria's research on cognitive development. Luria (1976) and his team of psychologists discovered that, as literacy is mastered, significant changes in the basic structure of persons' cognitive processes result—"and result in an enormous expansion of experience and in the construction of a vastly broader world in which human beings begin to live" (p. 163). Even short-term education, Luria and his cohorts determined, lead to this psychological shift and to the "formation of a new inner world" (p. 159).[16]

Nowhere is the shift toward an inner world more cinematically prevalent than in art-cinema narration's protagonists, who can often be found "expressing and explaining their mental states" or embarking on some sort of "dissection of feeling" (Bordwell, 1985, p. 208). The more frontal *object* of focus prevalent in the *masala* films (given its inherent im-

---

15. Ong (1982) echoes this in his assertion that, thanks to writing and print, "the present-day phenomenological sense of existence is richer in its conscious and articulate reflection than anything that preceded it" (p. 155).

16. A disproportionate number of Luria's (1976) nonliterate subjects were incapable of analyzing their own psychological features or subjective qualities: "As a rule, they either refused to name positive or negative qualities in themselves or dealt with the question by describing concrete and material aspects of their lives"; meanwhile, those who were "actively involved in progressive social life and with at least some education" participated in the process of "singling out and evaluating personal qualities" (pp. 147–148).

plication of an engagement with another) gives way here to a *subject* of focus—to an introspectively idiosyncratic (and sometimes self-absorbed) "I." Consequently, we find a character like Antonius Block in *The Seventh Seal* (1957) articulating his own existential angst to his confessor; and Guido in *8½* (1963), who, plagued by childhood memories, familial guilt, and fantasies of domination, ultimately "reaches a boundary situation with respect to the purpose of his life" (p. 208). We see the internal inconsistencies of Lidia in *La Notte* (1961), as Bordwell likewise notes, and the self-questioning of Anna in *Les rendezvous d'Anna* (1978) (p. 207).

Might we not safely postulate, then, that decidedly personal explorations of *la condition humaine*—perhaps even, by extension, psychoanalysis—are on some level motivated by literacy? In effect, it is literacy that has paved the way for the "psychological acting" and pursuit of an "interior drama," which directors like Bresson candidly favor (Schrader, 2001). Maybe literacy accounts, too, for why so many viewers, including literate ones, find art films pretentious. The foray into the self, especially when overwrought or crudely imagined, can appear cold, off-putting, and narcissistically motivated (cf. McLuhan, 1964). Moreover, some literate viewers may prefer an epistemically oral film because of their desire to regain a togetherness that writing, as an isolating endeavor, has in part undone. As Henri-Jean Martin (1994) observes, "Written discourse incited the individual to adopt a cold view of the world and his fellows, a view detached from contingencies and repressing sensitivity" (p. 510). Such an individual interacts less with other people, Martin intimates, than with written materials that essentially cut her off from other people. The inward turn, in other words, can ironically breed a kind of *disconnection* from the nontextually derived presence of others, an alienation from one's fellow "social" creatures, even a dehumanizing of them.

The phenomenological exploration that art cinema revels in—via "'exhibit[ing] character,'" providing an "'inquiry to character'" or presenting characters who "slid[e] passively from one situation to another" (Bordwell, 1985, p. 207)—comes with an additional cognitive encumbrance. For, this kind of exploration—this depth psychology as a concerted *act*—requires a "severing of clock time from psychic time" (Kahler, 1973, p. 191) and a competency for enduring and relishing *subjective* time. Subjective time significantly detaches the individual further from the group, however. It breeds—or, at the minimum, demands that a spectator willingly embrace—a kind of isolation that may well be anathema to the orally inflected spectator for whom "judgement bears in . . . from outside, not from within" (Ong, 1982, p. 55). As Luria (1976) discovered on the basis of the peasants whom he interviewed, judgment and evaluation of the self are, from the oral standpoint, perceived as extrinsically motivated enterprises, shaped foremost by what *other people* say.

The act of interrogating one's own feelings and memory, of inspecting the mind's various folds and diverse corrugations, is conceivably not only an aim of art-cinema narration (as Bordwell points out) but also the outgrowth of a literately inflected *mentalité*. Writing has made this formal disturbance possible, just as it has generated the concern with personal crisis and alienation and permitted the psychic sortie with which art-cinema narration so frequently flirts. One might even contend that, only when memory can be disentangled from the *act* of memory, does the projected Self (with a capital S) emerge. We interrupt ourselves quite literally to bring us ourselves, and in the process we are reconstituted.

Thus we might wonder: Is it literacy that has given rise to what Pasolini (2001) termed the *free indirect point-of-view shot*, which acts as a kind of inexplicit interior monologue (p. 47)? Has it ushered in, too, the first-person style of filmmaking that Bruce Kawin (1978) labels *mindscreen*, whereby a cinematic sequence appears to be narrated in the first person, emphasizing the "subjectivity—almost the solipsism—of private experience" (p. 12)? We should probably also draw attention to the "childization" of perspective evident in art films like Ray's *Pather Panchali*. Although similar in intent to the Romantics' exaltation of the child "for his unjaded, fresh perception" (Wellek & Warren, 1956, p. 242), such formalistically deformed perspectives are decisively *discontinuous*. They render time as much the subject of a story as the vehicle for the story's telling—an aesthetic manipulation that owes much to writing and print.

One might even liken such art films to existential fragments, diachronically shorn from the epic of oral life. Orally inflected narrative cannot afford to concentrate on individual presence in the present, after all, indifferent as such presence is to ancestral connections. Telescoping the past with the present, as we have already covered, is essential in an oral economy, and any move toward a discrete "pastness of the past" is contingent on "a historical sensibility which can hardly begin to operate without permanent written records" (Goody & Watt, 1968, p. 34).

I need note that depth psychology additionally promotes a divorce from the *divine* as the external arbiter of affairs. As we witnessed earlier, this is not a disassociation common to Hindi popular film. The "strict separation of divine attributes from the natural world, and from human life" (Goody & Watt, 1968, p. 54)—which indubitably one sees in art-cinema narration—very likely derives from a literately engendered capacity for succession from the group, including, importantly, the ancestral realm. Indeed, neglect of literacy's sway on this aspect of cosmic relations has led, as Goody and Watt warn, "to much misunderstanding of the non-empirical and magico-religious aspects of [oral] culture" (p. 54).

True, many of the most renowned films of the French New Wave do view the past explicitly "through the eyes, the languages, and the rhetoric of the present" (Higgins, 1996, p. 22). Nonetheless, they do so

subjectively, the implication being that the past is no longer "part of a coherent cosmogony that leads (chrono)logically to the present" (p. 22).
What this perforce speaks to is the *double-remove* of New Wave cinema
from the oral habit of mind: first, from the oral percipient's acute need to
conflate the past with the present; and second, from a more elemental
sort of literate inflection that fosters the production of chronologies, of
history as a linear accumulation of causes and effects (Havelock, 1963,
p. 169). In this way, the existence of New Wave films may be due no
more to the films' conceptual and historical rooting in literary modernism than to their being (as indeed literary modernism is) a continuation of a chirography- and print-induced movement that has permitted
individual experience "to replace collective tradition as the ultimate arbiter of reality" (Watt, 1957, p. 14). One might thus propose an etiological
alternative: that art-cinema narration's overarching subordination of
communal *action* to individual *reaction* results from a process that has
been at work since at least the Renaissance.[17]

Detachment from the oral economy and the resultant increased indi-
vidualization of personal experience certainly help to explain the cinematic emergence of what we might call the "mundane hero": the mid-
dling bureaucrat; the directionless nurse; the jejune gangster who never
grows up; even a collectively monotonous *beau monde*. These kinds of heroes—neither flat, nor inflated—only arise out of the possibility of the
subjectivity previously discussed. As Jyotika Virdi (2003) acknowledges,
"The creation of characters that are like 'real people' requires the acceptance of 'subjective individualism,' in which characters do not merely
represent class, caste, or a social role" (p. 41). Significantly, she states this
as a means of describing what *hasn't* been a dominant form of filmic representation in India. Art-cinema narration of course regularly and radically dissociates itself from characters that can only "represent" or that
eclipse locale, as well as from actors whose star potential overrides their
ability to inhabit a character. True, the species did have its own entrenched set of "stars": Yves Montand, Jean-Paul Belmondo, Marcello
Mastroianni, Liv Ullman, to name a few. But Orr (1993) makes explicit
that these were "figures of displacement, not icons of seduction. There
[was] little crossing-over of the spectator into the image, into *their* image"
(p. 57). In other words, the species downplayed "larger-than-life" personae in its pursuit of a verisimilar world where the human would be
"just one fact among others" (Bazin, 2001, p. 24).

Psychoanalytical film theory of course suggests that seductive screen
figures (the sort art-cinema narration was shunning) promote a specta-

---

17. According to Brian Stock (1996), the literacy-related "growth of interest in subjectivity, individuality, and the interior life" actually emerges earlier, during the Middle Ages
(p. 130).

tor's slippage into a star's image. Desire—here envisioned as the pursuit of that which a spectator lacks—is centrally bound up with the act of looking at a star on the screen and "gives rise to what Metz calls the 'perceptual passions' of narcissism, voyeurism and fetishism" (McDonald, 1995, pp. 86–87). One wonders, however, if the act of looking, with all its theoretical implications of pleasure and sadism, may have additional raisons d'être that are *not* exclusively motivated by psychosexual desire. Perhaps in not attending to spectatorial agency as such agency is bound up with issues of literacy, we have overemphasized levels of narcissism and sexual compulsion. Indeed, for some viewers the *lack* of a relational merger with a star may signal a story's lack of serviceability, removing the experience as it does from the empathetic and participatory realm of oral inflection. Consider, for example, that Homeric audiences "submitted gratefully to the hypnotism of another" and "to the paideutic [educational] spell" (Havelock, 1963, pp. 147, 159). Although here Havelock is describing a listener's relationship to a poetic performer, the statement's applicability to the realm of the film theater, where spectators are brought under the hypnotic spell of stars, certainly seems tenable.

Perhaps nothing endangers, even "kills," the hypnotic spell more than the invincible *anti*-hero, that is to say, the protagonist whose departure from social norms does *not*, for the sake of communal conservation, require that he be either reformed and reinstituted into the status quo or physically expunged by a film's end. Thus, Antoine Doinel can remain a lost and troubled waif up to his last freeze-frame, just as woman A and a man X can remain fixed in their labyrinthine last year at Marienbad. Such characters can appear fresh and affecting, but probably only to spectators who are not seeking in a hero "a major conservator of culture" (Ong, 1967, p. 205).[18]

Sometimes, of course, it is a director of the art film who intentionally and self-consciously sets out to kill the hypnotic spell—often by deploying Brechtian techniques. In such cases, detachment is used as a narra-

---

18. Sometimes in literately inflected material, an antihero's existential rationale will be tangibly linked to the technologies that have produced him. As Ong (1967) details,

> when the possibility of storing detailed verbalized knowledge becomes virtually infinite, the hero . . . is replaced by his opposite, the antihero, who, instead of storing knowledge, comes ultimately to reflect wryly on the vast quantities of it which are stored and on the storage media themselves, as do Samuel Beckett's typical technological-age antiheroes Murphy or Malone or, more particularly, Krapp, mulling over the hopeless electronic reproduction of his own earlier voice in *Krapp's Last Tape*. (p. 205)

Ong's observations here could just as easily apply to many of Godard's films, to Fellini's *8½*, even, in a sense, to *Citizen Kane* (1941), in which a journalist attempts to piece together the puzzle of an individual's life based on written records, newspapers, art objects, even film itself.

tive device ("distanciation," Brecht calls it). Action severed from sound, characters speaking into the camera, jump cuts, and other sorts of intrusions are used to disrupt the illusion of a continuous story. Through these means the viewer is implicated for anticipating or desiring the sort of emotional involvement that, in Brecht's (1964) estimation, ultimately thwarts legitimate human inquiry. Godard's films perhaps best illustrate this mode of screen storytelling. They are, in the words of Susan Sontag (2001), "regularly broken or segmented by the incoherence of events and by abrupt shifts in tone and level of discourse" (p. 312). Interestingly, Kazmi (1999) makes a well-intentioned, if corporately quixotic, plea for a Brechtian reconfiguring of Hindi conventional cinema. But Brechtian engagement problematically calls for an explicit *dis*engagement from a story, which the orally inflected percipient may find impractical, perhaps even infeasible. (Why this is so I address more fully at a later stage.)

The stretched or heightened consciousness that art-cinema narration delights in, and that Brechtian detachment purportedly enhances, is of course envisioned as a *positive* thing—as an expansion of human thought with all that thought's social and economic perquisites. But such freedom, as I earlier intimated, comes at a price. Any withdrawal into one's own brings with it "special strains of its own" (Ong, 1967, p. 135). The reason bears repeating: The isolation that is mandatory for the relishing, perhaps even possibility, of depth psychology also can trigger an increase in neurosis. Retreating into the self may result in a flowering of the internal world, but it can just as easily rouse feelings of segregation as a psychological and existential weight. As Ong remarks regarding the literate individual's displaced ken, the human being becomes "a kind of stranger, a spectator and manipulator in the universe rather than a participator" (p. 73).

This ontological condition certainly reverberates in modernist cinema where, more often than not, heroes and heroines are fashioned as cut-off and alienated entities. In fact, in a 1961 sociological survey, one of the two major features said to characterize the French New Wave was the nature of its heroes—as generally "isolated from society, living a life 'amputated from any background collectivity'" (Higgins, 1996, p. 19).[19] But the same could be said of Antonioni's Italian protagonists who, "blocked by their inability to confront and understand themselves and their environment," tend to "bend and collapse under the weight of their own anxiety" (Kolker, 1983, p. 142). Much, too, has been made of the alienation motif in Bergman's films. In *The Silence* (1963), as one example

---

19. The other feature highlighted was setting, which was felt to be "unremittingly *contemporary*," existing in a kind of autonomous present (Higgins, 1996, p. 19). Perhaps setting's autonomy from the past speaks further to the French New Wave's departure from an orally inflected requirement for ancestral engagement.

among many, characters "torment themselves, seeking guidance and comfort in a world from which God is absent" (Kemp, 1996, p. 572).

Kolker (1983) suggests that this particular expression of personal impotence emerged as a "negative inheritance of neo-realism" (p. 134). That is, neorealism's incapacity to depict despair in a nonpitying fashion led ensuing directors to merge their own experience with that of their characters. In short, "the sense of removal from the world—figuring itself finally in a general neurasthenia, a numbness and fragmentation of the spirit—became a major character trait, and in some cases, a worldview" (p. 135). But I wonder if this also marks an accelerated progression toward the internalization of events that Kahler identifies apropos the history of the novel. After all, such inwardly turned despair is rarely, if ever, present in the *masala* film.

To say that literacy is in part the catalyst for private torment may seem far-fetched, but consider for a moment the relative absence of that feeling or condition in oral communities. J.C. Carothers in fact paired literacy with a growth in feelings of guilt and unworthiness based on the comparative *lack* of such feelings among the nonliterate individuals with whom he did fieldwork (McLuhan, 1964). Guilt, as Ong (1967) elaborates, comes "with a sense of one's interior as one's own" (p. 135). Because societies that are more orally inflected are by necessity more exteriorly oriented, they also are more prone toward *public* pressures. Thus shame, rather than guilt, is the guiding principle for their conduct. As a result, "Introspective characters paus[ing] to seek the etiology of their feelings" (Bordwell, 1985, p. 208) might not be sufficiently relevant to elicit any kind of response. In being too broadly disconnected from other individuals and the community at large, too obsessed with what is arguably an aggrandizing of the infinitesimal, such characters would more likely appear wholly disconnected from *what it means to be human*. In this way, orally inflected narrative's "mythic" semblance may be no less (or more) mythic than is the art film's psychoanalytical parsing of the self.

REALISM, RESTRAINT, AND DISENGAGING
FROM THE VOICE

Contingent on—or perhaps coterminous with—this shift into the realm of the innermost self is an eventual (one might even say necessary) withdrawal from the heavy, or amplified, characters that permeate orally inflected film. Communal recollection of course requires that characters and their journeys be repeated and recycled, as well as kinesthetically, aurally, and emotively spectacular. (These are, after all, the best means by which to ensure knowledge's successful enlistment to memory.[20]) What this invariably impedes, however, is that quality of appearance known as *verisimilitude*: the projection of life, not in an inflated manner, but as it "really" or "realistically" (supposedly) is—or, what Allan Tate calls the "putting [of] man wholly into his physical setting" (cited in Watt, 1957, p. 27).

If neorealism portends the arrival of art-cinema narration, it is, I suggest, principally because of that movement's *literally inflected drive* to "never mak[e] reality the servant of some *a priori* point of view" (Bazin, 1999, p. 203). Verisimilitude, after all, is one of the salient features of the English novel during its rise, several hundred years before the advent of film (see Watt, 1957). Literally centuries before modernism, let alone art-cinema narration, in other words, the slow, sometimes awkward fidelity to human experience was already materializing. Plot was becoming subordinate to the primacy of individual experience; description was growing more particularized and more taken with foregrounding the backgrounds of both space and time.

Of course the pursuit of reality in the case of the neorealist filmmaker did not begin with the written word. Rather, it began with the *photograph*, which was thought to possess the special power to "record the world 'objectively'" (Kolker, 1983, pp. 46–47). Presumably able to capture what reality really *is* (as opposed to what people merely *think* about reality),[21] the photograph marked for the neorealist the least interventionist way of revealing truth. Bazin (2001) referred to the "is" of this photographed reality as an "image-fact," as

> a fragment of concrete reality in itself multiple and full of ambiguity, whose meaning emerges only after the fact, thanks to the imposed facts between which the mind establishes certain relationships. Unquestionably, the director chooses these "facts" carefully while at the same time respecting their factual integrity. (p. 23)

Helplessly embedded in Bazin's statement against cinematic serfdom is a corollary to his proviso (and a somewhat ironic one at that). For verisimilitude must at every turn maintain a mark of particularity, of originality; it must be a singular, original representation of the real. In this sense, it is a reality that *can never be legitimately repeated*, not even as two identical image-facts, given that the second image-fact immediately becomes servant to an *a priori* point of view. Thus, art film cannot sup-

---

20. Barbara Herrnstein Smith (1998) maintains that the classical canonical author's endurance owes something to his or her being "repeatedly cited and recited, translated, taught and imitated, and thoroughly enmeshed in the network of intertextuality that continuously *constitutes* high culture" (p. 1575). How this corresponds (or doesn't) to more orally inflected requirements for the successful transmission of story is certainly an area worthy of future exploration.

21. Critic Felix A. Morlion, cited in Kolker (1983, p. 46).

port two *Bicycle Thieves,* or several versions of *Hiroshima mon amour* and *Loneliness of the Long Distance Runner* (1959). There only can be one unique specimen of each.

True, we may get trilogies like the Apu Trilogy, as Bordwell notes, or serial biographies like that of Antoine Doinel; but their formal organizations are committed to a verisimilitudinous continuation of characters, not to prescriptive recreations. Perhaps this is the true stimulus for Rosselini's statement that everyone has "his own neo-realism" (cited in Liehm, 1984, p. 129). Now, much as was the case with the development of the novel, any attention by the filmmaker to "pre-established formal conventions" is perceived only as endangering artistic success (Watt, 1957, p. 13). Hence art film's abandonment of (Havelockian, not Brechtian) epical properties, which hinge on replication and reiteration. Similarly, formulae and stock characters are renounced, as are those "highly secondarized" codes of cinematic convention (Metz, 1982, pp. 149–163)—tantamount to clichés—which, being fixed and economical, are essential oral carriers of content.[22] True, stock characters, being larger than life, fundamentally steer a narrative away from verisimilitude and toward myth, and so they might merit forsaking. But ironically, even *vraisemblance* as hitherto established will require abandonment, for only through the projection of something *inimitable* will a narrative be said to be capturing the "real." Consequently, it is only here, within the confines of a literately inflected universe, that any legitimate "anxiety of influence" (Bloom, 1997) exists. Anguish over one's work exhibiting too much indebtedness to, or an echo of, one's predecessors' plays little to no part in *masala* culture, with its generally collective, and ergo *collectively owned,* orientation. Only individuals operating out of a literate habit of mind conceptualize the word not as an utterance but as something fixed in print and prime for ownership.[23] In fact, typography *encourages* the mind to believe that words are original, creative expressions that have independence (McLuhan, 1962).

In order to emphasize the novelty of the "vagaries of real life" or those "trivial moments" of the dedramatized life, art filmmakers of

---

22. Deleuze (1986b) refers to the cliché as a "sensori-motor image of the thing" (p. 20). Hence, *opsigns,* which "break the sensory-motor schema, and where the seen is no longer extended into action" (p. 335), are of necessity opposed to clichés. They also are, as Deleuze points out, a major presence in art film.

23. Ray's Apu Trilogy foregrounds the significance of writing *in* films alongside its epistemic contouring *of* films. In that trilogy's movies, creative expression in categorically *alphabetic* terms (i.e., as book learning, book writing, and book reciting) is paramount. In *masala* films, on the other hand, if the written word enters at all, it does so more for general (and often simultaneously aurally articulated) informational reasons, or as representative —as in a film like *Shree 420 (Mr. 420, 1955)*—of the national project of literacy. In this way, the dramatized skill of literacy still retains an aura of being collective as an endeavor.

course turned to *technical* innovations for help: unusually long takes; unexpected abrupt cutting (Bordwell, 1985, p. 206). Although these techniques may have provided more flexible means of expression (p. 206),
they could only do so insofar as they remained unconventionalized. In
this way, the catch-22 of literate inflection comes fully to light: Any excavation of reality was conjointly a *creation* of reality, given the perpetual
need to be utterly distinct. To some degree, this explains the compulsion
once neorealism was fully tapped for modernist filmmakers to dig
deeper, to dig elsewhere, to seek an increasingly multifaceted, heterogeneous reflection of existence (more symbols, less clarity)—anything that
would denote further departure from the already pictorially established;
anything to deform one's own narrative into a state of inimitability.

Despite that modernists exalted representations that were comparatively de-dramatized, one might argue that such representations were in
fact *more* dramatic due their being pictorially independent and distinct.
As Zavattini (1953) himself asserted, if a woman were going to be shown
buying a pair of shoes, all that the director needed to do was "to discover and then show all the elements that go to create this adventure. . . .
[I]t will even become 'spectacular.' But it will become spectacular not
through its exceptional, but through its *normal* qualities" (p. 146). The
drama, in other words, was migrating elsewhere—shifting out of the
realm of oral expectation and more toward the wont and aspirations of a
mentalité that no longer needed, as a conserving gesture, to pay obei-
sance to traditional materials. To label the orally inflected characteristics
of narrative *ab*normal, however, would be misguided; preferable, I think,
is to cede to the literate inflection of Zavattini's perception of "*normal*
qualities."

Readers familiar with Hindi popular cinema may be unsympathetic
to this portion of my argument, critical of the constrictive manner in
which I have been discussing verisimilitude. After all, Bollywood films
have a history of employing neorealist techniques. As Mishra (2002) observes, the 1952 First International Film Festival brought the films of De
Sica and Rossellini to Indian film producers' attention, and the consequences of that exposure are palpable in films like *Mother India* and *Roti,
Kapada aur Makaan* (*Food, Clothing, Shelter*, 1974).[24] Yes, location shooting
and natural settings were incorporated into these Bollywood films; but
they were incorporated in ways that were incompatible with the holistic
motivations that Zavattini (1953) describes. These movies neither fore-
went a reduction of story "to its most elementary, simple . . . banal
form," nor showed things "as they happen day by day—in what we
might call their 'dailiness,' their longest and truest duration" (pp. 145–

---

24. Mainstream Hindi films through the 1960s were also strongly influenced stylisti-
cally, and to some extent philosophically, by Soviet films.

146). I propose that they *couldn't*—not if they wished to engage the Indian film-going masses. In the oral conception of things, a story reduced to its most banal form *is* banal, and there is little essential or poetic to discover in the ordinary.

Of course Zavattini contended that, when neorealism is effectively realized, banality vanishes "because each moment is really charged with responsibility. Every moment is infinitely rich. Banality never really existed" (p. 148).[25] But those "infinitely rich" moments, which Zavattini finds in the films of Rossellini and De Sica, hinge on two characteristics that are *never* imported into the Bollywood film, but that are fundamental to neorealist films like *Open City* or *Umberto D.* (1952). One might even say that these characteristics—quiescence and quietude—*define* the "where" and "what-ness" of neorealistic reality as it was later to be imported into modernist films, whether as a verisimilitude of behavior—or of space—or of time.[26] Until now, quietude and quiescence have gone insufficiently commented on by theorists in terms of the cognitive demands they make on spectators. But a one-to-one mapping of art-cinema narration and Hindi popular cinema underscores the pair's indispensability to art film, as well as the manner by which Hindi films carefully modulated neorealistic elements to accommodate oral facility and expectation.

Here it is worth reiterating the last chapter's explanation of the orally inflected visual narrative's relationship to stillness and silence. Films like *Amar Akbar Anthony* and *Raja Hindustani* (*Indian King*, 1996) eschew such attributes at all costs; for, if expression is fundamentally tied to the *voice*—and, in the case of film, to visually formulaic extensions of oral rhetoric, such as syntagmatic kinesthesia and nonironically amplified camerawork—what can quiescence and quietude possibly *say*? What value can there be in narrative wordlessness, in a lack of movement or a slowed-down world? Epic and folk narratives are capable of silence or pausal depth, to be sure, but they include that experience primarily as utterance. (In other words, the silences typically serve as "institutionalized cues that help to channel audience reaction," Foley, 2002, p. 128.) A concerted departure from that kind of utterance, quietude and quiescence mark, in effect, the *absence* of a story, not a compelling route to its depth.

Consequently, in narrative that is heavily orally inflected, we find nothing akin to the lyrical narrative vagrancy found in Satyajit Ray's *The World of Apu* (1959), or to that film's general preference for climactic moments devoid of kinetic aplomb. Ray stipulated, in fact, that "crucial mo-

---

25. According to Deleuze (2001), this is a trait most comprehensively pulled off by Ozu, for whom "everything is ordinary or banal, even death and the dead who are the object of a natural forgetting" (p. 99).

26. Bordwell (1985) isolates these different types of verisimilitudes as they appear in art-cinema narration.

ments in a film should be wordless, if possible" (cited in Nyce, 1988, p. 5). Nowhere is his commitment to that aesthetic philosophy more apparent than in his domestic drama *Charulata* (*The Lonely Wife*, 1964), where an "elegant seven and a half minutes without dialog" begins the film and is meant to show "the genteel suffocation of [a] young wife's life as she moves within her mansion" (Heifetz, 1993, p. 72).[27] According to Kolker (1983), Ray's general concern is with "building images of faces and landscapes, of faces in a landscape, and with detail, textures, and spatial relationships that define events more quietly than sentimentality and melodrama" (p. 92). Critics often consider this kind of storytelling to be the exemplar of cinematic *purity* (as Kolker does) because of its refusal to "yield to the softening of cliché" (pp. 92–93). But given what we have uncovered regarding the necessity of clichés in the oral economy, such an attitude is most certainly born of a literately contoured *mentalité*.

Ray is only one of numerous art-film directors who deploy quietude and quiescence with something close to deference. As Orr (1993) waxes, "De Sica, Olmi, Pasolini, Rosi . . . Wajda, and Rohmer all celebrate the triumph of the image, its luminous intensity, *its priority over the spoken word*" (p. 45, emphasis added).[28] The gaze in these instances shifts *into* the image, binding with it in a different—and, in some respects, aberrant—fashion. Only the percipient existentially able and willing to *disengage* from the voice, however, will likely participate in a "whatness" of things, whether broken pots, wire fences, plates on a table, pylons that carry the hum of electricity, or water bugs scuttling weightlessly across lily pads. (In this way, the exoteric nature of orally inflected viewing—its "star"-gazing, for instance, its propensity for kinetic arousal—is once again shown to be no less fetishistic or idle as a mode of engagement.) Art cinema can afford customary, dilatory detachment from the human face precisely because there is no longer an epistemic need to prioritize the domicile of the spoken word. Thus, a film like Bresson's *Pickpocket* (1959) can document "through the disconnected movements of hands

---

27. One of Ray's artistic Bengali predecessors, the novelist, playwright, and poet Rabindranath Tagore, expressed similar sentiments. In a 1929 letter, Tagore insisted that

> [the] principal element of a motion picture is the "flux of the image." The beauty and grandeur of this form in motion has to be developed in such a way that it becomes self-sufficient without the use of words. If some other language is needed to explain its own, it amounts to incompetence. If music can achieve profundity without words of the cadence of a melody, then why should not this "motive form" be considered as a distinct aesthetic experience? (cited in Rajadhyaksha & Willemen, 1999, p. 225)

28. Similarly, in the Indian art film *Uski Roti* (*Our Daily Bread*, 1970), we find a "slow, unrelenting" pace that functions on the basis of stark images that "hold in them the distilled essence of sorrow and solitude. Silences enfold you, force you to face yourself" (Vasudev, 1986, p. 101).

and arms in train stations, streets, and barren rooms, the career of a small-time Parisian thief" (Kolker, 1983, p. 158), and touch can now become "an object of view in itself," a hand eventually "tak[ing] on a role in the image which goes infinitely beyond the sensory-motor demands of the action" (Deleuze, 2001, p. 98).

And if a director *is* inclined to concentrate on the face, only in the literately inflected realm will that face be present principally to manifest the "sacred solitude" that Schrader (1988) identifies apropos Bresson's work. Only from this epistemic arena can the expressive qualities of a face exist *solely for the sake of* the expressive qualities of a face. If a film's puissance lies "in what is not exposed, in the silent exchanges of looks and the unchanging expressions of faces" (Kolker, 1983, p. 159), we need to factor in the decidedly "textual organization of consciousness" (Ong, 1982, p. 154) that permits it this residence.

Correspondingly, literate inflection breeds a "whatness" of place, such as one finds in the disquietingly sere landscapes of Antonioni, or the vaporously volcanic ones that Rosselini sometimes favors. In narrative heavily contoured by orality, on the other hand, rarely, if ever, does an urban landscape take precedence over a protagonist's search—as happens in *Paisan*; and never—again in *Paisan*—is a protagonist's loss undercut by a "re-creation of the emptiness and random violence of a wartime city" (Kolker, 1983, p. 58). Similarly, set or décor as elements of montage seldom become "the very basis of the narrative and visual texture, the very source of the dramatic impulse" (Liehm, 1984, pp. 64–65), as indubitably they can, and often do, in art-cinema narration.

Absent, too, from the oral storytelling environs is art cinema's predilection for "empty spaces, without characters or movement"; for "interiors emptied of their occupants"; or for the "deserted exteriors or landscapes in nature" that Deleuze (2001) so extols of Ozu's films. Deleuze, of course, may claim that a shot of a vase or a bicycle as a still-life speaks to its being a representation of what *endures*, of "the unchanging form of that which moves" (p. 102); but endurance is a narratively circumscribed property, and one that, in the oral episteme, is fundamentally tied to the movement of information *through* time, not to information's becoming petrified *as* time. What is absent from orally inflected narrative, then—what *must* be absent—is precisely that Deleuzian prospect for unassimilated moments of "pure seeing," for visions "disconnected from the commonsense coordinates of their standard usage and practices" (Bogue, 2003, pp. 109–110). Once again, my claim is not that oral peoples can't function in silence or that they have no aptitude for seeing "purely." (I am dealing here exclusively with traits that epistemically proceed from a *storytelling* matrix.) But given that quiescence and quietude are largely absent from the oral storytelling matrix, we need to rethink Deleuze's assertion that narrative is *only secondarily* a product of a structure of space and time (Bogue, 2003): Cinematic space and time are, in fact, fundamentally structured by the pressures that orality puts on narrative.

For this very reason, we find no penchant in Bombay cinema for gaps in conversation, for long drawn-out silences and conversational *temps mort* (Bordwell, 1985). These are commonplace in art-cinema narration, of course, because of the way they reflect a temporal verisimilitude. Take, for instance, the "'dead' spaces of waiting for an event [which] become in Antonioni's films as vital and vibrant as the 'event itself'" (Orr, 1993, p. 25). Better yet, consider a scene from Marguerite Duras' *Nathalie Granger* (1972), where we watch

> two women in medium shot, busy in the kitchen, and we also see close-ups of their faces. Most striking are the extreme closeups of their hands, slowly sweeping the crumbs from the surface of the table. The scene is slow, hypnotic, and silent, the image rich and ambiguous. What emerges is a brutally blunt but, paradoxically, soothing account of the rhythm, the repetition, the mindlessness of housework, the very antithesis of social change, a movement that is no Movement. . . . [I]ts very plotlessness overturns narrative and visual expectations. (Higgins, 1996, p. 136)

Whereas the primacy of *masala* storytelling is housed in a shared, "spoken" language, here the spectator is being deliberately severed from that language via diegetic dead time.

For Higgins (1996), the "utter silence" of this scene from *Natalie Granger* additionally operates as a sign of a "particularly feminine mode for the Duras of 1972" (p. 136). Emphasizing that this is *Duras'* mode is prudent of Higgins, given that gender depictions may not always be able to escape the psychodynamic and performative demands that orality places on story. What Duras offers, we might say, is a literately inflected representation of the feminine, one that demands of its spectators a restrained, disciplined type of looking that may not be in the oral percipient's purview. Neil Postman (1982) puts great emphasis on how patience and self-control, which any silent reading mandates, are highly learned and *unnatural* skills. Reading, he proclaims, "is, in a phrase, an antisocial act" (p. 27).[29] Perhaps for the oral spectator, then, quietude and quiescence—even when gendered—are similarly perceived as *anti-social*. After all, they are antipodal to the agonism with which orally inflected audiences often engage with goings-on on the screen. In that sense, those darkened theaters in which "it is understood [that] we are supposed to be silent" (Telotte, 2001, p. 25) may be to some extent the

---

29. H. Bloom (1994), of course, extols the reader who "does not read for easy pleasure or to expiate social guilt, but to enlarge a solitary existence" (p. 518).

creation of a literately inflected sensibility. Only the individual inculcated into the habit of mind that reading fosters imagines that we should never "raise our voices above a whisper [in a theater], for here it is the *movie*'s role to talk and ours to listen" (p. 25).[30]

We need only turn to an anecdote from Satyajit Ray to confirm this. In Ray's moviegoing experience, "there were always some people [in Indian audiences] who would feel obliged to join in," and who would, in doing so, render the viewing process a group performance, thereby depriving a film of its beauty (Robinson, 1989, p. 85). For this reason, when in *Pather Panchali* the aged auntie Indir Thakrun dies, Ray, by his own admission, *avoided* representing her funerary procession in its wholly traditional form. Deliberately he excised the mourners' chanting of the mantra as they transported Thakrun's corpse to the cremation grounds. Instead of voices rising in unison to proclaim *Ram nam sat hai* (God is truth), Thakrun's disembodied voice sings a doleful ballad that has, by this point, become her leitmotif. So, although Ray was intent on making his film life-like and sans artifice, he was willing to relinquish authenticity, in order to keep his inferred audience at a distance and to mitigate its emotional response and public engagement with the text.

Perhaps no art-film director gives emphasis to the variance between orally and literately inflected storytelling better than Pier Paolo Pasolini. Pasolini is renowned critically for his deployment of *frontality*—a trait that I discussed at some length in Chapter 2. There, I claimed that frontality, as a style of representation modeled on devotional engagement with an icon, was unambiguously bound up with oral inflection. On the surface, Pasolini may appear to be using frontality in an identical way. For, as Noa Steimatsky (2003) explains, "The frontal assault of [Pasolini's] camera on the profilmic yields an image that seems to press forward onto the screen and endow the subject matter with [a] corporeal presence" that invites a sacral contemplation (p. 256). Pasolini of course drew inspiration for his frontal style from the Christian, not the Hindu, tradition, and more specifically from Byzantine and medieval portraiture. But religion is negligible when it comes to what really distinguishes Pasolini's use of frontality from Bollywood's; and the delimiting features are those already put forth in this section: realism, quietude, quiescence.

---

30. Baz Luhrmann, director of *Moulin Rouge* (2001), articulated something similar vis-à-vis his encounter with Indian movie audiences. As Meenakshi Shedde (2006) summarizes of his experience: "The audience was singing aloud the songs of the film, chatting, answering mobile phones—the viewers' interaction with the film onscreen was utterly amazing. Respectful silence is not at all integral to the way Indians express their appreciation of the cinema" (p. 24). This, as Shedde points out, is a way of watching films in great contradistinction to the French who "watch films in a theater as if they were in a cathedral —with awe and reverence" (p. 24).

"Pasolini's attachment to the 'things of the world' and to their incarnate images is," says Steimatsky, "manifest in the twofold commitment to the 'realist' and the 'reverential,' deeply intertwined in Pasolini's thinking, the one contaminating the other" (p. 254). Even this statement may seem to pertain to the *masala* film, which also blends the real with the reverential. But Pasolini additionally practices a "deliberate severing of sound and image," a "ceremonial isolation of voices," and, most radically, "moments of complete silence" (p. 259). Pasolini seeks out contemplative *detachment*, in other words, which is altogether distinct from the *attachment* that the Hindi popular film—by virtue of its never aurally or kinetically abandoning its viewer—exercises. In this way, conceivably, Pasolini's images lack the cultural intelligibility that Ravi Vasudevan claims drives the frontality of Hindi popular film. *Darsana* (beholding the divine) may sometimes be a solemn, private, spiritual affair in the context of religious observance; but the particular brand of "seeing" that the Bombay cinema imports from it is stimulated by the *communal* connection (not heightened disconnection) central to an orally inflected tale.[31]

Although Bordwell might attribute muteness and motionlessness to the loosened causality of art cinema and to its desire to open gaps that reflect contingency and the "realistic" tenuousness of life, the fact remains that this motif of absence-as-presence is inextricably tied to the ability to depart from the human voice. Only those who have been cognitively conditioned into the kind of reflection that quiescence and quietude mandate may find (or desire to find) value in disengaging from the tangible, situational externalities of plot.[32]

True, sometimes art films *aren't* muted. At times, they may ardently shun restraint, playing up and even celebrating the visually excessive. But this visual amplitude, as Bordwell (1985) intimates, is *still* beholden to a cinematic universe of "unfocused gaps" and "plausible improbabilities," of aimless wanderings and chance encounters (p. 206). A film like Fellini's *8½*, for instance, which revels in artifice and the carnivalesque, is at the same time a meandering "reflection upon memory and desire" and a personally motivated flirtation with "some modernist effects of memory and perception" (Kolker, 1983, p. 87). The motivations for its immoderation are hence almost the converse of those of orally inflected

---

31. Ozu also is singled out for his primarily frontal composition. Unlike Pasolini, Ozu creates a disparity or "overemphasis of the everyday" in his films via an employment of *irony* (Schrader, 2001, p. 305). For reasons detailed below, irony is generally nonapparent in the Hindi popular film.

32. Once again, orality serves a productive resource for explicating the Deleuzian severing of movement-image from time-image. If indeed speech in modern cinema became "detached from the sphere of public action" and thus became "its own 'image,' the sound-image" (Restivo, 2000, p. 178), it is likely that this was because percipients were capable of, or desirous of, detaching themselves from the sphere of public action.

film, where, beyond permitting indulgence in conspicuous consumption, visual and dialogical plenitude underscore a kind of *muscle memory* of events. In this way, the comment that Fellini's directorial alter ego, Guido, self-reflexively makes in *8½* about his own film—that "everything is in it"—applies just as well to the orally inflected film, but only if stripped of *8½*'s *ironical* self-awareness of excessiveness. (Just why this is the case becomes clear in the ensuing section.)

And so, it is not simply that art-cinema narration reflects a "different sort" of reality. Reality, once more, has been afforded the opportunity to develop into a new, more interiorized, more restrainedly real sort. And because this particular reality has been shepherded by literacy, one should not presume that that reality—even in its most outwardly "simple," "unaffected," or "accessible" form[33]—will be intellectually available, performatively engaging, or perceived as more "authentic" or "real" by all. Authenticity, like its counterpart artificiality, is to some extent *cognitively inspired*. We might even say that, narratively speaking, the artificial is that which is *pre*known (i.e., born of what literates might term the impersonal vacuities of caricature and formula); and if distinction from the preknown is conspicuously tied to literacy (as reflected, for instance, in *vraisemblance*), then we should be more sensitive to percipients who find themselves more comfortable engaging with the universe of the preknown. For them, orally inflected narratives may be exhibiting just as much attachment to the existential; but because this attachment exists and is manifest in the realm of surface plenitude, amplification, rhetorical redundancy, and the exoteric, it oftentimes goes dismissed or

---

33. The first two terms were used to characterize *Pather Panchali*—*simple*, by Ephraim Katz (1979) in *The Film Encyclopedia*; and *unaffected* by the *Video Movie Guide*. The third characterization appears on the jacket of *Wend Kuuni* (*The Gift of God*, 1983). Although *Wend Kuuni* (from Burkino Faso) is a film whose attributes evince heavy indebtedness to literacy, its director, Gaston Kaboré, claims to have made a film "immediately accessible to villagers seeing a movie for the first time." Unfortunately, I have been unable to locate any study addressing how villagers actually engaged with the film. The issue is in some sense resolved by Manthia Diawara (1989), who maintains that African films are not oral but "use the material of oral tradition to reflect the ideology of the time and not [the ideology] of the oral tradition. . . . Orality is the *subject* of the film because it incorporates an oral rendering of a tale which it later subverts" (p. 201). Such films herald the creation of a new film language, in other words, one that combines oral tradition's heritage with a contemporary African voice (Chirol, 1995, p. 50). *Wend Kuuni* in fact bears much in common with *Pather Panchali*, in terms of its *deceptive* simplicity. Like Ray's film, Kaboré's is consumed with routine and mundane activities of living: Life moves slowly, in an ethnographically envisioned way, absent of agonism or oratory. Further, the heavy presence of irony, symbolism, and tacit political and ideological transgressions adds to its literate inflection, as does its certifiable open-endedness. These traits are of course remiss in the African oral tradition where, as Diawara (1996) points out, a return from a journey, as a denouement, "symbolizes the return to the status quo" and a reinforcement of traditional values: "In oral traditions, the story is always closed so as not to leave any ambiguity about interpretations" (p. 215).

does not get recognized as deep or legitimate by high literates. One might even say that, to a nonliterate viewer, a Bollywood film may be *more real* and *more purposeful* than a film like *8½*. But because film scholars, like all humans, wear the collective spectacles of their subculture (Bourdieu, 1993),[34] until now this fact has gone largely obscured. Surely it is not a stretch to contend that a scholar's judgments may be as constrained as they are liberated by literacy. (Much as Bordwell, 1989, admirably acknowledges, "It would be disingenuous to pretend that I am neutrally surveying critical activities. . . . I am a member of the group I am studying, [and] my categories come to a large extent from my own group," p. xii.) Film intellectuals, through no fault of their own, have been trained into a mindset that prepares them to negotiate, and thus perhaps to elevate, quietude, stasis, the mundane, the unmotivated, the stripped-away, the abnegation of artifice's "easy" pleasures out of a respect for the veracity of the inward turn.

No doubt for this same reason Bollywood films, as an academic enterprise, have been frequently pigeonholed as vehicles of fantasy or gotten conscripted by ideological agendas. If scholars sometimes overread the *masala* genre or lambaste it for having "brainwashed the public and destroyed its ability to appreciate good cinema" (Garga, 1996, p. 242), this is likely because they are reading the genre through a high-literate lens. In this way, more may be revealed about the respondent than the text. For instance, is it possible that our recent academic infatuation with postmodernism has led to our grafting too brazenly onto orally inflected materials concepts like pastiche and bricolage? Such postmodern phenomena often entail, if they do not quite dictate, a consciousness on the part of the reader, a critical expectation of and facility for recognizing pastiche *qua* pastiche, bricolage *qua* bricolage.[35] (Homeric epic might otherwise qualify as pastiche nonpareil.) For similar reasons, we need to be cautious about applying terms like "intertextuality" to orally inflected narrative. Although one can certainly call Bollywood films intertextual, they are only so in the manner that *all* language is intertextual. The term, as it is used in the current critical vernacular, provides no real meaningful latitude here, as it applies too stringently to written texts, to literature and "modern poetic language" (Kristeva, 1984).

---

34. Pierre Bourdieu (1993) states, "The illusion of the 'fresh eye' as a 'naked eye' is an attribute of those who wear the spectacles of culture and who do not see that which enables them to see" (p. 217).

35. Larkin (2005) seems to echo this point in his consideration of Nigeria's *bandiri* music, which locally reworks Hindi film songs. The "bricolage of culture inherent in [such] a phenomenon," he cautions, should not be misread as a "free-floating event" (p. 306).

The problematic interstices between how postmodernists and typical viewers interpret films are colorfully addressed by Paul Lippert (1996), in his discussion of science-fiction films:

> Although the former embrace concretely glowing schematizations as symbols of conceptually glaring cultural prognostications, the latter struggle to maintain an existential footing on the narrative path. Dazzling one another in their kaleidoscopic dance of antifoundationalist imagery, the postmodernists fail to see the significance, indeed, even proclaim the "obsolescence," of narrative as it is known to the average person. But for the audience, it is the narrative that grounds the experience of images in the human lifeworld, which is where experience ultimately originates. (p. 268)

This is not as much of a digression as one might initially think. For, Nandy (1998) suggests something similar when he opines that Hindi popular film "does not require sophisticated analytic schemes of the kind that an Indian postmodernist might cherish. It is often vulgarly blatant" (p. 8) We might argue, thus, that the postmodernist's intellectual repudiation of expectations of coherence, and its concession to play and fragmentation in storytelling emerge in part from a *mentalité* heavily shaped by the legacy of print. How else to explain such an exuberant renunciation of traditional narrative form? Form, in the postmodernist circumstance, no longer needs to serve as a vehicle for content, as it must for members of oral societies.

If anything, such interpretive fissures speak to the broader, more intricate applicability of orality-literacy theory to film, in terms of how literate percipients read, read into, and recreate oral texts. But *can* it work the other way around? That is, are oral percipients as able or willing to read or read into literately inflected texts? Or is the perceived vanishing of the split between high and popular culture (as contended by postmodernists) somewhat illusive—*elusive*, in any case, to those who do not possess the epistemic capital to engage actively with literacy's legacy of recombinant texts? Certainly Easthope's (1991) explicit mention of the textual one-way street of postmodernism—with high cultural forms embracing material from popular culture, but the solidly popular seldom incorporating features of high culture—hints at an asymmetry. Consider for a moment how elusive quietude and quiescence might be, given that both these norms imply that a story is going *somewhere else*, that the story no longer resides (or needs to reside) expressly in the words or the words' visually rhetorical counterparts. Where then does the story go? Where *can* it go? How is it even possible for a story to go somewhere else in light of the two-dimensionality of the screen? Bring literacy into the fold and the answer becomes deceptively simple: *Inside*. Not inside the characters on-screen but *inside the viewer*.

TEXTUAL POLY-SEE-ME (SEE-ME-NOT) AND THE RISE
OF THE IMPLIED AUTHOR

According to Bordwell (1985), art films dramaturgically loosen up narrative cause and effect for diverse reasons. Causal gaps may be consciously inserted in order to provide an authenticity of sentiment or as a formalistic stance against Hollywood; they may be there "to exhibit character," or to "emphasize insignificant actions," or to "suggest an impersonal and unknown causality" (pp. 206–207). Irrespective of the director's motivation, viewers are clearly forced into situations where they must tolerate more permanent lacunae (p. 206). Such gaps make an especially consistent show in the cinema of the French New Wave, which is rife with "holes, blank spaces, aporias of all kinds, jumps and cuts, proliferating *mises en abyme* and figures of infinite regress" (Higgins, 1996, p. 15). Bordwell (1985), for instance, calls attention to the ambiguities of the opening sequence of Alain Resnais' *La guerre est finie* (*The War is Over*, 1966), which, being induced foremost by a "strongly subjective cast of the narration," thwarts our easy comprehension of events (p. 213). Or take *Bicycle Thieves*, where a peripheral event like getting caught in a rainstorm is rendered structurally central as an event. Sometimes the gaps may be more subtle—solicitations, say, that the viewer "notice how behavior and setting can give the character away" (p. 208). Indeed, art-cinema narration has developed an entire "range of mise-en-scène cues for expressing character mood: static postures, covert glances, smiles that fade, aimless walks, emotion-filled landscapes" (p. 208). Occasionally "the very surroundings may be construed as the projections of a character's mind," as in films like *Juliet of the Spirits* (1965) and *Repulsion* (1965) (p. 209).

Sometimes these narrative breaches are intended to project what *isn't* there. In *L'Avventura*, for example, a Bazinian "image-fact"—here in the form of a long take that is supposed to reflect the character Anna's absence—"casts doubt not only on what is seen but on who sees it. If Anna is out of sight, out-of-frame, none the less particular ways of framing her absence reinsert her as the unreal object become active observer" (Orr, 1993, p. 91). Other times, the ellipses are grounded (or not grounded, more accurately) in the fourth dimension. In the films of Bergman and Resnais, as well as of more recent directors like Wim Wenders and Andrei Tarkovsky, "durational time," as Orr (1993) tells us, "is mesmeric, hypnotic, a magnet to the gaze . . . directionless, indeterminate. One is tempted to call it a visual approximation to the subjective experience of time as suspended, lingering, listless, waiting to be enlivened by spectacle, by the sudden, unexpected act" (pp. 24–25). What we have here, in a sense, are temporal extensions of conversational *temps mort*—not to mention cinematic cues that "have alternately been lauded and deplored" (Higgins, 1996, p. 15).

Art film's juxtapositional handling of images, its laying of individual shots "gapingly" one against another, is a trait exhaustively explored by Deleuze. Indeed, if modern cinema offers a challenge, he says, it is for the director to start with a single image and "to choose another that will induce an interstice *between* the two. It is not a process of association, but of differentiation, as mathematicians call it, or disparation, as physicists call it" (cited in Bogue, 2003, p. 171).

On the surface, such textual alterations may seem formalistically temperate, especially to the spectator who has been steeped in literacy his or her entire life. In fact, these holes bear marked resemblance to the seductive flashes or "erotic gapes" that Roland Barthes (1975) contends are constituent of the best, most "writerly" (*scriptible*) literature. Such literature's meaning and potency, he argues, arises from its premeditated staging of "appearance-as-disappearance"—from a textual see-me/see-me-not-ness that engenders a *jouissance*, or sexual bliss, that a more passive "readerly" (*lisible*) type of literature cannot (p. 10). Places of indeterminacy, from the Barthesian vantage point, allow for a heightened spectatorial engagement precisely because they propel a percipient along a path that is *not* mentally predetermined.

But engagement with such nuanced and unarticulated cues, with such ill- and even undefined silences, heavily depends on a spectator's psychodynamic capacity and willingness to enter into dialectical *negotiation*. For, erotic gapes—or "deliberately weak links," as Deleuze (1986a) terms them in cinema (p. 210)—implicitly require that part of the storytelling be nested in a kind of thought oriented toward interpreting what, say, the silence of an aimless walk or the stillness of a bucolic place might signify. After all, with speech what "is" is rendered and given; in silence, what "is" *isn't* rendered and hence calls for private formulation. (This accounts for my previous emphasis on quiescence and quietude, since it is fundamentally in those two milieus that such deciphering is cognitively born.) Even *emotional* responses may require arduous accessing in the art film: "since nothing is obvious, the onus to generate emotion is upon the audience. Feeling must be discovered by the spectator" (Orr, 1993, p. 57).

Nowhere is this proactive mental (and emotional) engagement more solicited perhaps than in the oeuvre of Jean-Luc Godard. His textual universe verges

> on the absurd, or at least on the unmotivated fantastic, with actions defying both plausibility and efficiency. In Godard's *Weekend* [1967], for instance, St. Just reads aloud to the camera, garbage workers recite Engels, and Corinne eats her husband. . . . The tight verisimilar codes so important to the Closed Text are severed and replaced by ellipses and contradictory events. (Neupert, 1995, p. 139)

Such strategies of disruption render a story more akin to "a story-*man-qué*" (Chatman, cited in Neupert, 1995, p. 142) or to "a Nietzschean narrative about the absence of narrative" (Orr, 1993, p. 25). But what narratives like these unavoidably demand is that negotiations between characters shift to negotiations among characters—*and* screen—*and* spectator. And if the gap between them cannot be filled ("her look implies this . . . "; "his departure signifies that . . . "; "irony is intended in both . . . "), then the experience may be misinterpreted or, possibly, not experienced at all.

Likely the reader has surmised that such premeditated lacunae are nonapparent in Hindi popular cinema. Their absence is understandable, though, given that the ambiguity-cum-polysemy that such gaps induce and the honeycombed nature of the reality that ensues require that a spectator negotiate meaning on an abstract, nonoperational level—as a kind of "game-playing" or diversionary hide-and-seek. In fact, even literate spectators who do not want to do the work, or who suspect directors' gaps to be motivated more by faux artistry than intellectual intention, may find themselves disinclined to participate.

Luria's (1976) studies corroborate that such gaps require a spectator's engagement in a process of ratiocination that may be unattractive, even impracticable, to the oral individual. Consider that Luria's nonliterate subjects regularly refused to make inferences from syllogisms that were fashioned out of particulars directly connected to those subjects' own practical experience. Instead, they continuously repeated "different parts of the syllogisms as isolated, logically unrelated phrases" and did not perceive those various parts as "unified logical systems" (p. 106). At first blush, this may strike the alphabetic reader as peculiar, but the reasons for the subjects' behavior prove well founded when one factors in the utterance's tie to *action* in the oral economy. In the oral economy, words are situationally, not textually, bound; treating words as *independent* from activity might thus appear impractical, even nonsensical. When the utterance is capable of being put into writing, however,

> it can be inspected in much greater detail, in its parts as well as in its whole, backwards as well as forwards, out of context as well as in its setting; in other words, it can be subjected to a quite different type of scrutiny and critique than is possible with purely verbal communication. Speech is no longer tied to an "occasion"; it becomes timeless. Nor is it attached to a person; on paper, it becomes more abstract, more depersonalised. (Goody, 1977, p. 44)

The kinds of structures that call for a "free play" of mind apropos "logic" are obviously not consonant with the orally inflected individual's way of thinking or knowing. Literate society cultivates an intentionally and actively problematized semantic engagement, and it does so, as Goody and Watt (1968) propose, "by sacrificing a single, ready-made orientation to life" (p. 63).

In this way, those very textual elements which critics like Barthes and Umberto Eco (1979) venerate—erotic gapes, openness—might seem to the oral percipient existentially detrimental, divorced as those elements are from that ready-made orientation to life. This possibility is borne out further by the heightened resistance that the subjects in Luria's (1976) study displayed when it came to solving problems whose conditions contradicted those subjects' own practical experience. Unlike their more educated counterparts (whom Luria also studied), the nonliterate peasants remained committed to concrete thinking and operated "on the basis of 'practical utility'," refusing to define new concepts or to stray into thinking that was functionally irrelevant (p. 59).[36]

Notwithstanding that *The 400 Blows'* "seemingly haphazard linking of the film's actions" might be a creative directorial ruse to "decrease any expectation of homogeneous event-to-event repetitions" (Neupert, 1995, p. 87), some of its viewers might be disinclined (for valid reasons) to decode the impractical, and even idle, haphazardness of its text. Consider for instance the film's third scene, in which "Antoine forgets to buy flour, Mr. Doinel buys a fog lamp for the car in preparation for an automobile club outing, Mrs. Doinel shows her disgust toward her cousin's repeated pregnancies, and Antoine takes the garbage down"; as Neupert points out, "None of these acts ever develop in the film, so they are offered as representative events rather than the basis for any future scenes" (p. 87). The orally inflected viewer might ergo ask—or, more likely, *wouldn't* ask[37]—as to the purpose of such representative events. One of the fascinating by-products of the creative latitude taken by art-cinema narration, then, is an opening up of space for inadequate or incorrect readings—even for reading *into* material. But precisely because the oral episteme is linked to preservation, these are noetic alleyways that are likely to be avoided by nonliterate spectators.

Nowhere does erotic "free play" have freer reign than in those elements that are the pedagogical focal point of most literature and film studies classrooms: symbolism, metaphor, irony, and so forth. Readers (of this book) might summarily challenge that statement, calling attention to the prevalence of symbols in primitive cultures. However, as Dorothy Lee's anthropological fieldwork among the Tiv of Nigeria revealed, and as Edmund Carpenter (1972) rhetorically reminds us, "with nonliterate peoples generally, the symbol is regarded as an inseparable part of that which literate man believes it merely represents. Here the symbol participates in the

---

36. Vasundara Varadhan's (1985) fieldwork with nonliterate viewers of Indian government planning instructional films determined the same, that is, that nonliterate individuals appeared to "concretize [higher-level] abstractions in terms of their experience" (p. 120).

37. Generally, the nonliterate peasants whom Luria (1976) interviewed insisted that "it was senseless to 'define' or 'talk about' things that were perfectly obvious," including the obviousness of things *not there*: "The sun is the sun, everyone knows that." "There are cars everywhere, so people know what they are" (cited in Luria, 1976, p. 86).

total situation so that when the symbol alone is offered, it conveys—it doesn't create or evoke or apply—this value" (pp. 16–17). Symbols are not *riddles* in the oral milieu, in other words. In fact the sorts that typically appear in the *masala* film—a figurative representation of the Indian flag, a statue of Rama and Sita—operate far more as *totems*. The distinction between symbols and totems is vital here, and Susanne K. Langer (1942) cogently differentiates the two: Symbols, which require the distinguishing of a figure from its meaning, necessitate a mind's apprehending "*both* a literal and a 'poetic' formulation of an idea," whereas in the spontaneous envisagement in which the totem is rooted, "there is no such duality of form and content" (p. 150). Here, then, is the reason for why Raj Kapoor's Bombay films in the 1950s worked strenuously, as Virdi (2003) phrases it, to "narrow the gap between the symbolic and the real" through literal devices, such as a gold medal to signify integrity (p. 96). Meanwhile, a film by the likes of Werner Herzog can confront a viewer with a series of anomalous images that have "no immediate connection to the narrative: a crucified monkey; a kneeling camel; an old truck that goes endlessly around in circles" (Kolker, 1983, p. 257). The viewer, in these cases, is left having privately to decipher the symbolic import of the images.

This "poetic formulation" apropos the art film, this double register, also impacts a *single image's* semantic density (or its anti-frontality, we might call it). In such an image, multiple, often dialectically occasioned, meanings are conveyed because that image is working, more accurately, as a *net* of images. Percipients must thus be mentally able— programmed even—to accrue and catalogue the particular net of images and to deduce what those images are projecting representationally.[38] This can be especially difficult as an undertaking when one is expected to read an image for what its visual density is *implying* but not outright saying, such as when Antonioni creates an "objective correlative of an interior world" (Kolker, 1983, p. 149). Perhaps a better example would be Buñuel, who, in anticipating that spectators will divorce his characters' perversely unconscious desires from their conscious lives, invests his images "with a subjectivity that is always present and never explained" (p. 97). True, one might argue that the stock epithets common to the oral episteme possess a kind of semantic density. But much as is the case with oral poetry, "the metaphor is not there to increase semantic density of

---

38. Could this explain why Jean Vigo's *L'Atalante* (1933) could not find a public in its day? Although considered "prophetic" by critics at the time in terms of its forecasting where cinema would artistically go, *L'Atalante* was recognized as being a "difficult film for French audiences comfortable with a cinema based on dialogue. Vigo's visual density necessarily confused this audience" (Ross, 1989, p. 191). In other words, literacy might have had some bearing on the film's phasure, that is, on its not having coincided as a film with the conditions by which it could be spectatorially accessed (p. 191).

the text, but because it belongs to the arsenal of poetic ornaments" (Todorov, 1981, p. 24).[39]

And then there is of course irony, which may "burst out" of art-cinema narration, as Bordwell (1985) writes. Indeed, irony permeates the films of Ozu and Bresson (Schrader, 2001), as well as Godard's entire corpus; and the entire "organizing rhetorical strategy" of Resnais' *Hiroshima mon amour* is said to be "irony, carried out through foregrounding and subversion of contraries" (Higgins, 1996, p. 21). If we accede to Hayden White's labeling of irony as a mode that corresponds to "a stage of consciousness in which the problematical nature of language itself has become recognized" (cited in Higgins, 1996, p. 22), we should recognize that that stage, as well as language's purported indeterminacy, is fundamentally tied to the written and typographically fixed. As Ong (1982) explains, writing is "the seedbed of irony, and the longer the writing (and print) tradition endures, the heavier the ironic growth becomes" (p. 103). Certainly irony's wholesale absence from Hindi popular film helps substantiate Ong's assertion. Parody is of course omnipresent in Bollywood. But irony is a free-floating event and, thus, nonpreservative and nonsituational. It makes incredible demands on the spectator, who must seek out that which is not present but only implied, that which is "doubled" as (and in) language.[40] Thus, it is principally the literate *mentalité* which is geared toward what E.H. Gombrich calls "seeing as" (as distinct from a sheer perceptual "seeing") (cited in Andrew, 1984a, p. 173). Indeed, literate folks might maintain that only this ironic, seeing-as sort of storytelling reflects the essence of the poetical use of language, whereby a single word can become the site of "multiple resonances, the meeting point of several distinct 'chains of thought'" (Metz, 1982, p. 237); or where "two statements are made as if they were connected, and the reader is forced to consider their relations *for himself*" (Empson, cited in Culler, 1975, p. 126). But such translations call for a solitary act of *invention* on the part of the spectator, for a type of nonspontaneous Hegelian analysis that may not be in the orally inflected individual's purview. Indeterminacy, after all, requires that a percipient know *how* to look—not for what is there, but for what is *not*.

If high-literate folks prize more complex semantic engagement, very likely this is because it is the precious fruit of their long-term affiliation with literacy. And so, skills like detecting similarities between objects, or

---

39. Here Todorov was summarizing Milman Parry.

40. The nature of this doubling is illumined with economy by S.V. Srinivas (2005) when he observes that a film like Stephen Chow's *Kung Fu Hustle* (2004) does not require "a *Kill Bill* [2003] . . . type of smart reading of a convention that will produce quotations that are better than any existing 'original.' The fundamental difference between a *Kill Bill* and a *Kung Fu Hustle* is that the latter is characterized by the impossibility of disengagement from the object of parody" (p. 294).

drawing abstract analogies, or "reasoning about conditions divorced from practical experience" (Luria, 1976, p. 129) are prized in the culture of reading and writing, as is too the performance of "formal logical reasoning independent of content" (p. 130). Contrast that with what one nonliterate peasant told Luria's researchers rather dismissively when asked to explain a given syllogism: "We always speak only of what we see; we don't talk about what we haven't seen" (p. 109).

No cinematic technique would probably be more anathema to an orally inflected viewer, given his or her narrative disinclination toward seeing-as, than the art film's idiosyncratic use of flashbacks. Flashbacks are of course a staple of orally inflected narrative, as earlier I discussed, but the manner in which they are employed in art-cinema narration betrays their phylogenetic nucleus in literacy. Alain Resnais' *Last Year at Marienbad* (1961) serves as a veritable poster child for the modernist flashback, given the way the film's flashbacks subvert what the film's writer Alain Robbe-Grillet called "the linear plots of the old-fashioned cinema which never spare us a link in the chain of all-too-expected events" (cited in Goodenough, 2005, p. 15). In short, Resnais "dispense[s] with the signifying flashback which tells us where we are," opting instead to "constantly re-echo the role of the past in the present" (Orr, 1993, p. 26). In this way, he ostensibly presents the world "as it unfolds" as determined by the "present-tense consciousness of its characters" (Kawin, 1978, p. 79). Additionally, we could cite Antonioni, who "makes time inseparable from the spatial composition of his *mise-en-scène*," or Godard, who "constantly interrupts his own narrative as if visibly taking scissors to his film in front of his audience" (Orr, 1993, p. 26).

Higgins (1996) argues that the unscrambled flashback of modernist film intentionally offers, through its radically disjunctive and decontextualizing nature, "an even more intense subjectivization and dehistoricization of the past and memory" (p. 30). Here, then, is our evidence for the modernist flashback's epistemic link to literacy. For, in orally inflected film, the travel back—which is *always* contextualized—promotes collectivity through a diachronic extension of the self into the past (and also an absorption of the past into the present). Even though the flashback in these circumstances is generally manifest via a single consciousness (e.g., a mother recalling her college days; a vengeful son), it is *not* "subjectivized"; it does *not* isolate the viewer through subverting (in lieu of suturing) past and present. The implication is that the unscrambled flashback, in order to succeed, takes for granted a spectatorial tolerance of, and openness to, interpreting formalistic, manipulative plays with time—a hermeneutical positioning to which the nonliterate spectator may not aspire.

Deleuze unwittingly hints at the difficulty inherent in this interpretive activity—even as he applauds the modern film's ability to enmesh memory and perception in ways that blur temporal boundaries and reflect the nature of dreams (Bogue, 2003, p. 114); for, the "pure optical situation" that is forged from a merger of the virtual and the actual invariably converts an image into a *thinking* image. With a deferential nod to Noel Burch, Deleuze (1986b) speaks of the *superiority* of the "analytic of the image," which requires the whole image to be

> *"read,"* no less than seen, *"readable"* as *well as visible*. For the eye of the seer as of the soothsayer, it is the "literalness" of the perceptible world which *constitutes it like a book*. . . . [T]he camera is no longer content sometimes to follow the characters' movement, sometimes itself to undertake movements of which they are merely the object, but in every case it *subordinates description of a space to the functions of thought*. (p. 22, emphases added)

Deleuze's reference to this analytic underlines the difference—and perhaps potentiality for Derridean *différance*[41]—between rudimentary literacy and high literacy, with all that difference's cognitive and phenomenological implications. Orally inflected thinking, to reiterate, is grounded in the obvious and concrete; it is lodged in a practical assessment of reality. Grappling with, or extrapolating meaning from, an image's semantic density; interpreting a discrete symbol: these call for formal operations of problem solving, which, as Luria (1976) discovered, may present "major, sometimes insurmountable difficulties for [nonliterate] subjects" (p. 132).[42]

In this way, it is not enough to say that art-cinema narration *can* be studied; it *must become a thing of study*. This is of course in contradistinction to Sontag's (1961) plea against interpretation, which she claims is the "revenge of the intellect upon art" (p. 7). But in her eloquent praise of transparence—that "highest, most liberating value in art" which allows for "experiencing the luminousness of the thing in itself, of things being what they are" (p. 13)—she points to the greatness of directors like Bresson and Ozu and of films like *The Rules of the Game* (1939) and *Last Year at Marienbad*. Alas, these are precisely the types of directors and films that demand a literate inventiveness.

This need for interpretation is perhaps brought best to light by Satyajit Ray (1994) in his response to *The Rules of the Game*: "Although

---

41. The same might be said of the Althusserian "symptomatic reading," wherein one "concentrates not on the obvious features of the text itself, but on the silences, gaps and contradictions that reveal its problematic" (Macey, 2000, p. 374).

42. Importantly, Luria (1976) also discovered that an aptitude for performing "'theoretical' operations of formal discursive and logical thinking appear[s] after relatively short-term school instruction"; the significance of schooling, thus, lies not "just in the acquisition of new knowledge, but in the creation of new motives and formal modes of discursive verbal and logical thinking divorced from immediate practical experience" (pp. 132–133).

perfectly comprehensible on the surface, [it] is still a difficult and demanding film. . . . One has constantly to read between the lines and, like all great works of art, one has to go back to it again and again to discover fresh nuances of meaning" (p. 84). Ray's sentiment is echoed in Bordwell's (1995) avowal that the construction of art-cinema narration typically "becomes the object of spectator hypotheses: how is the story being told? Why tell the story in this way?" (p. 210). Bordwell goes so far as to say that the "procedural slogan" of art-cinema narration might well be "Interpret this film, and interpret it *so as to maximize ambiguity*" (p. 212). Though art film may consider unresolved ambiguity a sophisticated strategy for "indicat[ing] that art cannot provide any final truths" (Cook & Bernink, 1999, p. 117), such a strategy calls for a shift in perspective— one that moves from a "sensory and emotional experience of things," as Cynthia Freeland (1999) notes (albeit without citing orality or literacy), "to a more cognitive, intellectual appreciation," from a perspective *"within* the film to a perspective *about* the film" (pp. 72–73). The observer is expected, in other words, "to open a dialogue with the work, engage it intellectually and help complete it" (Kolker, 1983, p. 163). Kurosawa's *Rashomon* (1950), for example, leaves it up to the viewer to decide whether the death of one of its characters "is suicide or murder and by whom" (cited in Staiger, 1992, p. 192).[43] But having to determine what a story is *supposed* to be saying—or, as in the case of Bergman, whether it is intended as a parable, an allegory, or an exercise in surrealism[44]—cannot help but lift (or lower, as the case may be) spectatorial engagement into the arena of abstraction. Via an "elaborate concatenation of causes" (Ong, 1982, p. 57), the spectator is obliged to parse a work into a set of ideas. But the "sheer idea," as Havelock (1963) warns, is, due to its non-imagistic nature, a non-epic property, a *dissolution* of a story's vividness. Thus even the neorealist "fact-image," whose concrete reality is allegedly enhanced by its being nonmanipulated and unmediated, may pose problems. True, the image may be more "democratic" (Kolker, 1983, p. 147);[45] but by virtue of its rich ambiguity, it is so primarily for viewers who are already graduates of a *reading* democracy.

---

43. Staiger (1992) provides an illuminating overview of how critics during the art film's heyday conformed to "the art cinema interpretive strategy for accounting for ambiguity in a movie" (p. 190). Apparently, reviewers did not jump directly to that solution, but instead "work[ed] toward it, abetted . . . by several films for which editing practices solicited associations with modern art. Then reviewers began assuming (as they were already accustomed to doing for contemporary paintings) that technique *was* part of the subject matter" (p. 190).

44. These are journalistic reviewer responses to *La Strada* (1954), *Wild Strawberries* (1957), and *Seventh Seal* respectively, as catalogued by Staiger (1992, pp. 191–192).

45. Kolker wisely offers a corrective to Bazin, who "did not extend his theory of the image very far into a theory of narrative and of the way the spectator perceives the cluster

Bollywood films of course also require the development of a reading competence. However, that competence nests principally in cultural knowledge, and more particularly in what Thomas Hansen (2005) calls a "visceral familiarity with styles, songs and the legacy of older films" (p. 241). Much like Carroll's (1988) erotetic narration, then, high-oral inflection ultimately endows a movie "with an aura of clarity" (p. 181). Such a movie does not ask questions that it *refuses* to answer—although literate folks, in keeping with their programmed nature, may often attempt to prove otherwise. Given this, it might behoove us to digress for a moment, in order to recall Havelock's (1963) counsel to print readers who mistakenly attempt to "literize" oral narrative. Too often, metaphoric phenomena in Homer are guilelessly misread, he explains, and he offers as an example the "wrath" of Achilles, which transforms into "a divine demon . . . who saddles the Achaeans with a burden of pain":

> The sophisticated palate of a bookish culture, savouring the vigour of these lines, will be tempted to interpret this personification as "poetic" in the aesthetic sense, as an image which is consciously designed to replace abstract relationships of cause and effect by a substitute which is emotionally more powerful. . . . What we should say is: How necessary it is for the minstrel, if he is to offer a paradigm of cause and effect which our memory will retain, to present this as a series of acts performed by an agent with whom we can identify as we listen and repeat the lines. In short, a sophisticated language which analyses history in terms of causes and effects, of factors and forces, of objectives and influences and the like, is in the living oral tradition impossible because it is not amenable to the psychodynamics of the memorising process. (pp. 168–169)

The insinuation here is not that more literate readings of more oral texts are any less valid or vital; but orally inflected narrative, whether remote or recent, neither wants nor can afford to assign more and more responsibility onto spectators—in a sense, to *abandon* them. Alas, this is precisely what art-cinema narration does in insisting that viewers unwind the extraordinarily subtle threads of connotative expression—an act that viewers must undertake primarily *alone*. In complete isolation, a spectator must struggle to extract a theme, to mine for philosophy, to translate the Deleuzian "noosign," that "image which goes beyond itself toward something which can only be thought" (Deleuze, 1986b, p. 335). Without the literate inclination to unwind these threads, however, a sense of estrangement or alienation is bound to set in. And who can say that this

---

of images (and sounds) that tell a story in film. If Bazin had," says Kolker, "he might have seen more clearly that meaning is not transferred from 'reality' through the image, but produced by images in a narrative structure and perceived by a viewer who is always directed in some way by that structure" (p. 148).

type of alienation is any less legitimate than the existential sort the art film is so eager to communicate?

The upshot of the isolated reading is that film-viewing is rendered a highly *nonparticipatory* affair, with the storytelling experience expected to unfold exclusively within the self. Heckling characters, shouting at the screen, commenting publicly on the narrative as it proceeds—all in keeping with orally inflected participation—become signs of disrespect rather than of engagement. And so, once again, oral articulations give way to spectatorial quietude, to a reverential silence in the theatre and not just on the screen.

This expectation of mute viewership hints again at the meditative distance required of percipients engaging with a literately inflected text. Ironically, then, the narration often deemed most rapturous by the highly literate may strike oral spectators as the most lifeless and breathless. "The *unsummonab[ility]* of Welles, the *inexplicab[ility]* of Robbe-Grillet, the *undecidab[ility]* of Resnais . . . the *incommensurab[ility]* of Godard"—qualities that Deleuze (1986b) sees as cinematically restoring our world through their capacity to travel to "a point of outside beyond the outside world" (pp. 181–182)—may, in the oral conception of things, be considered unconstructively mired in the absence of story (and so in the absence of purpose and of psychic power too). The literate episteme quite literally *exults* in an unreliability that the oral episteme dutifully forecloses.

What this unreliability motif additionally points to is the central connection between literate inflection and the emergence of the *auteur*—or, perhaps more amenably, to the way in which the former ushers in the easier possibility of the latter. For, what calculated unreliability in storytelling animates is the existence of an *implied author*. As Gregory Currie (2006) incisively observes, "unreliability in narrative makes no sense without appeal to the concept of an implied author. . . . The implied author, we might say, is an absolute presupposition of unreliability, the narrator merely a conditional one" (p. 208). Unreliability demands that spectators be alert to the director *behind* the film, in other words, to the artist who is, in a manner of speaking, sending them messages "in code." This sort of camera consciousness puts serious and potentially insurmountable cognitive demands on a viewer, however:

> [I]ncrease the distance and you increase the difficulty. By distance [Currie] mean[s] the disparity between what you want to convey as a first impression and what you want the audience to catch on to on further reflection. The greater the distance in this sense, the greater the subtlety and complexity of the reasoning that the audience will have to go through to cover the gap. (p. 206)

Instead of identifying with characters in a film, spectators are forced via that gap to identify noetically with the director's overarching "discourse-vision."[46] The director *inserts* herself into the picture, metaphorically speaking, *writes* herself into the viewing process, and by doing so, purposely forces the percipient into a position of "distrusting the presentational field" (Kawin, 1978, p. 86).

Ultimately, it may be this lack of epistemic distance in Bollywood films that accounts for their appearing "relentlessly exhibitionistic" (Mishra, 2002, p. 122). *Masala* films are bereft of subtext—even of a subconscious, one might say. When one factors in the exigencies of expressly oral ways of knowing, however, the reason for that lack of distance becomes transparent. An outwardly shared form of storytelling must be *epistemologically frontal*; it cannot afford to be indirect or abstruse, or to possess undertones that are in danger of being missed. Only art-cinema narration, as a literately inflected narration, can afford through its various double-registers to present an independent philosophy of mind (which directors, one might argue, only secondarily hope will be universally shared). As a result, it may be much easier to become an art-film auteur than a *masala*-film auteur, given that only the former has the literately inflected luxury of creating, much as with the inwardly turned novel, "the whole compass of the work out of himself" (Kahler, 1973, p. 58).

What this also perforce recommends is that the auteur theory as a reading strategy largely relies on texts that have been contoured by literacy for its existence. Indeed, Andrew Sarris, who imported the concept of the auteur to the United States, elaborated its criterion of worth in terms of "a theory of *literary* production" largely because of the self-consciousness typically associated with the modernist text (cited Mishra, 2002, p. 90). "The way a film looks and moves should have some relationship to the way a director thinks and feels," Sarris exclaimed (p. 90), in effect suggesting that a director's thinking and feeling ought to become part of a film's "interior meaning." For that reason, it was only natural, as Mishra astutely observes, for Sarris to

> valorize art cinema over and above the popular because the controlling eye of high modernism directors (Bergman, Fellini, De Sica, Satyajit Ray, for instance) is more readily discernible in works that have a self-conscious aesthetic intention and where, for obvious reasons, there is considerable directorial control. The kinds of visual and semantic unities achieved by art cinema made the use of auteur/director (behind whom always stood the figure of the literary author) less problematic and certainly more rewarding in the critical/evaluative arena. (pp. 90–91)

---

46. The term, as far as I am able to recall, is Deleuze's own.

Given the excavation undertaken in this chapter, it seems equally imperative that scholars acknowledge the etiological root of a loosened pragmatics that *permits* the unreliability and self-consciousness that amplify auteur-ship. Directors of orally inflected narrative certainly *can* be auteurs, but much as Havelock (1963) points out regarding the oral epic, "The poet [is] in the first instance society's scribe and scholar and jurist and only in a secondary sense its artist and showman" (p. 94). Because there is far less expectation of a spectator having to gauge some private, individualistically assigned theme or purpose, the spectator's identification rests primarily with the story and its performing agents, *not* with the story's director. This is a point partly borne out by Mishra's (2002) analysis of the works of two directors who qualify for him as Bollywood auteurs, Raj Kapoor and Guru Dutt. In their films, Mishra adduces, "the auteur arrives as an already constructed star" (p. 122). In other words, the auteur in Indian popular cinema "surfaced only when there [was] spectatorial involvement in him through the spectator's prior identification with him as actor" (p. 97).

Conversely, art-cinema narration—which operates as an intellectual extension of its creators—has leeway to come, as Staiger (1992) guardedly puts it, "with the compliments of the auteur" (p. 194). My aim here is not to denigrate art film as a species; rather, it is to reiterate that, although early 20th-century literature may have been the species' central source for "models of character causality and syuzhet construction" (not to mention for the philosophical concession that art can never be as complex as life [Bordwell, 1985, p. 208]), the demands that its particular honeycombed structure foists on the spectator—demands that unequivocally foreground the auteur—are linked to a literacy-generated inheritance of mind.

The competence cinéphiles possess to engage with art film aesthetics was never—and *is still not*—due to some inborn mental superiority. The stretched consciousness that art films interpretively require is too profoundly a historical consequence of chirography and print. True, the ability to experience the films' pleasures may be routinely perceived as an ascendancy of mind; but that is more likely a reflection of, to coin a term, *cognicentricity*, of a bias that arises from the possession of cognitive skills both induced and cultivated by institutionalized literacy.

Although the conscious authorial impetus for creating art films may have been to flout the expectations set up by Hollywood or to challenge France's outmoded "Balzacian" directors, underlying this challenge was an almost certain unwitting *anti*-oralism—or, at the least, an unconscious forsaking of attributes that felt superannuated. After all, art-cinema narration was never trying consciously to counter Bombay cinema—a species whose plenitude and exhibitionistic leanings are *even more* antithetical to art cinema's particular "canon of realistic motivation" (Bordwell, 1985, p. 206)!

There is a scene in Ray's *Pather Panchali* that enchantingly reflects the tensions between the demands of the oral *mentalité* and the self-regarded pre-eminence of the literate habit of mind, and it is with it that I would like to bring my excavation of the oral and literate attributes of visual narrative to a close. Villagers are gathered round an open-air stage performance—not because they are riveted by, say, the subtle psychological interplay of two characters in a drama by Ibsen (a playwright whom Ray highly admired), but because they are fully engrossed in a staged rendition of an Indian folk tale, one that fully complies with the modes and morphology of oral performance: broad gestures, flatulent rhetoric, simple emotional patterns, stylized fights. Furthermore, the representations are of noteworthy kings and amplified demons, and the costumes of the traveling group are as loud and iconic as the actors' deliveries are bold and agonistic.

Ray devotes a substantial amount of screen time to this folk play-in-progress, although as "ideal readers" we are probably not expected to be drawn into the heavy and extrospective melodrama. Rather, our delight presumably comes in watching its inelegance and rough ungainliness: the stilted deliveries and mechanical gesticulations, which may be poignantly sweet but are not (to literate minds) narratively savory. Indeed, Ray films this nighttime theatrical performance using composition and angles that seem almost to resemble those of Hindi popular cinema, and in this way he is perhaps commenting on, if not outright mocking, films that employ similar anachronistic tactics of storytelling. Perhaps, then, the contrapuntal shots of the child protagonist, Apu, who is watching the spectacle from the makeshift bleachers, are intended not only to move or captivate us (because Apu is so dazzled, so utterly bewitched), but also to instruct us, to engage us in a tiny, socially conscious, Brechtian lesson on the repercussions of "theatrical-operatic" traditions (given that Apu is so dazzled, so utterly bewitched).

With almost magical exactitude, this scene lays a finger on the pulse of the characteristics of oral narrative and performance, as well as the frequently misinterpreted rationale that literate minds ascribe to such *jatra* (folk) forms. In miniature, the scene captures a touching irony that permeates the movie unbeknownst to Ray. For *Pather Panchali*, in its nostalgic emphasis on the joys of childhood, in its wistful celebration of a pre-consciousness of youth—and ergo of a preliterate, precognitively adult state of being—celebrates and venerates an innocence and incorruption that it obstinately struggles *as an artwork* to overcome, even to obliterate.[47]

---

47. See Ray (1994). Despite his admirable pedagogical desire to reach the untutored peasant, Ray displays a very literate—if not, on occasion anti-oral—sensibility.

To be sure, *Pather Panchali* is also a culturally mediated text shaped by regional demands and expectations, and for me to argue otherwise would be reckless. Indeed, I feel a certain intellectual discomfort in attributing to orality or literacy particular formalized tropes that have long been identified as *culturally* motivated. Suffice it to say that the issue of how epistemic structures intersect, overlap, or come into conflict with culturally determined conventions, styles, or traditions apropos storytelling aesthetics is an area that merits further exploration. But if underlying rules and discursive systems are discernible, and if there are interpenetrated features that appear distinctly motivated by particular ways of knowing, then it seems pound-foolish to ignore them for the sake of adhering to the program of cultural relativism. This seems especially the case given what this chapter has disclosed about the likely incapacity for a significant proportion of spectators to engage profitably with a literately inflected cinema. If we agree that in the modern setting literacy ought to be taught (something I think few today would dispute), do we not then acknowledge, however indirectly, the superiority (the pragmatic desirability) of the literate habit of mind and all its cognitive and narrative perquisites? In this sense, it is perhaps debilitating, if not once again foolish, to purport that *no* socially inequitable hierarchy exists when it comes to narrative content and form.

4

Between the Oral and Literate Epistemes:

Re-"Mixed Cinema," 1950–2000

The encounter with a work of art is not "love at first sight" as is generally supposed, and the act of empathy, *Einfuhlung,* which is the art-lover's pleasure, presupposes an act of cognition, a decoding operation which implies the implementation of a cognitive requirement, a cultural code.

—Pierre Bourdieu (1984, p. 3)

In this Tower of Babel, one has to find a way to be seen and heard with the kind of films one makes.

—Shyam Benegal, explaining his crossover to mainstream Hindi cinema (cited in Datta, 2002, p. 45)

RE-"MIXED CINEMA"

Let us pause to consider some of the theoretical gains of the last two chapters. For one, the literate episteme—even at this embryonic stage—seems to liberate art-cinema narration from any presupposition of its being categorically superior, or even any good. Literately inflected films may require a higher level of viewer complicity in order to be understood, but that does not lead ex cathedra to their excellence as texts. And although as a species art film may have reached its apogee during the 1950s and 1960s (Bordwell, 1985), disinterring its literately inflected morphological traits prevents the species from being temporally sealed off. After all, we can find pronounced degrees of literate inflection in the

works of contemporary directors, like Wong Kar-wai and Terrence Mal-
ick. Literate traits are even palpable in a strand of films from the silent
era. Indeed, it seems important to note that the period of modernist filmmaking with which we were so preoccupied in the last chapter was in
actual fact *neo*-modernist. As John Orr (1993) explains, the modernist period was more accurately "a Nietzschean *return* to the modern, to the
earlier moment of high modernism between 1914 and 1925," when directors like F.W. Murnau, Carl Dreyer, Luis Buñuel, and Sergey Eisenstein were working (p. 2). In other words, directors like these had already begun investing their films with a greater polysemy that required
the spectator to elaborate a story more fully in his or her mind. On the
basis of works like Murnau's *Sunrise* (1927), we need wonder, then, if the
onset of sound precipitated the need for a *reconstitution* of a literately inflected cinema that was already in development (see Nayar, 2009).[1]

At the same time, being able to funnel 1950s–1990s Bombay cinema
through the orality-literacy paradigm productively snarls the sorts of
snide, totalizing claims that have sometimes been leveled against the
masala film and its audience—such as that "Reality is shunned, because
the mass audience mind remains equally dormant and unresponsive to
change"; or that "The difference between the art cinema and commercial cinema is simply the difference between good cinema and bad—between serious films and degenerate 'entertainment.'"[2] Perhaps application of the oral and literate epistemes to visual narrative will help
impede such indiscriminate conflations of industry and text, not to
mention the too easy polarization of "Eastern" and "Western" aesthetic
sensibilities.[3] As Ramaswami Harindrinath (2005) asserts, "it is no longer
valid to either consider entire populations in developing regions as a
monolithic group of audience, or to make clear cut distinctions between
'Western' and 'non-Western' audiences on the basis of geographic locality." The same could surely be said of "Western" and "non-Western"
artists.

True, one might contend that the literate episteme is at heart a reflection of a specific and culturally hegemonic *context* of literacy, one typically partnered with modern Western society or, more precisely, Western

---

1. Michel Chion (1999) reminds us that speech and the voice figured prominently in
silent film. Movies were in fact "chatty," with characters' lips moving constantly. It was
simply that audiences couldn't hear the words. In this sense, the films were *deaf* more than
silent. He also calls attention to musical accompaniment—a movie house staple from the
outset—as well as to sound effects created live in some halls and to commentators who interpreted the intertitles for nonliterate audiences.

2. This first statement is from Firoze Rangoonwalla (cited in Vazzana, 1994), the second from Chidinanda Dasgupta (cited in Datta, 2002).

3. See Nayar (2005), where I argue this very point concerning postulations made in
film studies textbooks.

liberal education. Certainly, we need to consider the possibility that conventions like the pyramidal plot, which became fully standardized in 19th-century European fiction, were *not* the exclusive literately contoured norm of story construction during the period. Could a colonialist way of thinking have led to a disregard and even quashing of other, indigenously developed forms of literately inflected storytelling? Here, I am thinking of the distinct philosophical emphasis in Sanskrit drama on *rasa*. Introduced in an ancient treatise, the *Nātyaśāstra* (1996), *rasa* is an aesthetic relishing or state of rapture that takes place *within* spectators (not only emotionally but mentally as well). What if *rasa* had developed into an alternative, but no less progressively writing-influenced aesthetic than the one that Aristotle (1967) is famous for having articulated in *The Poetics* apropos plot construction?[4] Unfortunately, the scope of this project prohibits consideration of the pressures that politics places on the historical evolution of aesthetics; but importing orality and literacy paradigmatically into narrative studies suggests exciting new terrain for ethnographic and cultural-studies readings of texts.

Exposing and dissecting the visible epistemic extremes of visual storytelling is one thing; trying to tease out the ways in which stories both contemporary and bygone, both synchronic and diachronic, circulate between and/or interpolate those extremes is wholly another. Nevertheless, my seemingly dichotomous set-up of the oral and literate epistemes demands that I take this territory into account, if for no other reason than to dissuade readers from thinking that what I am theoretically proposing is binaristic as a model. This is an accusation that has often been leveled against Ong, as I noted earlier, and I wish to circumvent the accusation in my own case by shedding some light on the complex and concomitantly flexible nature of the paradigm. Indeed, what more recent scholars offer in their "correctives" to Ong's work is less an opposition to his dichotomizing of orality and literacy (which, to some extent, they self-servingly graft onto his intellectual oeuvre) than a calling of attention to the insufficient recognition that he has given "to the reality of 'mixed' and interactive modes" (Street, 1984, p. 5). As Coleman (1996) exhorts, scholarship that conceptualizes orality and literacy as two poles gives the erroneous impression that any identifiable mixed or middle

---

4. As Abhinavagupta writes in his 10th-century commentary on (and hence elaboration and modification of) the *rasa* theory, "those people who are capable of identifying with the subject-matter, since the mirror of their hearts has been polished through constant recitation and study of poetry, and who sympathetically respond in their own hearts are known as sensitive readers"; and "*Rasa* is nothing less than the reader's reaction to, his personal involvement with, literature" (cited in Patnaik, 1997, pp. 49–50). Might this insistence on training reflect an evolving commitment to the sensitivity of art's being born of study, or is it more a contemplatively driven response, born, as the author says, of constant recitation?

ground is but "a symptom of transition . . . a residual holdover from orality or (alternatively) . . . a herald of literacy" (p. 5). Authors who follow the model of a "Great Divide," so critics like Coleman charge, invariably miss or misrepresent "lively variations and crossover influences that become visible when we abandon technological determinism and place events within a larger cultural context" (p. 15).

In the introduction I stated that the present project, as a historically and materially rooted archaeology of knowledge that asks (and excavates) "what has made possible different knowledges" (Macdonell, 1986, p. 82), points to the theoretical inaptness of categorizing orality as premodern. Furthermore, the project undermines any proposition of a definitive cultural "shift" from orality to literacy, which is something scholars who have concentrated their energies on written texts in the West—and here Ong must be included[5]—have sometimes indirectly advocated. Thus, this chapter materially demonstrates that multiple storytelling epistemes do coexist and can even interact in the technologically visual realm. As a route to illustrating the existence of what one might call *epistemic differentials*, it considers some extant strands of "mixed cinema," which formalistically circulate between the epistemic extremes introduced in the preceding chapters.

The term *mixed* is of course a bit of a misnomer, given that the literate episteme is envisioned here not as the polar opposite of the oral, but rather as evidence of a single (which is not to say sole) discursive system that has emerged from a human capacity to relinquish an exclusively oral way of knowing. The inference here is that the film landscape does not slough off epistemically older forms so much as it adds to them; the landscape becomes an accretion of old and new forms—a veritable *masala* of epistemically contoured narratives, we might aver. At the same time, one cannot refute that texts circulating between these two epistemes may, in some circumstances, be diachronically reflecting an *evolution* of storytelling form. Although an orality–literacy schema for visual narrative (see Table 4.1) makes room for the singularity of, say, a postmodern narrative that plays with notions of hybridity and identity, it also concretizes a certain semantic *progress* to Art. The gradual shift toward inwardness, for instance—which even Hegel (2006) identified as reflecting a later stage of art's historical development—is, after all, what permits the heavy irony that pervades the postmodern text.

---

5. See, for instance, *Rhetoric, Romance, and Technology*, where Ong (1971) argues that contemporary popular culture, in its use of formulary devices (like clichés and catch phrases), does *not* "function as a storage and retrieval device" because such devices are "no longer deeply grounded in practical living" (p. 296). Certainly Bollywood film suggests deeper or, at the least, more variform roots.

TABLE 4.1. THE ORALITY–LITERACY PARADIGM FOR VISUAL
NARRATIVE AS EVIDENCED IN HINDI POPULAR CINEMA
AND ART-CINEMA NARRATION

The Oral Episteme of Visual Narrative	The Literate Episteme of Visual Narrative
Structure and Form	*Structure and Form*
• Episodic narrative form, including flashbacks and digressions • Repetition, recycling, formula privileging • Spectacle (flat surface—a "cinema of attractions") • Narrative closure (no ambivalent or open endings)	• Deformed plot (pyramidal or consciously depyramidized) • Originality, verisimilitude • Anti-spectacle, foregrounding of the background • Lack of narrative closure (ambivalent endings, open endings)
Visual, Verbal, and Aural Tone	*Visual, Verbal, and Aural Tone*
• Agonistically toned (e.g., inflated violence, melodrama) • Heavy, amplified characters and settings • Frontality • Syntagmatic kinesthesia • Plenitude, redundancy (e.g., visual, material, and dialogical excess) • Use of rhetorical devices (e.g., clichés, proverbs) • Noninterpretive, unambiguous meaning (e.g., privileging of oaths, totemism in lieu of symbolism)	• Quiescence and quietude • Understated, nuanced characters and settings • Semantic density • Syntagmatic nuance and subtlety • Restraint (or nonclichéd use of visual excess) and nonredundancy • Concerted formalistic "deformation" of language • Ambiguous meaning, meaning that must be extracted (e.g., subtext, symbolism, irony)
Worldview and Orientation	*Worldview and Orientation*
• Manichean worldview • Nonpsychological orientation • Nonhistorical (synchronic, synthetic, experiential telescoping) • Unself-conscious (e.g., presense of parody but not irony) • Fulfillment of audience expectations • Participatory • No anxiety of influence (imitative, no concept of plagiarism) • Focus on social suturing, preservation of the status quo • Collective social orientation ("we" inflected)	• Nonpolarized worldview (grayness) • Psychological orientation (introspective) • Historical (diachronic, discontinuous, psychic time) • Self-conscious (e.g., irony) • Subversion of audience expectations • Private engagement • Heavy anxiety of influence (desire for idiosyncrasy, concept of plagiarism) • Interrogative with respect to society, querying the status quo • Individualistic orientation (subjectivity, "I" inflected)

I am not, in invoking progress, insinuating a state of mind that is "improved" or "superior"; nor am I suggesting that we are working toward some finite target that, in the Hegelian conception, is destined to lead to an end to art. Obviously, I am more aligned with the Foucauldian proposition that discourse is discontinuous. But this does not foreclose the possibility that storytelling can simultaneously reflect a certain phenomenological (and phylogenetic) conditionality, one that dictates how Homer, without the resource of writing, would probably *not* have elected to foreground irony in his storytelling, given irony's inherent instability; nor would he have likely constructed a narrative awash in the kind of dense, indeterminate symbolism that Romantic poets like Keats and Shelley would come to relish. As Suzanne K. Langer (1942) reminds us:

> Just as verbal symbolism has a natural evolution from the mere sugges-
> tive word or "word-sentence" of babyhood to the grammatical edifice
> we call a language, so presentational symbolism has its own character-
> istic development. It grows from the momentary, single, static image
> presenting a simple concept, to greater and greater units of successive
> images having reference to each other; changing scenes, even visions of
> things in motion, by which we conceive the passage of events. (p. 145)

In other words, the literate episteme is an unavoidable testament to a certain historical progression, but it is not a progression—perhaps *succession* is a better word choice—that is teleogically determined. New technologies are continuously remediating visual storytelling, after all. Readers ethically troubled by this theoretical overture may find comfort in Claude Lévi-Strauss's (1963) observation that "What makes a steel ax superior to a stone ax is not that the first one is better made than the second. They are equally well made, but steel is quite different from stone" (p. 230).

There is of course no existing framework for assessing the spice-mix of visual storytelling as inflected by literacy, and so we are left as well with a lexical gap for discussing this rich, polymorphous—and also, admittedly, messy—epistemic in-between. Hence, my bald appropriation of the term *mixed cinema*, which was coined by André Bazin.[6] Bazin (1967) employed the term for the purposes of discussing the cross-pollination of theater and literature with film, which, as he saw it, could stimulate aesthetic refurbishment or, at other times, induce "barren hybrids" (pp. 60–61). (For example, Bazin suggested that *Citizen Kane's* "novel-like style" was owed in part to the influence of the works of James Joyce.) Co-opting and reorienting Bazin's concept of mixed cinema—*re-mixing* it, as it were—will not only potentially reinvigorate the term's use, but will more vividly draw attention to the orality–literacy para-

---

6. See "In Defense of Mixed Cinema," in *What Is Cinema?* (Bazin, 1967).

digm's panoptic latitude, as well as its pedagogically constructive potentials.[7] Re-mixing cinema may also help to highlight why "the history of entertainment and popular forms and of elite forms must be written together, as a series of negotiations and accommodations" (Andrew Ross, summarized in Chakravarty, 1996, p. 246).

For the sake of continuity and in order to narrow my focus more fruitfully, I will, in considering "mixed" cinematic forms, pull my evidence principally from India. Cinemas beyond India indisputably disclose epistemic likenesses when appraised in light of the orality–literacy paradigm. However, in resuming with the subcontinent as a case study, I will hopefully put to rest any misapprehension on the part of readers that all Indian cinema can be bifurcated into the high-oral and high-literate, or worse, that I categorize the "Indian cinema megalith . . . as two things: the 'Hindi movie,' and 'Satyajit Ray'" (Rajadhyaksha, 1996, p. 678)—with "Ray stand[ing] alone as the only valid cinematic voice in a desert of Indic schlock" (Heifetz, 1993, p. 72). This is especially critical given that these "two things"—Bollywood and Ray—were instrumental to my earlier excavation of the oral and literate epistemes.

Scratching the surface of this large and critically dense middle ground will, once more, help to reinforce that the oral and literate epistemes are *not* underscoring some oppositional discourse. In order to accomplish this goal most profitably, I limit my examination to three particular strands of mixed cinema within the Indian context: The first strand is India's "middle-class cinema," which emerged from within Bollywood prior to the arrival of television, and which departs from *masala* films in some notable and consistent ways. (That class and literacy often go hand-in-hand is no doubt axiomatic.) The second strand I investigate is India's self-styled *middle cinema*, which materialized intentionally and self-consciously in the 1970s as a storytelling form separate from—and even hostile to—*masala* film. Finally, I address 21st-century Bollywood, which is evincing significant, if subtle, changes in terms of its films' semantic positioning. By this I mean that a certain degree of literate inflection is currently seeping with popular consensus into a segment of mainstream cinema. Although most Bombay film superhits continue to reflect the triumph of texts that exhibit high oral inflection, a handful bear the markings of a socially sanctioned push toward the lit-

---

7. This "in-between" applies no less to print stories than to visual stories. It would be interesting, for instance, to extend Janice Radway's (1984) study of romance novels and their readers into the realm of orality–literacy theory, given those novels' general formulaic nature and possession of a meaning "not only unambiguous but *already known*" (p. 198). In fact, Radway posits that the "romance-reading experience, in short, appears to provide both the psychological benefits of oral myth-telling and those associated with the reading of a novel" (p. 199). The reasons (or comforts) of such "mixed" novels might prove to be no less epistemically than psychologically motivated.

erate episteme. However, much as the existence of those first two strands of Indian cinema mentioned above intimates, there have *always* been options to *masala* films in India, whether as alternative species, or offshoots, or intriguing reworkings of the genre.

MIDDLE-CLASS CINEMA THROUGH THE
ORALITY–LITERACY PARADIGM

Middle-class cinema, a 1970s subspecies of Bollywood film, was apparently *not* a particularly demanded sort of filmmaking.[8] According to M. Madhava Prasad (1998a), this cinema of socioeconomic identification (p. 163) was more an attempt on the part of producers to appeal to the middle-class substratum of Indian society, often by highlighting that substratum's remove from the more chimeric aspects of the national cinema. (Bollywood, in other words, yearned in the creation of this storytelling offshoot to conceive of itself as Bolly*woods*.) Generally speaking, middle-class cinema addressed "the middle-class subject as a beleaguered entity, facing a threat to her/his identity from the encroachments of the rest of society, in particular the glamorous world of popular culture, and the politically awakened masses" (p. 25). The films accomplished this largely through employing "images of authenticity and realism as a point of contrast to the illusions of popular cinema" (p. 171). Hence the production of films like *Guddi* (*Darling Child*, 1971), in which a star-obsessed schoolgirl is exposed to the deflating realities of the Bombay film industry, and *Anand* (1970), where a middle-class cancer victim "rises above the conflicts that surround him and reunites a divided world by dying" (p. 165).

Prasad is one of the few film analysts to have ideologically probed this category of Hindi popular cinema. His interests lie foremost in unpacking the species vis-à-vis its petty-bourgeois subject, for the broader purpose of "foregrounding the political dimension of the problem of textual *form*" (p. 20). But middle-class cinema can be just as rewardingly unpacked on the basis of the oral–literate dimensions of textual form. (In fact, according to scholars like Brian Street, 1984, one can hardly isolate the skill and practice of literacy from any discussion of bourgeois modernity.[9]) *How* the middle-class cinema addressed its subject matter, I

---

8. Partha Chatterjee (2006), somewhat to the contrary, argues that, had these films "not done reasonably well consistently, there was no way that any of them could have survived the dog-eat-dog world of box office-driven, crassly commercial Bollywood."

9. Street (1984) goes on to say that "the introduction of literacy is always accompanied by the introduction of new forms of social organisation"; as a result, "differences in thinking processes cannot . . . be attributed to literacy *per se*" (p. 103). What this of course implies is that the reverse is equally true: that the new forms of social organization may be a direct

argue, significantly hinged on its audience's capacity or desire to retreat from the oral episteme—or, more accurately, to branch away from that episteme without losing complete connection to the Bollywood product as a cultural form. Consider, for instance, Prasad's (1998a) observation that the middle-class cinema was "founded on the twin distinctions of primacy of narrative and the ordinariness and authenticity of the world represented" (p. 164); and that, rather than submitting to an alternative cinematic reality, this cinema confronted the "popular cinematic image and expose[d] its falsehood, its unworthiness as an object of emulation" (p. 174). One might conjecture that this breed of cinema bore a moderate kind of "writerly" awareness of the Bollywood formula, at the same time as it readily participated in and reworked the formula from *within*.

We can draw with even greater precision on Prasad's analysis, in order to demonstrate tangibly this species' subtle move away from the oral episteme. For instance, Prasad (1998a) readily identifies that, although the middle-class film retains its overarching identification with the traditional family unit, the romantic couple "emerges *into relative autonomy*," and the "sources of conflict shift from the economic and moral domains to the *realm of the psychic*, where envy, ambition, pride and other disruptive emotions reside" (p. 181, emphasis added). At first glance, these might appear to be exclusively industrially motivated (in that the retreat was *from* the Indian masses). The parallel withdrawal from a mythological telescoping vis-à-vis ancestral relations, however, as well as the turn toward more inward explorations via a concern with the psychologically motivated self, heralds a concomitant detachment from the face-to-face nature that high-oral inflection necessitates. A spectator must be epistemically inclined to grapple with characters that are less polarized and less exteriorly oriented, in other words.

The middle-class species' presentation of character is, understandably, conventionally read as reflecting that socioeconomic class's wrestle with issues of modernity and a desire for self-segregation. In other words, the foray into the psyche was ostensibly a means of getting away from illusory depictions of India (and perhaps from India itself); and for this reason, so Prasad (1998a) claims, the middle class "was more amenable to the exclusivist aesthetic enclosure produced by the narratives of domestic conflict than the national integrationist role delineated in the narratives of martyrdom" (p. 186). But enclosing oneself domestically may have as much to do with a growing existential inclination to *parse the self* as it does with a desire to retreat into a safely self-homogenizing arena. In other words, spectators were withdrawing no less from

---

consequence of literacy. Benedict Anderson (1991) seems to acknowledge this—or, perhaps more accurately, defers to McLuhan's theoretical acumen—when in *Imagined Communities* he conceptually reconfigures capitalism into *print*-capitalism.

the nationalist project than they were from the exoteric proclivities of highly orally inflected narrative (which, one might argue, Prasad's allusion to "the violence of martyrdom" insinuates). The middle-class cinema's parallel omission, or weeding out, of other types of agonism—such as of the *masala* film's loud, clichéd camera work—substantiates this point. Even in all-out farces like *Chupke Chupke* (*Hush-Hush*, 1975), the *masala* film's frenetic style of cinematography and editing is conspicuously absent. Distinction for the middle-class viewer may have come less in differentiating oneself merely through taste than through cognitively learned habits and inclinations that became earmarked *as* taste—in part because those tastes were not as unilaterally negotiable.

As Foucauldian analysts are careful to point out, when it comes to the development of particular knowledges, practitioners are often not conscious of the rules (Macdonell, 1986). But certainly we can now conjecture that, when Partha Chatterjee (2006) describes the middle-class Indian cinema as that "gentle, 'thinking and feeling cinema,'" which deals with middle-class values, he is unwittingly acknowledging its subtle departure from the more exoteric norms identified with the oral episteme. So, too, is Mihir Bhattacharya (2006), in describing middle-class cinema's most renowned director, Hrishikesh Mukherjee (indeed, Mukherjee directed all the films mentioned thus far) as offering a "kind of intermediate regime in modernity," a middle path in the "arc of realism" that extends from "the formula-torn cliché-tormented world of Bombay films," to the defamiliarization and "new representational regime" evincible in Satyajit Ray. Bhattacharya further portrays Mukherjee as a director whose "plot lines are clean, his characters coherent though perhaps neither very deep nor complex, his songs mood-contextual, his dialogue respectful of the cadences of common speech, his narrative logic resolutely tied to common sense." One might argue Mukherjee was simply generating narratively clean (not to mention, morally clean) Bollywood films. But Bhattacharya's continuing homage to the director hints at something more—or, rather, suggests that cleanliness as a filmic quality may have been the unconscious byproduct of expectations molded by literacy. One sees "cleanliness," after all, in Mukherjee's capitulation to tidy, orderly plot lines and in his predilection for narrative *logic*. And there are other traits to indicate a rising literate inflection, such as in the way he inserts his formulaic themes into "a fresh, recognisable, *ordinary* setting"; in his favoring a more *sedate* acting style and comparatively *nuanced* performances; and finally in his gesturing toward an "emerging desire for *verisimilitude* and coherence" (emphasis added). Intriguingly, Bhattacharya comments that films like *Anand* prove that the novel's "rather exceptional demands" on readers are capable of being met in the cinema.

That middle-class cinema turned with more regularity to literature, specifically Bengali literature, as a source for narrative material

(Prasad, 1998a) seems of consequence here. Adapting literary texts for the screen does not lead implicitly to those adaptations being more epistemically literate. (Certainly there are novels—and, more recently, graphic novels—that display storytelling ways of knowing that are more in keeping with the oral episteme.) But could middle-class cinema's more committed turn to print fiction have had its roots in a growing interest on the part of a book-reading public for more literate traits of narrative? Bengal, incidentally, has long been identified as the historical seedbed of Indian intellectualism and the home of the artistic elite that developed the "first regional literary language of India" (Wolpert, 1991, p. 185). Perhaps this is what ultimately underpins Bhattacharya's contrasting of Mukherjee's commendable "intermediate cinema" with those "pot-boilers churned out by Indian studios," which Bhattacharya colorfully denounces for their "loose plots (spanning generations), disjointed episodes (parallel and subsidiary plots), melodramatic ranting and moralizing . . . coincidental events . . . sketchy characterization (mood swings, episodic motivations), tawdry symbolism . . . and so on." Judgments aside, this description's heavy echo of the oral characteristics of visual narrative is hard to disregard, as is the connection between oral exigency and the "folk culture of the day" that Bhattacharya cites as the source from which these traits extensively derive.

The terms *middle-class*, *bourgeois*, and *modernity*, we might propose, have been employed as catchall phrases that customarily collapse bourgeois socioeconomic advances that reconfigure identity with educationally endowed shifts in cognition. The formalistic moves in Mukherjee's films may not be toward the *extra*ordinary, or even the narratively *out*-of-the ordinary, but they do signal a willing immersion into a moderately literately inflected mimetic representation of the world.[10] In this way, middle-class cinema may be epistemically analogous to the 18th-century British novel, which, as Ian Watt (1957) proposes, reveals an early inward turn. That prose genre's move several centuries earlier toward an individualist reorientation and pursuit of a Cartesian truth, compounded

---

10. Of the middle-class films I have seen, one in particular stands out in terms of its more literately pronounced norms. *Dastak* (*Knock*, 1970), which Prasad (1998a) explores at some length, possesses a verisimilitude and individualized voyeurism (as distinct from the collective voyeurism of Hindi popular film) that at times renders it semantically dense. As an idiosyncratic form of social noir that blends song and melodrama with staged social realism, *Dastak* employs thematics that, as Prasad detects, introduce issues of female subjectivity, via working through a fittingly claustrophobic *mise-en-scène*. It also makes serious, if crude and obvious, attempts at symbolism. Although Prasad considers the film part of middle-class cinema, Rajadhyaksha and Willemen (1999) consider it an early example of New Indian Cinema (see below). I cannot help but wonder if this discrepancy concerning categorization is due to *Dastak*'s comparatively higher literate inflection.

by its growing fidelity to human experience and individualized personality, are similarly palpable in middle-class cinema—and also similarly
palpable *minus* semantic density, especially the sort produced by Barthesian erotic gaps. Films like *Aandhi* (1975) and *Abhimaan* (*Pride*, 1973) may
be quieter than standard Bollywood fare, but they still reflect little-to-no
complete quietude; they may be historically situated, but only blandly so;
and although they may suppress spectacularity, they do not disaggre-
gate themselves from frontality. Furthermore, these middle-class films
consistently eschew open endings, social subversion, and any what-ness
of things, and in this way renounce any need for percipients to engage in
a highly ambiguous, symbol-reading realm—or with what we might
now term those *higher-order* literate characteristics of visual narrative
(see Table 4.2).

Crucially, these films do not seek or demand that they be probed for
an authorial philosophy, a type of activity that would make much more
strenuous demands on the intellect, forcing a kind of spectatorial distance that was possibly not the wont or in the epistemic purview of the
Indian middle-class population. In the words of M.L. Haina (1986)—
who otherwise reads this brand of cinema through the lens of petty-
bourgeois class identity—middle-class cinema catered "neither to the
semi-literate and the pedestrian taste nor to the educated critically dis-
cerning perception" (p. 133);[11] rather, its appeal was to that section of the
middle class that was "put off by the grossness of commercial cinema,"
but equally "baffled by what they regard[ed] as the 'artiness' of the New
Wave films" (pp. 133–134).

True, one could argue that the incremental nature of this retreat
owed less to a middle-class unwillingness to engage with higher-order
literate norms than to a reluctance to abandon wholesale the familiar
territory of Bombay film. Turning one's collective back on Bollywood
might have been perceived as a desertion of one's own indigenous popular culture. The solution, perhaps, lay in distinguishing oneself more
literately *from within*. But that is of course an aesthetic and narrative activity suffused with paradox: How does one legitimately literize a highly
orally inflected form like the *masala* film without eschewing the very storytelling qualities that have come to define its cultural distinction?

One innovative way that the Indian bourgeoisie managed to contest
the *masala* species without actually forsaking it was through film magazines. *Filmfare*, a publication that was read "primarily by the English-
speaking middle class" (Prasad, 1998a, p. 172), was extremely popular
during the height of the middle-class cinema period, and readers would

---

11. Haina actually uses the term *middle cinema* in his writing, but he is careful to distinguish the films he discusses from Indian New Wave cinema (which more typically goes
by the label *middle cinema*, see below).

TABLE 4.2. THE "HIGHER-ORDER" LITERATE CHARACTERISTICS
OF VISUAL NARRATIVE
Based on Their Absence in Both Hindi Popular Cinema *and* Middle-Class Cinema

- A *personal*, not shared or collective, experience—one created out of the "self" of the director—that hence requires interpretation
- Meaning (i.e., truth, reality, etc.) as possessing the capacity to exist underneath or behind the visible; the existence of *inner amplitude*
- A tendency toward the *polysemic*, toward a diversity of meanings
- An *unstable* relationship between viewer and film

regularly submit comments and criticisms to a column called "Readers Don't Digest." There, they bemusedly critiqued the assorted inconsistencies and flaws in popular films, objecting to the

> non-linear conception of time that is characteristic of Hindi film narratives. Another reader observed the Hindi film-maker's indifference to historical accuracy: in *Baharen Phir Bhi Ayengi* [1966], the Chinese war of 1962 is shown but a character refers to the narrative present as 1965. Sociological accuracy was also demanded: "Funny that Dharmendra becomes a News Editor and still stays in a hut." Other readers pointed out formal inconsistencies: in *Vaasna* [1968], "Surprising that Padmini, narrating the past to her son, remembers the comedy sequences in which she didn't figure." (p. 172)

Prasad reads the column as serving pedagogically to train middle-class viewers "to anticipate a Hollywood-style realism" (p. 172). Perhaps that is giving too much credit to Hollywood, however, for such a reading minimizes what the very act of reading (and of writing, and of reading *through* writing) was encouraging in terms of narrative expectation. Yes, one could argue that the realist aesthetic had already been largely packaged by an unequivocally Western brand of literate inflection (a point buttressed by the fact that these were readers of an *English*-language magazine and so readers who were already likely engaging educationally with English literature). Then again, realism had by this time developed a strong presence in Hindi literature, such as in the stories of Premchand which were—and still are to this day—a Hindi classroom staple.

If *Filmfare* "provided opportunities for a kind of disdainful engagement with the popular which sustained the existing industry by making available the supplementary pleasures of readerly superiority" (Prasad, 1998a, p. 172), it succeeded because *reading itself* had molded this comparatively small spectatorial body into anticipating and privileging historical accuracies, narrative consistencies, perhaps even a kind of pictorial isolationism. Chirography and print had feasibly detached readers from the existential need or desire for high-oral inflection. No wonder, then, that certain strands of Hollywood might have come to feel more epistemically comfortable or pertinent. Nevertheless, middle-class viewers obviously still participated in (and possibly thoroughly enjoyed) the indigenously imagined, communal nature of the *masala* film, and this may have led to their feeling internally conflicted. Hence, they sought critically to quash their own relish of this "lesser" breed of storytelling through the "readerly superiority" that Prasad assiduously references.[12]

MIDDLE CINEMA THROUGH THE ORALITY–LITERACY PARADIGM[13]

The label *middle cinema* is hardly exclusive to India. Self-proclaimed middle cinemas exist in several outlying geographical locales, including Egypt (Armbrust, 1996) and Hong Kong (Cheng, 2006). In these contexts, the term is typically employed to distinguish films that fall between the perceived kitschiness of popular cinema and the off-putting esoterica of art film. We might even speculate that the designation has come unconsciously to reflect an epistemic realm comfortably lodged halfway between orality and literacy—one generally removed from an entirely oral conception of the world-as-storytelling, but minus the higher-order literate inflection that marks art-cinema narration. In this sense, such international species of middle cinema may be more formalistically akin to the type of middle-class cinema discussed in the preceding section.

In the subcontinental context, however, things get complicated. When scholars speak of Indian films that display a serious and engaged commitment to a Bazinian *realist aesthetic*, they are typically addressing India's "middle cinema." To confuse matters, the term is often used interchangeably with others, like "New Cinema," or "New Wave Cinema," or "parallel cinema." Many of these labels were once historically rooted, but have since acquired a broader application. As such, directors

---

12. Correcting facts and disputing a film's lack of historical accuracy speak to an educationally endowed knowledge competency, although not necessarily to the higher-order goals that distinguish "high literacy" (see Resnick, 2002). Of course, this may more accurately reflect the nature of the films themselves: One can't easily comment on a poor employment of subjectivity if there isn't any subjectivity there in the first place. Because no study has yet been done to measure the effect of alphabetic literacy on film spectatorship, these can only remain hypotheses.

13. Extant scholarship on middle cinema offers various readings. For a general-historical framework, see Rajadhyaksha and Willemen (1999), Aruna Vasudev (1986), and Thoraval (2000); for political-ideological readings, see Prasad (1998) and Chakravarty (1996); for biographical works on specific directors, see Datta (2002), among others.

"as diverse as Basu Chatterjee with a penchant for conventional narrative on the one hand and Mani Kaul, who wishes to dispense with narrative altogether," get lumped together, and the term "becomes redundant and problematic" (Chakravarty, 1996, p. 237). In order to avoid that sort of indiscriminate melding, this section deals briefly with two particular subsets of Indian middle cinema: those films that emerged out of the Film Finance Corporation (FCC) and "turned realism into a nationalist project" (Datta, 2002, p. 27); and the "'middle-of-the-road' cinema of the independently financed, commercially designed art-house movie" (Rajadhyaksha & Willemen, 1999, p. 26), which materialized subsequent to FCC patronage.

The genesis of both these cinemas begins with a 1968 manifesto that advocated for an author-cinema that would be state-sponsored. The FCC became the eventual sponsor of this independent filmmaking, which was to serve as an "instrument for the promotion of national culture, education and healthy entertainment" (Rajadhyaksha & Willemen, 1999, p. 26). The result was a sector of government-supported cinema that the popular press—in clear allusion to the French *Nouvelle Vague*—christened the "Indian New Wave" (p. 165). These films differed appreciably from those of the middle-*class* cinema in terms of the extent of their realist program—or what Prasad (1998a) describes as their "developmental aesthetic" and "aura of individual artistic achievement" (p. 190). In a collective determination to turn away from Bollywood's "formulaic sentimentalized representations of hero and glamorous heroine, from the pleasures of spectacle as in song and dance, and action, and from mandatory happy endings," these directors followed in the neorealist tradition, casting unknown, and thus unglamorous, actors to play authentic characters residing in authentic milieus (Datta, 2002, p. 35). Thus, many films of the period unfolded in rural settings and were "focused on age-old customs and social taboos and practices" (Chakravarty, 1993, p. 246). Mani Kaul's *Uski Roti* (*A Day's Bread*, 1970), for instance, integrated its subaltern characters into a "dusty, flat Punjabi countryside" (Rajadhyaksha & Willemen, 1999, p. 402).

According to filmmaker Girish Karnad, this "ruralist drive" was influenced by several factors: first, filming in villages was comparatively cheap, not to mention that it coincided with the post-independence conviction that the "real India" was to be found in the villages; second, filmmakers had been significantly influenced by Satyajit Ray's trilogy as well as by homegrown *literary* works, novels mostly, from which many of their films would be adapted (cited in Datta, 2002, p. 27). In other words, the realism that these films evoked was not without an indigenous predecessor. The genre of the realist novel had appeared on the Indian cultural scene long before, in the final quarter of the 19th century (Mukherjee, 1985). (Indeed, the oral–literate tensions between contemporaneous strains of Indian cinema from 1950 to 2000 were no less evident in *book* tastes during that earlier colonial period.[14]) To be sure, the unprecedented absorption with history that surfaced at the turn of the century may have been induced by a broader exposure, via the study of English, to Victorian writers and foreign cultures (Mukherjee, 1985). This is paralleled later in scholars' frequent assertions that Indian spectators in the 1970s were becoming increasingly influenced by an overt consciousness of "world standards" in cinema (Chakravarty, 1993, p. 85). Perhaps, then, the decisive turn toward the verisimilar was owing to a literately inflected epistemic readiness to struggle with the deformed film language and "internalised yet distanced kind of realism reminiscent of Robert Bresson" (Rajadhyaksha & Willemen, 1999, p. 402)—and which one finds in spades in a film like *Uski Roti*.

No doubt, this helps elucidate the makeup of the audiences that these realist films attracted. Despite subaltern representations *on* the screen and a putative wish on the part of directors to reach the underclasses (Chakravarty, 1996, p. 246), it was, as Prasad (1998a) explains, the urban spectator who was typically "invited . . . to witness a world other than its own" (p. 161). Sangeeta Datta (2002) similarly draws attention to the national aesthetic program's "formulation of an enlightened audience" (p. 30), as Chakravarty does to the audiences' being city-bred, English-educated, and middle class. One wonders, as a result, if the radical, literately inflected orientation away from mass culture evinced in *Uski Roti* was what led to its being both "violently attacked in the popular press for dispensing with familiar cinematic norms and equally strongly defended by India's aesthetically sensitive intelligentsia" (Radhyaksha & Willemen, 1999, p. 402).

Not only do these scholars' statements regarding spectatorial trends clarify who the audiences were for this particular species of filmmaking; they call attention, too, to a spectatorial inclination that overwhelmingly departs from orally inflected cinema—namely, the desire to participate in a *verisimilar* world that is categorically *other than one's own*. Take, for instance, the sharp exoduses from oral inflection that can be pulled from

---

14. One could argue of course that this move toward the realist novel was a reflection of a hegemonic *context* of literacy—exposure, in this case, to the storytelling forms circulating in, and part and parcel of, Western culture. But Meenakshi Mukherjee's (1985) descriptions of readers' novelistic preferences during the period suggests a more complicated scenario, one very likely epistemically underpinned by orality and literacy. "The earnest novels of purpose," after all, "were never as popular or numerous as the lavish novels about heroism and adventure, love and romance, that captured the popular imagination of late 19th-century India. Elements of fantasy and intimations of history are inextricably tangled in these works. Chronicles merge with legend, events lapse into magical happenings, and kings who lived once-upon-a-time cast their spell upon those who ruled at a specific period and over a definite area. The spectrum covered by these novels is not only wide but also colourful" (p. 38).

Uski Roti alone: its formidable presence of quietude and quiescence; its relishing of ordinariness and, indeed, of altogether *minor* happenings (Thoraval, 2000), which compel us not only to interpret what is happening *in* the film, but to scramble for a perspective *about* the film. Doubtless it will come as little surprise to the reader that *Uski Roti*'s director openly professed admiration for directors like Bresson, Ozu, and Tarkovsky, as well as for Bengali director Ritwik Ghatak, whose own films reference the mythological in distinctly literate ways.[15]

In other words, although this new cinema was, as Chidananda Dasgupta argues, a "creation of an intellectual elite that [was] keenly aware of the human condition in India" (cited in Datta, 2002, p. 18), its creations helplessly, perhaps even haplessly, reflected that human condition through an expressly literate and thus exclusivist way of knowing. Once again, we find one of the paradoxes of film narrative construction brought center-stage: How is one to represent oral people *to* oral people without submitting to orally inflected attributes?

My objective here is not to impugn directors for their literately derived inspiration and stylistic co-option, or for their possessing an "intellectual conscience" (Thoraval, 2000, p. 148). In fact, one need be just as sensitive to the invisible transnational culture that *literacy* generates, without either capitulating to knee-jerk charges of repressive elitism or disavowing—out of an ideological commitment to anti-imperialist compulsions or aims—the double-directedness of such creative flows. (Here, Marx's ambivalent feelings about literature and art merit mentioning. Marx was in no way immune to an appreciation of aesthetic achievement; but, in light of his political philosophy, the creative arts did sometimes prove befuddling territory, as one can gauge from reading his excerpted writings [with Engels, 1947] on the subject.) At the least, it seems constructive to identify why films like *Uski Roti* tend to stay "within the class rooms of the film appreciation courses, or at best [get] exhibited at international festivals abroad" (Raina, 1986, p. 133).

According to Rajadhyaksha and Willemen, it was Shyam Benegal's debut film *Ankur* (*The Seedling*, 1973) that launched the ensuing "middle-

---

15. As Vasudev (1986) notes, Ritwik Ghatak uses mythology but "mythology internalised, never obvious, never used for simple identification" (p. 25). There is undoubtedly interesting work to be done on the unusual, and oft extraordinary fusions, of the oral and literate as evidenced in Ghatak's films. This is especially so in light of his (unsuspectingly) paradoxical desire to *reach* the masses through use of melodrama and epical structure—albeit in combination with Brechtian notions of politicized storytelling and dialectical filmmaking techniques of the type typically associated with Sergei Eisenstein. What makes Ghatak's films so interesting and unique, I posit, is the veritable *clash* that he produces onscreen between high-oral and high-literate aesthetics. (If such an assertion strikes readers as a sorry reduction of a filmmaker's oeuvre to a single perspective, I would agree, in the sense that the desire here is to offer an ancillary, not substitutive, lens for reflecting on the nature of narrative.)

of-the-road" cinema in India. Benegal's film differed from its state-sponsored predecessors in a seminal way: It was not state-sponsored. *Middle
cinema,* in other words, is in some respects a contraction of *middle-of-the-
road cinema,* a term that was intended to distinguish financing structures
more than cinematic form or content. Derek Malcolm, for instance, refers
to middle cinema as those "films that communicate with the audience
and pay for themselves (through box-office returns)" (cited in Datta, 2002,
p. 31). Perhaps a clue apropos epistemic availability is to be found in his
clause *films that communicate with the audience,* for it may well be that the
type of storytelling that *Ankur* exhibits additionally operated from a more
accessible "middle ground," a more readable "*terra cognita,*" apropos the
orality–literacy continuum. In fact, one might argue that Benegal's body
of work actually reflects or mediates *between* varying increments of literate inflection. For, as I show momentarily, some of his films display the
"gaping" realism of high-literate inflection—that is, heavy connotative elements, subjectivity, open-endedness—while others follow a naturalist-
realist premise that is more firmly entrenched in the epistemically oral tradition. Perhaps this accounts for the mixed reviews Benegal's oeuvre has
received, with some critics pointing to his auterist inconsistency (in the
negative spin) and others to his auterist diversity (in the positive).

Ankur, for instance, is famous for its definitive absence of closure,
which distanciates the viewer from the goings-on on the screen. In brief,
the film ends with the protagonist, Lakshmi, a deaf-mute laborer's wife,
turning "on her former [landlord] lover with a passionate speech calling
for a revolutionary overthrow of feudal rule. In the last shot, a young
boy throws a stone at Surya's [the landlord's] house and then the screen
turns red" (Rajadhyaksha & Willemen, 1999, p. 416). *Ankur* is often additionally lauded for its "narrative baseline [which] is one of the strongest
features of the film" (p. 64), as well as for its "detailed exploration of
characters and their motivations, the contradictory impulses they are
governed by, the stray glances and gestures, landscape details, marvel-
lous use of folk music and natural sound" (p. 66). But it is generally that
ending which has drawn the film its greatest critical approbation—perhaps because the resolution is a crystallized moment of high-literate inflection (in a film that is arguably more modest, epistemically speaking).
Prasad (1998a), for one, insists that the power of *Ankur's* climax, "which
has provoked so much comment," derives from "the sense of relief and
pleasant surprise we feel when we are rescued from the *ménage-a-trois*
[of landlord, servant-inamorata, and servant's husband] and placed on
the side of the oppressed for the brief space of [that] stone-throwing incident" (p. 203). But such a congealed *suspension* of narrative (in its refusal to surrender to the status quo) is largely the birthright of a print
culture and, in an orally inflected storytelling world, would be tantamount to self-annihilation.

Benegal's *Nishant* (*Night's End*, 1975) ends in a fashion even more *in medias res*, offering the spectator what Prasad (1998a) confirms is "a considerably less secure position of contemplation than *Ankur*" (p. 203). The destinies of its multiple characters remain to the end unclear, ambiguous, and incomplete, such that spectators are left having to surmise—presume—infer; they must fill in the existential blanks, so to speak. But, alas, these are activities with profound ties to a literately inflected psychodynamic engagement with narrative (accounting in some measure, perhaps, for *Nishant*'s comparative lack of box-office success). To be sure, numerous other factors govern a film's box-office success: storyline, performances, technical sophistication, stylistic and political sensibilities, not to mention the *zeitgeist*. But if we are speaking on the basis of storytelling *norms*, then we have no recourse but to draw attention to the critical role that the open ending plays in middle cinema. Consider that lack of closure is just as fundamental to films like *Aakrosh* (*Cry of the Wounded*, 1980) and *Ardh Satya* (*Half Truth*, 1983), which were directed by Govind Nihalani, Benegal's former cinematographer. In fact, in these latter films—disturbingly rich and ambivalent portraits of individuals caught between the crosshairs of corruption and civic impotence—the fates of the characters are left so completely devoid of closure that spectators are even expected to draw *philosophical* conclusions about what the stories *in toto* could possibly mean. Sometimes, as in the case of *Aakrosh*, a story can feel more discontinued than open ended. Could such unresolved resolutions bespeak a subconscious insurgence on the part of the films' directors against Bollywood's tightly sutured endings, which homeostatically conflate history with myth?

Quietude and quiescence also have a steady presence in this species of filmmaking. This is so even in a more moderately literately inflected film like Benegal's *Kalyug* (*The Machine Age*, 1981).[16] Although *Kalyug*

---

16. Although *Kalyug* does display periods of quietude and quiescence that call for connotative spectatorial address, the film on the whole exhibits a more moderate form of literate inflection than the majority of Benegal's oeuvre. The kind of decoding *Kalyug* calls for is far less literately inflected than, say, a work like *Nishant*. Indeed, as Kishore Valicha (1988) observes, *Kalyug* has "all the trappings of popular narrative cinema. There are killings, intrigue in high places, a good deal of glamour, even a disco song" (p. 104). Thoraval (2000) theorizes that the film opts "for a 'Hollywood' kind narrative [*sic*] accessible to a larger audience" (p. 162). Although these qualities do not imply *a priori* a more oral inflection, they perhaps hint at the film's greater differential remove from high-literate inflection—and also possibly why the film is one of Benegal's least celebrated (Gopalakrishnan, 2003). The film is a modernized corporate retelling of the *Mahabharata*'s epical battle incidentally, and its narrative structure is a complicated reflection of that. What Thoraval (2000) objects to is that "we don't see a very convincing attempt by Benegal to measure up to the 'epic' cinema of Ghatak and Kumar Shahani" (p. 162). This, I argue, is because Benegal's epical tale, despite its periodic need for connotative readings on the part of spectators, is in fact ironically *more* in keeping with the constraints and characteristics of authentic primary, or oral, epic.

calls for comparatively less decoding, still it is a film where "social isolation is established" via scenes of a character silently contemplating his
city, and a "moment of claustrophobia potently conveys the sense of an
individual caught in the web of larger forces" (Datta, 2002, p. 130). Irony,
too, has been identified as a recurrent trope in Benegal's movies. Although scant in middle-class cinema, no doubt because of the "game-
playing" demands that it makes on the spectator, irony is critically acknowledged to be one of the major devices driving Benegal's *Trikaal*
(*Past, Present, Future*, 1985) (Datta, 2002).

Some scholars actually *distinguish* Benegal and his contemporaries
from middle-cinema directors. Bhaskar Sarkar (2001), for instance, applies the term exclusively to filmmakers who came into prominence
in the 1980s *after* Shyam Benegal—directors like Nihalani and Ketan
Mehta—who Sarkar contends "evince more accessible, audience-friendly
styles. . . . [T]hey continue to make socially conscious films without eschewing the pleasure factor, in a vein closer to Bombay's *masala* products" (pp. 163–164). Suffice it to say that the terms and definitions continue to be fuzzily applied. Still, comments like Sarkar's illustrate an
academic awareness of the *differentials* of narrative accessibility, which
orality and literacy are able in part to explicate—and in a manner that
appropriately problematizes any notion of a "pleasure factor." Although
incorporating elements of melodrama or music (as Mehta has) or quick-
ening story pace (as Nihalani has) may appear on the surface to connect
a film to popular artistic traditional forms (and, ergo, to circumvent
alienating traditional audiences), *how* these particular traditions are employed (i.e., how they are inflected) is of immense consequence. Melodrama, for instance, if isolated from the oral episteme's network of attributes and acted on as a discrete mode (e.g., ironized or ambiguated),
may no longer serve the orally inflected viewer, at least not in terms of
his or her ability to engage *meaningfully* with a story. Nihalani inadvertently confirms this in his explication of middle cinema's radically alternative incorporation of mythological figures: "unlike the commercial
cinema which uses mythological references to support the status quo
which they promote, we refer to mythology to support an action for
change" (cited in Vasudev, 1986, p. 48). The difference here—at least
from this project's vantage point—is between an orally inflected *use* of
mythology (for preserving and, accordingly, *promoting* the status quo)
and a literately inflected *ab*-use[17] of mythology (whereby myth is inter-
rogated for the purposes of effecting change).

For certain, one could argue that middle cinema generates its own
clichés, such as its own brand of Manichaeism, whereby the subaltern is
portrayed as eternally innocent and victimized, and the system as eter-

---

17. The word, etymologically speaking, quite literally means a *moving away* from use.

nally wicked. One might even assert that there is a veritable *formula* to literately inflected cinema, given the cinema's foregrounding of those attributes that constitute the literate episteme. This might explain why the distinct cinematic movements or styles that function in this realm necessarily come and go, recreate themselves, eventually yield to other movements: because, in becoming imitations of themselves, they are irrevocably *drained* of their novelty. Such was the case incidentally with middle cinema's early ruralist drive. As Sumita Chakravarty (1996) describes, "Soon the practice of trooping out to the villages with camera and crew itself hardened into a predictable genre" (p. 246). Perhaps in becoming too identifiable—too generic—the films eventually become unconscious reminders of the oral recycling and redundancy that high-literate communities are programmed to disdain. Although in the oral schema thematic co-option and continuation are existentially sought, literate creations—including species like "New" Cinema—call for a continuous *differentiating* of the self from others.

But what if this dissimilitude that I am heralding is really nothing more than my own subliminal glorification of literacy, a callous employing on my part of value-laden terms to differentiate the highly oral less favorably from the highly literate? How different, after all, is each episteme really when it comes to, say, recycling? Yes, Bollywood has a notorious history of borrowing, stealing, or at the least getting "inspired by" Hollywood, Hong Kong, and its own antecedents (Kadapa-Bose, 2009). (We need only recall Raj Kapoor's iconic 1950s version of Chaplin's Little Tramp, complete with black bowler hat, hobo sack, mustache, and shuffling walk.) But is that really so different from a filmmaker like Satyajit Ray finding a mentor in Vittorio de Sica, or Shyam Benegal one in Satyajit Ray, or (to keep the chain going) Mrinal Sen finding aesthetic sustenance in Glauber Rocha and Federico Fellini,[18] or Martin Scorcese in Akira Kurosawa, or Quentin Tarantino in Martin Scorsese? The distinction, I would say, lies in the *roots* of the behavior and, to be sure, in the ethical response to such appropriations: In the oral episteme, the blatant use by one text of another text's lines, storylines, or props is regarded as neither anxiety-inducing nor inappropriate, but instead as warranted and essential, since it is only through such retransmission of effects that knowledge persists through time. In the literate episteme, contrarily, such borrowings circulate in a culture intensely conscious of plagiarism, given that knowledge is always known to exist elsewhere in permanently fixed forms; thus originality becomes the harbinger of good

---

18. It need be acknowledged that Mrinal Sen, in his deployment of a vast array of influences (including not only Rocha and Fellini, but Truffaut, Solanas and Getino, and Bresson as well), has "consistently and unambiguously downgraded notions of artistic 'originality'" (Rajadhyaksha & Willemen, 1999, p. 211).

storytelling, and one sets great store as a director in acknowledging influences, and, as a viewer, in being able to identify an "homage" that connects an original work to a preexisting one.

MILLENNIAL BOLLYWOOD THROUGH THE
ORALITY–LITERACY PARADIGM

During the late 1980s and early 1990s, the *masala* film putatively began to wane in popularity. As Thoraval (2000) explains, the reasons for the formula's casualty of reputation were due to a

> loss of interest by a large part of the public who were tired of the repetitive themes shown in the films, the plagiarism from video clips, the nonsensical formulas, etc. . . . While in the two previous decades, it had been possible for a film to hold its own in a single hall in Bombay for 40 weeks at a stretch, now the movie halls, often in a pitiful state, were often empty. A few new multiplexes were constructed in the upper class areas in some big cities but these were used more to show American than Indian films. (p. 130)

I myself am resistant to the claim that the *masala* film form became altogether scorned. A judicious look at the top hits of the 1990s makes it fairly apparent that the *masala* film was still very much spectatorially prized. Films like *Maine Pyar Kiya* (*I Fell in Love*, 1989), *Saajan* (*Husband*, 1991), and *Aankhen* (*Eyes*, 1993) are just a handful of films from those years that garnered "superhit" and even "all-time blockbuster" status. These may have constituted the type of movie that came to be increasingly disdained by India's more upscale audiences, that is true; but that did not lead *sine qua non* to a waning in popularity of the species. More accurate is that India's state-run television, Doordarshan, "opened its doors to private producers," with television's ensuing "hugely popular, glossy soap operas [taking] away the cinema audience" (Datta, 2002, p. 38)—or, the *middle-class* cinema audience, at least. Benegal himself calls attention to this change in percipient body when he declares that, in the late 1980s, even *non*traditional cinema "lost its entire audience to television" (cited in Datta, 2002, p. 11). The *masala* film's loss of reputation might be less the issue here, then, than the increasingly stratified audiences that were reconfiguring what rendered narrative material reputable—or, at the least, popular.[19]

---

19. Perhaps this was part of Benegal's rationale for crossing over into mainstream Bollywood with his release *Zubeidaa* (2001), a move for which he was both saluted and censured. When asked at the time why the industry was incapable of making "mature films" (Joshi, 2002, p. 121), Benegal answered, "we have a fairly large section of the population that is still either barely literate or illiterate. . . . [A] lot depends on the audiences them-

Besides, even into the new millennium, films like *Gadar: Ek Prem Katha* (*Mutiny: A Love Story*, 2001) continue to display that familiar spicy blend of elements—or what Anil Sharma, *Gadar*'s director, describes as a "rooted-in-the-soil flavour" (cited in Saxena, 2001, p. 3). According to Sharma, such seasoning is still crucial to a film's success in small-town and rural India. Although some readers might interpret his qualifier to mean that the films require an overt visual presence of rural India and discrete village mores, I propose that those alone are insufficient. It is no accident that *Gadar*—a film set during the time of Partition—also displays considerably high levels of agonism (of both the melodramatic and violent varieties), nondiegetic amplification, slapstick digressions, flashbacks, totemic iconography, and a deliberate Manichean worldview. Indeed, these very traits may have assisted it in becoming 2001's top film, and one of the nation's all-time earners (www.boxofficeindia.com).

Regional "top-grosser" lists also reveal that *masala* films still to this day find dedicated audiences. Bihar's "top 20" list, for example, includes *Indian* (2001) and *Soldier* (1998), films that, beyond speaking to that province's preference for stars who reflect more subaltern personae, do so *through* a more oral storytelling gestalt. (Bihar, it need be pointed out, is one of the least developed, most economically troubled regions in India, and also home to the nation's lowest literacy rates.)

By the same token, there have always been films produced within the Bollywood system that exhibit a higher literate inflection than the standard *masala* film. Some even manage, beyond critical approbation, to succeed at the box office. Gulzar's *Maachis* (*Matches*, 1996), for example, tells the tale of a Sikh youth from rural Punjab who joins a league of terrorists as a matter of vengeance against a corrupt political system. The film employs both verisimilitude and a regional authenticity that ironically distances it from any so-called "rooted-in-the-soil" flavor. Additionally, it is comparatively quiet, restrained, and anti-spectacular. Gulzar generally produces films that are more literately inflected—not to mention, more politically charged. (That he is also a lyricist, playwright and poet is no doubt significant.) Granted, many of his films do not do exceptionally well at the box office—but *Maachis* did.

So, too, did Ram Gopal Varma's *Satya* (*Truth*, 1998), which explores, via *vraisemblance* and psychologized characters, the murky goings-on of the Bombay underworld. The film is extremely violent and action-oriented, and all the syndicate bad-guys are obliterated by the end; but *Satya* relies much less on iconic stars and avoids the platform moralizing

---

selves, the audiences' acceptability—what they accept and what they don't accept. . . . All these factors contribute to the kinds of films that are made in that given society" (cited in Joshi, 2002, p. 121).

typical of more conventional *masala* films. Here we find instead periods of quietude and quiescence, strong symbolism, powerful deployment of irony, and even an initial intent on the director's part to abstain from musical numbers (they were added at the last minute for fear of alienating the masses).[20]

Undoubtedly, the literate inflection of these films could be viewed as the realist aesthetic of middle cinema becoming absorbed or co-opted by Bollywood. More and more filmmakers, as Datta (2002) observes, "clearly use the style of parallel film-makers and concede their debt to this style of cinema. Ram Gopal Varma openly acknowledges Benegal's films (in particular *Kalyug*, 1980) as a primary influence on his form and treatment of *Satya*" (p. 12). Other critics argue that such leanings toward "realism" arise out of the culture's emergent awareness of real-life villains, thanks to a mounting exposure to media (Chopra, 2001b, p. 46). But why that would apply to villains, and not to other social groups or communities, renders that assertion still open for debate. More likely, the subject matter provides license and leeway for directors to contour their storytelling with a more personal idiom without endangering commercial success. By this I mean that it is no accident that the films bearing higher literate inflection that *do well* at the box office are often terrorist- or gangster-oriented and, consequently, highly violent. Although they possess fewer melodramatic upsurges and rely less on clichés, they concomitantly surrender to a paradoxically extreme agonism of mimetic events.

One exception to this all-around concession to violence is Kamal Hassan's *Chachi 420* (*Auntie 420,* 1998), an adaptation (and also, arguably, a more literately inflected version) of the Robin Williams comedy *Mrs. Doubtfire.* Despite *Chachi 420*'s periodic forays into a highly oral slapstick, the film is set in a verisimilar Bombay and, in many ways, takes a more middle-class cinema-type approach to critiquing the Bombay filmmaking universe (its protagonist works as a choreographer in the film industry). It is witty, nonformulaic, and performatively restrained, although these qualities in no way stipulate, or call for, a "seeing *as*" on the part of the spectator. Perhaps for this reason the film manages, as one website commented, to be a film "for the masses as well as the classes" (www.apunkachoice.com). Smartly choreographed interplay between characters, combined with a certain verisimilitude that kindles pathos, makes the film, in a word, Chaplinesque.[21]

---

20. Interestingly, at one point in the film a character didactically proclaims, "The problem [in India] is not law and order, but education. This is a country with a vast population, but the literacy level is so low. We must educate them. The problem will get solved on its own then."

21. Hassan's Tamilian film *Nayakan* (Leader, 1987) is another highly engaging and affecting story, this one about the rise and fall of a criminal underworld godfather. Realist

Finally, Mani Ratnam has made some very successful Bollywood films that display what Shyam Benegal grants is Ratnam's clear interest in a "cinematic grammar" that eschews the Bollywood "theatricality, histrionics and rhetoric" to which audiences are generally accustomed (cited in "Cannes," 2002). Quietude and verisimilitude are characteristically integral to Ratnam's oeuvre, including in films like *Roja* (*The Rose*, 1992), *Bombay* (1995) and *Guru* (2007). But such films are also sans any neorealist ambition to burden an audience with a what-ness of things, or with a deformation of cinematic language that calls for a spectatorial pursuit of meaning via private dialectics.

Plainly in a nation as large and spectatorially broad as India's, it would not behoove the critic to claim that the Bombay industry was altogether shifting in any single direction. Nevertheless, in recent years profit margins, and so, too, the public eye—and, along with that, the *academic* eye—have largely swung the direction of a newly emerging type of Bollywood film: one whose address is to "a cosmopolitan middle class" (Jain, 2005, p. 86). The reasons for this emergence are typically, and appropriately, pinned on India's recently privatized marketplace (Jaikumar, 2003, p. 27),[22] which has led to the resurgence of the middle class as a *theater*-going public. Although only a comparatively minor slice of the nation's whole population (around 10%), the middle class constitutes a collectivity somewhere in the region of 300 million (as large, in other words, as the entire U.S. population). This comparatively moneyed class with a purchasing power tied to the cinema is especially evident in the nation's urban centers, in cities like Bombay and Delhi. As Raminder Kaur and Ajay Sinha (2005) describe:

> The predominance of young lower class males in cinema halls up and down the subcontinent as was the case in the decade of the "angry young man" no longer applies. Nowadays one is likely to see families driving into the multiplexes[23] in their flashy BMWs, or studious conference-goers and curious travellers trying to get to the bottom (and indeed, the top) of Indian cinema. (p. 29)

This more affluent audience is also a more media-savvy and globally aware constituent of film-goers for whom "compatibility between [the]

---

images and nonfrontality combine with comparatively restrained performances. Peculiarly, the film's aurality generally bears a higher grade of oral inflection than the film's visuality (its fight scenes, for instance, are disproportionately inflated via sound effects). Perhaps this accounts for its capacity to absorb spectators who might otherwise not engage so readily with a more literately inflected diegesis.

22. Economic liberalization became an acknowledged national project in the 1990s and continues at exorbitant speed to change the economic and commercial sectors of India.

23. The recent appearance of multiplexes in India's urban centers has dramatically impacted the breadth of entertainment options, including a recent spawning of the niche film.

need for conspicuous consumption and the dominant consensus on 'Indian values'" is central (Jaikumar, 2003, p. 27).

Bollywood's burgeoning overseas market has also had an effect on India's film industry, proving in some circumstances to be more profitable to producers than the Indian home market (Ganti, 2004, pp. 38–39). Indeed, Hindi films can sometimes earn as much as 25% to 50% of their revenue from overseas (Walunjkar, 2006). The past decade's dominance of "family entertainers," which are generally rife with romantic sensibilities and cosmopolitan gloss, is often attributed to this newly tapped segment of the economic market. As Yash Chopra, one of the most successful filmmakers of this romance subgenre, explains, "Indians abroad are attracted to well-made family films based on human relationships which remind them of their roots" (cited in Aiyar & Unnithan, 2003, p. 41). Could it also be that, for nostalgic reasons, Indians abroad prefer to see the more *orally* inflected nature of the formula preserved, albeit with both the violence and any unsettling struggle with communalism, poverty, and corruption pared away? Despite the higher literate inflection of *Satya*, after all, that film did *not* do well with Indian spectators abroad.

Without question, this only complicates further the nature of the act of literacy. Although people may have the *capacity* to engage with more literate texts, they may find oral engagement more affecting, or they may prefer to retain their connection to the oral for sundry personal, psychological, or sociocultural reasons. (This is not to recommend that all Indians abroad are highly literate, by the way.) To bedevil the issue further, one need ask if such family entertainers appeal to consumer classes, both at home and overseas, because their nostalgic idealism vis-à-vis India is not impinged upon by a violence that self-consciously lends itself *too* readily and obtrusively to the potpourri quality of more highly orally inflected texts. In other words, there may be a secondary reason for this desire to diminish, or narratively detach from, violent agonism—at least according to what the history of written narrative suggests. Coarse physical violence, which is fundamental to much oral epic, becomes "residual through much early literacy, [and] gradually wanes or becomes peripheral in later narrative" (Ong, 1982, p. 44). As Ong explains, "As literary narrative moves toward the serious novel, it eventually pulls the focus of action more and more to interior crises and away from purely exterior crises" (p. 44).

No doubt the family entertainers' concomitant erasure of indigence is what leads contemporary analysts like Sheena Malhotra and Alagh Tavishi (2004) to refute Nandy's claim that Bollywood films are best comprehended through the metaphor of the urban slums. These authors instead maintain that "the most successful Hindi films of the 1990s have been glossy, easy to digest, eye-candy versions that make those [crude, lower middle-class] sensibilities palatable" (p. 27). Indeed, in this "new" romantic universe, the Hindu gets conflated with the wealthy, and the poor, who do not fit that constructed norm, get marginalized (p. 19). If one factors in the oral and literate epistemes of visual narrative, however, Nandy and his challengers prove *equally* correct. Even if many of the family-entertainer films shun the violence commonly associated with *masala* films—and concomitantly vacuum away the existence of the subaltern citizen—representation of the self *on* the screen should not be confused (or conflated) with accessibility *in front of* the screen. The inflated evocation of wealth in these movies (opulent mansions, fancy cars, an across-the-board material magnificence and munificence) still undergirds these movies, just as conspicuous consumption did Homeric epic. Although arguably kowtowing to NRI fetishism, the films still articulate that fetishism through a frontality that frustrates any requirement that meaning be mined, mulled over, or studied. Although violence may be tempered, if not altogether abandoned in these films, violence's agonistic partner, melodrama, still fundamentally drives the narratives—more so certainly than it did in the middle-class cinema of the 1970s.

Similarly, this new breed of family dramas—at least in terms of its films which have obtained hit status—shows little of the deference to realism that the middle-class cinema was subtly, if awkwardly, attempting. Perhaps that is why the first of the breed, *Hum Aapke Hain Koun . . . !*, was no less successful in Bihar than in Bombay or Baltimore. Still beholden to a high-oral inflection, the film effectively bridged the gap between the cognitive requirements of less literate viewers and the upwardly mobile Indians and NRIs eager "to lap up rosy pictures of Indian society" (Ravinder Kaur, 2002, p. 208). The same could be said of a film like *Kuch Kuch Hota Hai* (*Something Happens,* 1998), which glamorizes the cosmopolitan lifestyle, while also eventually surrendering to "we" inflection and a safeguarding of the status quo.

Many of these domestic films, in other words, are *not* significantly different from their *masala* predecessors—at least not in terms of their epistemic attachment to orality and the demands that that particular way of knowing places on identity construction in films. But the movies have admittedly updated themselves, in order to accommodate newly emergent (and lucrative) spectatorial trends. Here, then, I must agree with Virdi's (2003) judgment that the films' "iconography of abundance" is less an innovation than a celluloid re-casting: "In the romance genre the Non-Resident Indian . . . is Hindi cinema's new aristocrat. Iconic of new wealth the NRI replaces the *zamindar* (landed wealth) and Kunwar *sahibs*, scions of the princely states from previous decades, who now stand effaced from popular cinema's social landscape" (p. 202). Once again, these romance films have perhaps been the most economical way to straddle a greater socioeconomic swathe of audiences: from those who are in pursuit of a quixotic, upscale reflection of the self (through a nostalgically venerated formula that perhaps even engenders a kind a formalistic reactionaryism), to those whose engagement with the form is bound up with aesthetic-cultural motivations formidably shaped by cognitive ones.

And yet, there is indisputable evidence that in this new millennium epistemically literate impulses *are* subtly working their way amenably— that is to say, *popularly*—through Bollywood. Earlier romance films, for instance, typically possessed brazenly bad villains (dons, diabolical dads, sinister entrepreneurs); some of today's films, on the other hand, display a patent "lack of a villain and, consequently, the absence of the state and its representatives (police officers, judges, etc.)" (Ganti, 2004, p. 40) who are generally trotted out to intercede on the state's behalf. Obviously, the disappearance of the villain implies that a film's dramatic tension has migrated elsewhere, that its source now derives from somewhere else. Ganti observes that, in the case of films where villainous *class* differences have been removed, the narrative becomes "internalized and centers on the conflict between individual desire and duty to one's family" (p. 40). The characters in *Veer-Zaara* (2004), for example, are more restrained and more psychologically motivated than their antecedents. Perhaps that's what accounts for the film's occasional lapses into quietude, for its aural "pauses" during which we watch characters silently grapple with their own physical and emotional, if not quite existential, states. The film's politics, too, are on some level progressive (a female lawyer; parents who accept a communally mixed marriage); but the film's intimations of literate inflection are nonetheless mostly surface phenomena that do not seriously penetrate or intervene with the oral accessibility of the text. The film's quietude, for example, is never connotatively motivated, and the more muted performances eventually submit to a telescoping of individual personalities into a collective self. In a sense, what we see here is a kind of literately inflected dimpling on an otherwise orally inflected narrative.

Films like *Lagaan* (*Once Upon a Time in India*, 2001) and *Mangal Pandey: The Rising* (*The Ballad of Mangal Pandey*, 2005) also deserve mention for the manner in which they reorient (and subtly "literize") the epical expanse of the *masala* Hindi film by consciously setting out to create films with express links to folklore and mythologized history. In fact, *Lagaan*'s transnational success, so Priya Jaikumar (2003) argues, "may be attributable to its adaptation of Hindi cinema's formal and thematic elements (such as song and dance, Indian values versus a mercenary modernity) to familiar Western tropes (of a single-stranded narrative and psychologically motivated characterization)" (p. 25). In other words, *Lagaan*, while preserving many of the standard conventions of the *masala* film, tightens its plot line so that it is more in accordance with Freytag's pyramid. *Mangal Pandey* reproduces *Lagaan*'s gentle shift toward characters that display moderate leanings toward internalized conflict, and its more classical Hollywood style of camerawork and editing. One might argue that *Mangal Pandey*'s style is less intrusive than both highly orally *and* highly literately inflected narrative, in that the film neither "tells" its story agonistically nor "shows" it via covert messages that a spectator must privately extract. What this produces, interestingly, is a film more akin to a toned-down oral spectacle—a restrained orally inflected epical film, one might say, not unlike *Braveheart* (1995) or the biblical epics of 1950s Hollywood. Here, a patina of historical and psychological authenticity overlays a technically superior oral-epical template, efficaciously bridging the anticipated expectations of both oral and literate audiences. For the former group, the narrative (thanks to its oral underpinnings) can still function *as* folklore; meanwhile, the latter group understands itself to be narratively engaging *with* folklore. (This is in important contradistinction to more literately inflected epical films like the Coen Brothers' *O Brother, Where Art Thou?* (2000) or Ang Lee's *Crouching Tiger, Hidden Dragon* (2003)—*literate spectacles*, we might call them—which are awash in ironic distancing and self-conscious play.[24])

Meanwhile, recent Hindi popular films that are *not* expressly family entertainers display an even greater move toward, or more serious grappling with, literate inflection. More daring, for instance, are *Jaane Tu . . . Ya Jaane Naa* (*Whether You Know or Not*, 2008) and *Dil Chahta Hai* (*The Heart Has Desires*, 2001), which operate on the basis of comparatively self-possessed, subdued, and more lifelike characters who are tied to earth. As Jaikumar (2003) observes of *Dil Chahta Hai*, "The young men are rich, but not in the manner of recent Hindi films. . . . They have comfortable relationships with their parents, who are not portrayed as complete autocrats. . . . The men do not entertain the archetypal do-or-die approach to friendship, family, or love. The film explores some shades of gray in relationships" (p. 26). Here again we observe a heightened penchant for internalized dramatic conflict—a conflict that is particularly

---

24. *O Brother*, for instance, concurrently punctures and deflates its own grand rhetoric through incessant joking, multiple allusions to literature, and a full-fledged ironic distancing. And although *Crouching Tiger* is set in legendary times; sweeps across vistas with epical splendor and iconographic excessiveness; and incorporates flashbacks as a storytelling device, it also engages in a highly *self-conscious* play apropos its oral antecedents. Directors like Lee and the Coen Brothers engage with oral epic-ness or myth as a narrative strategy or motif. They *literize* the form in ways that blur, if not outright sever, the form's connections to orality, that is, to the genre's initial noetic *raison d'être*. *Crouching Tiger*, for instance, is a film *to look at*, not to participate in; a *dream* of the past rather than an epical connection to it. One might even interpret it as a symbol of inwardly turned folks trying to get back to their primordial or elemental state of being, but, ultimately, at the same time, revealing their incapacity to do so.

significant in this case (at least by orality–literacy standards) because of
its less explicit bond to the preceding generation. (Indeed, even films
that remain heavily spectacular, such as *Om Shanti Om* [2007], reflect this
shift away from the overtly intergenerational.) Much as Desphande (2005)
keenly detects, "the new hero, for the first time in the history of Hindi cinema, is someone without a past and consequently without memory"
(p. 187). Desphande argues that these changes are "directly related to the
changing economics of film production and distribution, and an expansion of its market not just beyond the shores of India, but also to other allied industries such as music, satellite television, and so forth" (p. 187).
But could they not signal a synchronous ability (and psychodynamic
agility) on the part of percipients to participate in a safe and nonjeopar-
dizing detachment from the realm of the ancestors? Such attachments to
"the hero's past, his childhood, [and] the circumstances of his birth and
upbringing" (p. 202) are a precondition of more orally inflected narrative,
after all, given that, for oral peoples, the self (and the Self as a "historical"
phenomenon) is only preservable and recallable *through* narrative.[25]

At the same time, *Jaane Tu . . .* and *Dil Chahta Hai* remain largely outwardly directed as texts, never traveling so far inward as to induce, extend into, or permit the likes of serious *anti*-spectacle or understatement
(something that *is* the case for *Satya*). Nevertheless, what both films lay
bare is a recent trend toward less *aurally* agonistic storytelling. Indeed,
some of the more recent hit romance films, like *Kabhi Alvida Naa Kehna*
(*Never Say Goodbye*, 2006), and even a stylized action film like *Don* (2006)
to some extent, display a relative mutedness, accomplished via a comprehensive erasure of nondiegetic sound effects that operate as aural
clichés; of deliveries that are amplified and histrionic; and of a too heavy
reliance on verbal clichés. A "quelling" of the aural dimensions of the
orally inflected text, we might aver, is conspicuously transpiring in a
strain of hit Hindi films—although without any parallel shift into a territory where complete formulaic discontinuity and subjectivity reside.
Could it be that these films represent a return to a subspecies of *middle-
class* cinema within the larger context of Bollywood? This time, however,
because of the super-gentry urban and overseas markets, instead of

---

25. Desphande (2005) cites family entertainers like *Hum Aapke . . .* , *Dilwale . . .* , and
Kuch Kuch . . . in order to substantiate his claim. He posits that their characters no longer
have childhoods because "the consumable hero has no history. . . . More precisely, he has
no history that he cares to recall" (p. 202). I argue that the intergenerational commitment
that ties individuals to collective memory in these films remains a, if not *the*, overriding
force—which is not the case in a film like *Dil Chahta Hai*. Still, Desphande's point about the
films' deliberate and recurrent extrication of characters from their own histories cannot be
disregarded. We might ask if, coterminous with an etiology based in sociocultural ruptures
facilitated by consumerism and the appearance of new markets, these films' motif of detachment also subtly reflects how persons *with* written histories no longer require that the
memory of the self (as tied to the past) bears repeating in every film.

functioning as an untrendy minority, the subspecies regularly ranks in the annual lists of top grossers and box-office successes.

How else to explain an anomaly like *Black* (2005)? This film, which explores the decades-long relationship between a Helen Keller-type student and her unflagging elder-statesman teacher, skirts some of the more entrenched conventions of the Hindi film formula genre. For one, it sacrifices song numbers altogether and prioritizes a more character-driven form of storytelling. At the same time, *Black* holds fast to spectacle, deploying its own strange brand of German expressionism (high-contrast lighting, jarring visual techniques, stagey sets) and a heavy-handed symbolism, both visual and aural. The aim, in a sense, is to *look* like an art film, but to be devoid of the characteristics that mark high-literate inflection (e.g., foregrounding the background, erotic gapes that compel a "writerly" reading). In fact, many of the attributes particular to the oral episteme are acutely present in *Black*: storytelling via flashbacks; noninterpretive meaning; amplified "flat" settings against which the (comparatively less amplified) characters act. Although dramatic and successfully tense at times, *Black* functions more in the *guise* of an art film—is aping art-cinema narration, in some respects. Perhaps it does so for an audience that cannot, or that is unwilling to, engage with the kind of literately inflected norms that conventionally drive the art film; or, perhaps it's fairer to say that the film operates much like the films from the early German expressionist period, especially those of the Kammerspiel or "chamber-drama" genre, which introduced a type of amplified subjectivity via expressionistic techniques, while still managing to tell stories that were narratively intelligible.[26] One wonders if this production impulse replicates that of select producers in the early American film industry, who likewise sought "to produce motion pictures that articulated exclusive, 'highbrow' cultural values and yet . . . appeal[ed] to a broad, cross-class audience" (R. King, 2005, p. 6).

Rang De Basanti (*Paint It Yellow,* 2006) displays a comparable leaning toward literate inflection, albeit of an intriguingly different cast. Unlike *Black*, which renounces the song and dance of Bombay film in order to align itself with its own conception of art film, *Rang De* remains loyal to the musical tradition of Hindi film. However, it injects its song and

---

26. Offbeat or crossover films that stray too close to the high-literate episteme, such as the small, intimate film *Raincoat* (2004), normally flop at the box office. Nevertheless, such films have engendered a following as well as notoriety for going against the grain of conventional Hindi film-making practices. See, for instance, the "semi-hit" *Life in a . . . Metro* (2007). In fact, a manifesto produced by some of the earliest proponents of this recent multiplex breed, including the directors of *Bombay Boys* (1998) and *Hyderabad Blues* (1998), verbally acknowledged their desire to distance themselves ideologically (and aesthetically) from Bollywood *and* art cinema. As they bluntly put it, films were to be "set after 1947 (partition); director of Indian origin or content of Indian origin, no Bollywood, parallel or arthouse, no gratuitous songs, dances, or foreign locations" (cited in Desai, 2003, p. 52).

dance numbers into a tighter, more pyramidal plot (even given the en-
semble nature of its cast). Furthermore, *Rang De . . .* actually engages
with Indian history *as* history. History must eventually take second stage
to *mythologized* history, true; but *Rang De . . .* generally suppresses melodramatic excess in order to exact a more verisimilar performative style.
Inarguably the film acquiesces to an orally inflected climax and denouement, making it formalistically (in terms of orality–literacy theory, at
least) quite in line with Hollywood's commercial formula. The film is obviously intended for spectators who appreciate a less formulaic narrative (less amplified, less nonhistorical), but who at the same time do not
wish to extend too far from a genre that has cultural saliency, or too seriously into the subjectivity and self-consciousness of a film like *Ankur*.[27]

MIXED CINEMA AS A CINEMA OF COMPROMISE

What the films discussed here hopefully demythicize are those popularly conceived notions of what intrinsically or ideologically constitutes
"entertainment." Is *Rang De Basanti* any less entertaining or pleasurable
because it is more inflected by literacy? Wouldn't a percipient's qualita-
tive measurement of entertainment depend in significant measure on his
or her educationally endowed competence to negotiate an orality–literacy continuum? Many other questions—some vital to the body politic—
emerge because of the exposure of these variously mixed cinemas. How,
for instance, will the clefts between rural-urban and educated-unedu-
cated audiences continue to reshape and splinter or speciate Hindi popular film? Will the result be a more democratic appeal to heterogeneous
audiences, or a deepening of the extant rifts between "the masses and
the classes"? And what of the influence of the aforementioned overseas
sector with its *sui generis* interests and heftier "ad-venture" capital? Although the South Asian diaspora may stimulate greater attention on the
part of producers to production values and the mitigation of oral storytelling components, "crossing overseas" also harbors the potential danger of producers losing sight of the less prosperous (and often nonliterate or marginally literate) viewing body at home. At the same time,
might focusing on that less prosperous population endanger the development of an indigenously Indian *art* cinema? Or is the flowering of a
more vibrant art cinema now an inevitable, given the rise of the educated middle-class on the subcontinent?

---

27. *Rang De . . .* was trying, not irrelevantly, to appeal to an educated urban middle-
class audience, especially students, and especially students jaded by corrupt politics and in
pursuit of nationalist renewal. Some of those students are even given room during the end
credits to speak on their role and responsibility vis-à-vis the nation.

Art films may receive the international awards and approbation, but it is the *popular* films that have always been perceived as Indian cinema's binding force. Film critic Iqbal Masud once asserted that Indian New Wave films, cloaked as they were in the language of Godard or Bresson, were "removed from the [Indian] people," and "a form of abstraction"; commercial cinema at least retained some "connection between the director and the audience" (cited in Chakravarty, 1996, pp. 236–237). But trying to create a popular film that will reach *across* the socioeconomic divides—that will succeed with both front-stallers and multiplexers, in both the interior and the metropolises—is, as Farhan Akhtar, director of *Dil Chahta* . . . , concedes, the veritable Bollywood Holy Grail (Chopra, 2006).

Nevertheless, Bombay is home to directors like Mani Ratnam, Kamal Hassan, and Raj Gopal Varma (in the present) and Raj Kapoor and Guru Dutt (in the past), who have exhibited a willingness, even an eagerness, to create a *cinema of compromise*, that is, a cinema that refuses to relinquish the imaginative development of a director's own artistic (even auteurist) drives, while also respecting that a significant portion of the Indian audience is burdened by nonliteracy or semi-literacy. In fact, I term this a cinema of compromise based on a comment made by Mani Ratnam, who granted that India's arts, and accordingly India's masses, were heavily influenced by oral tradition. Hence Ratnam's readiness as a filmmaker to use (what readers of this book would recognize as) orally inflected munitions: "If using songs makes it easier for people to grasp what I'm doing I don't mind using that language. Think of it as a compromise—or as a method of communicating" (cited in "Cannes," 2002).[28]

Perhaps there is no director in the history of Bombay cinema who managed more effectively to straddle orality and literacy in a single film than Guru Dutt did in *Pyaasa* (*Thirst*, 1957). The film predates the contemporary scene by almost half a century, but it is cinema of compromise *par excellence* and therefore merits brief attention. Dutt's film is still touted by film critics as one of *the* most artistic, cinematic, poetic films to have emerged from India, let alone Bollywood; and the ways in which it managed to do this remain—at least in this author's eyes—both remarkable and mystifying. The film revolves around the travails of an idealistic, principled poet trying to survive in Bombay under the twin crush of penury and a lack of renown. Although unusually critical and bleak, *Pyaasa*'s tone is balanced out by "comic asides" and "popular songs" (Ganti, 2004, p. 150). Furthermore, the film is unself-consciously episodic in structure and heavily interpolated by flashbacks and songs. ("Sincer-

---

28. I would recommend that, across the waters, the Italian director Sergio Leone also succeeded in producing his own idiosyncratic brand of a cinema of compromise.

ity to the genre," as Mishra points out, "is a formal prerequisite of the Bombay auteur"; p. 122.)

But *Pyaasa* is also awash with poetical touches spun from semantic density and a deformation of language, both cinematographic and linguistic. As well, the film exhibits nuance; periods of high verisimilitude; an economy of emotion; not to mention, a denouement of subversion (one where the disenchanted poet and a prostitute renounce the city together for terra incognita). In some sense, the film foregrounds a literately inflected protagonist, a Wellesian figure cloaked in Romantic *sturm und drang*, who is dually struggling to extricate himself from, and get himself understood from within, an orally inflected form. The flashbacks, for instance, are more orally inflected in style and content than the poet's dismal present; and unlike the more stereotypical and inflated stock types that surround him, his "private" world is projected with a poetic subjectivity. This is especially the case when we are with him "in song" (indeed, Guru Dutt, much like Gulzar, is proof that a literately inflected cinema need not dispense with musical numbers).

It can be no accident that Dutt plays this protagonist, a poet at odds with a profit-mongering business elite that neither recognizes art for art's sake, nor acknowledges its own people's suffering. At the same time, Dutt exhibits a certain understandable anxiety at *being* a literately inflected artist/poet/writer in a nation-state concurrently struggling with fundamental issues of scarcity, illiteracy, exploited laborers, and urban squalor. *Pyaasa*, in other words, is a film as much *about* literate inflection trying to rupture through an oral episteme as it is about "not wanting to be part of an opportunistic and materialistic world" (Ganti, 2004, p. 150). It is a film whose auteur-protagonist struggles with the tension of satisfying his own literately inflected, auterist impulses, but for a spectatorial body who cannot possibly comprehend those impulses.

Although historically it may be that people who can only participate incompletely in a literate economy are ultimately reduced to less prestigious roles (Gozzi & Haynes, 1991, p. 221), Dutt, in an ironic twist, relegates himself to that position. He is a man driven to self-exile from the city because of his comparative epistemological sophistication. Could this be one reason why the film managed to succeed even with orally inflected audiences at the time? Possibly those audiences *did* align themselves with the status quo, and so experienced poignant *relief* at witnessing the poet and his prostitute-girlfriend abandon the civic collectivity, which could not afford such subversive and interrogative thorns.

If anything, *Pyaasa* is an exemplar text, not only in terms of how visual narratives can circulate within, between, and even complexly overlap the oral and literate epistemes for visual narrative, but for the way tensions *between* the two epistemes can sometimes induce some of the most innovative storytelling.

5

The Future of the Orality–Literacy Paradigm, Cinematically Speaking

I cast this project introductorily as a historical poetics, one whose aims were to concretize some of the structuring principles of film narrative and to explain why those principles might have surfaced or transformed under certain conditions (Bordwell, 1989). My approach in doing so has been highly integrationist, in that I have refused to "isolate 'narrativity' from other layers of meaning and from the total textual experience" (Ryan, 2004, p. 4), principally because I view narrativity, aesthetic appeal, and so forth, as indissoluble.

At the same time, I have demurred from reading these constructional codes and effects through any sort of ideal reader. In this way, *Cinematically Speaking* healthily precludes itself from any "lack of correspondence with the historical real" (Staiger, 1989, p. 364). Moreover, I have rejected that the reader-text relationship, or spectator-film relationship, is one that can—or that ultimately must yield to—a freezing of "the text or film into having either a singular use-value for all people or a use-value only for its historical moment" (p. 364). In such an instance, as Staiger indicates, "aesthetic appeal and personal interpretation are anesthetized into appropriate, sanctioned versions of reader-response" (p. 364). In the case of the orality–literacy paradigm for visual narrative, fortunately, anesthesia gives way to invigoration and gelid constriction to generative possibility. This is because infinite reader positions (and readings) are possible within the matrix, contingent as these are on how texts *and* viewers have been historically and also independently molded by literacy.

Based on these claims, one might be inclined to identify the paradigm with an Hegelian point of view, one where, as Schrader (2006) writes apropos film, the philosophy of Aesthetics is synonymous with the history of Aesthetics: "That is, the definition, the essence of Aesthetics, is nothing more or less than its history. The philosophy of Aesthetics equals the mutation of the Aesthetic ideal—understand the mutation, you understand Aesthetics" (p. 34). Though this may be a bit too stringent and uncompromising as a position, understanding *a* mutation (certainly there are others) means conceding—at least in the case of this project—to the technologies that have permitted our phylogenetic move toward a literate way of knowing. Again, it would be shortsighted, if not downright specious, to claim that orality and literacy are an aesthetics catchall; but there does seem to be a pivotal, empirical correlation between texts that film scholars repeatedly deem *canonical*, and the literately inflected skills elaborated in the preceding chapters.[1] To be sure, such canons come with deep political and ideological linings; perhaps for this very reason, it would be enlightening to discover what *nonliterate* viewers perceive as textually meaningful and what parameters *they* employ in defining or qualifying what makes for an authoritative text.

We need only look to the Western literary canon debates of the 1980s—or "brawls," as Lee Morrissey (2005) characterizes them—to witness how literately charged the act of canonization has been from the outset. Although battles over gender, race, and ethnic representation were fought in the humanities with scholastic zeal (and sometimes wrath), nobody decried the built-in irony that critical debate and canonical inclusion were exclusively confined to *alphabetic* readers. The observation may be axiomatic, perhaps even obtuse; but if the canon debates aimed to foreground the controversies concerning what constitutes representation, then the fact that orality *wasn't* talked about was surely a major elision.

My desire is not to degrade the importance of academic canons, cinematic or otherwise. (Doing so would be tantamount to disregarding where technologies have permitted us textually to go, given that this is in some respects what a chronological canon, even if only accidentally, is tracing.) Nor am I trying to make light of scholars who demanded a reevaluation of those Eurocentric and phallocentric positions, which were for so long historically privileged vis-à-vis canon selection. But those of us fortunate enough to participate in canonical critiques should at least recognize that any righting of representational inequity that takes place

---

1. See, for instance, Schrader's (2006) essay "The Film Canon" and the various *Sight and Sound* top-10 polls available on the British Film Institute's Web site. Although such lists are continually modified, their general gestalt leans toward a conspicuously high-literate inflection. Schrader's list of pre-eminent canonical films, for instance, includes Renoir's *The Rules of the Game*, Ozu's *Tokyo Story*, as well as films by Bresson, Godard, and Bergman.

in the classroom is, and can only be, taken up by those already bound up in the prestige and privilege of being part of a reading public.

But to return to the matter of my having characterized this project as a historical poetics: My concern with poetics and the principles by which films have been constructed has invariably resulted in my brushing aside other significant phenomena that shape film production and practices, such as economic patterns of distribution. Furthermore, I could easily be admonished for the narrowness of the hermeneutical lens that I have cast on narrative film. On the other hand, the paradigm spawns so many of its own Barthesian erotic gapes that I feel compelled to keep that restrictive lens on the subject just a little bit longer. That is, as a small corrective to what this project *hasn't* been able adequately to address apropos its own framework, what follows are some specific lines of inquiry that I can only hope scholars will take up more comprehensively in the future.

READERS, RECEPTION, AND RECEPTION STUDIES

Reception studies as an area of inquiry in film and media studies aims to elucidate "the consistencies *and the variations* of spectatorial activities and of readings" (Staiger 1989, p. 358). As Staiger explains of this vital extension of reader-response studies: "[T]he reader or spectator is recognized as historical and as participating in the circulation of available meanings. *Which spheres of cultural intelligibility* are available to a particular spectator is part of the research area that recognizes the historical and dialogical nature of film viewing" (p. 361). Despite its commodious theoretical parameters, reception studies has yet to take into account spectators who cannot *alphabetically* read; nor, by extension, have its advocates factored in how differentials in skills of reading and writing might impact semantic engagement. The oversight is not reception studies' alone. Robert Shuter commented in 1983 that, "Despite the prevalence of cultures in the developing world that are either completely oral or possess a high degree of orality, few field studies have been conducted on oral societies" (cited in Varadhan, 1985, p. 121). When it comes to the matter of oral peoples "reading" films, sadly Shuter's criticism holds true more than two decades later. (In the humanities, scholars are more generally geared toward examining orality's sway on ancient, classical, and medieval texts, or on folklore and ballads.) Varadhan's (1985) study of how nonliterate viewers in India engaged with family-planning instructional films gives emphasis to the need for extending the field. For, as she discovered, even in the realm of instructional narrative, one cannot assume nonliterate viewers will make the same noetic connections between scenes that literate viewers do. Nonliterate viewers employ a "different set of thought processes to derive meaning" (p. 103). Much as she avers, this mandates that we consider "the cognitive make-up of the receiver" vis-à-vis orality and literacy (p. 102). How, for instance, is mimesis differently experienced by spectators who lack literacy instruction? Can we learn something more nuanced about the art or illusion of mimesis based on what nonliterate populations perceive as mimetic?

Very likely the orality–literacy paradigm will be able to generate a more responsive reading, too, of the *transnational* filmic predilections of subaltern classes. An analysis of nonliterate or low-literate viewers that does not confine itself to discrete national borders or to other visible commonalities between peoples (e.g., gender, race, ethnicity) certainly appears justified. Such an ethnographic study, which in some sense reads against the grain of conventional sociological measures used for analysis, might expose a global audience that inhabits an (until now) unheeded transnational space. For example, how might the epistemes elucidate some of the cross-cultural correspondences one sees with respect to audience stratification and tastes? Consider the echo of the Indian context in what Hamid Naficy (2003) observes about the Iranian theater halls of his youth: "[T]he lower classes usually went to see Egyptian, Indian, and Persian song and dance melodramas, while the educated and the upper classes frequented foreign 'art films'" (p. 191). By all means, such moviegoing patterns would have been motivated in concert with sociopolitical and economic phenomena (such as concerning issues of status). Nevertheless, the epistemes of visual narrative might help us to negotiate aesthetic choices in a more calibrated—and perhaps even more pedagogically beneficial—way. Moreover, the epistemes have the potential to undo the reductionist grouping of peoples into categories of "traditional" or "modern." Scholars have conceivably misinterpreted (or only synecdochically read along economic, social or ethnic lines) particular beliefs and practices that are in actual fact appreciably motivated by orality.[2]

We might now be able to define more precisely what academics mean when they call holistic attention to the influence of "education" on percipients' engagement with visual storytelling. Too often that term is employed bereft of adequate materialization, in terms of just what—or how—education is producing or enhancing an individual's "cultural capital" (Bourdieu, 1984; also see Guillory, 1993). On other occasions, the

---

2. See Tamar Liebes and Elihu Katz's *The Export of Meaning*, which analyzes along ethnic lines percipients' responses to the television series *Dallas*—specifically the responses of Russian Jews, "Americans and kibbutzniks," and "two more traditional groups—Arabs and Moroccan Jews" (cited in Harindrinath, 2005). As Harindrinath fittingly warns, such a study "reproduce[s] a monolithic conception of ethnicity." I would add that it assigns to ethnicity traits that might be more suitably explained by literacy levels and access to education.

consequences of education are folded into, or opaquely subsumed by, other divisional systems such as class. Purnima Mankekar's (1999) ethnographic assessment of female viewers responding to India's popular 1980s mythological *Ramayan* serial serves as an effective example. Although Mankekar sensitively points to the nonmonolithicity of the category "popular" by rhetorically foregrounding that viewers' modes of engagement are multifactorially shaped (p. 196), somebody alert to the oral characteristics of visual narrative will surely recognize that her interviewees' "class-based" responses to the broadcast were driven as much by epistemic issues bound up with orality and literacy as they were by economic status. Upper-class viewers, for instance, complained that the *Ramayan*'s sets were "kitschy" and "gaudy"—or, in Mankekar's words, "inspired by the tinsel and glitter of *nautanki* [north Indian theater] performances" and the ripe iconography of calendar art (p. 191). These viewers deemed the serial "stagey" overall and the performances too heavily "stylized" ("very artificial," "too full of sermons," as one informant put it) (p. 195). On the other hand, "many lower-middle-class viewers [Mankekar] worked with described the sets as 'glorious' or 'magnificent,' and the serial's characters—antipodal to upscale viewers' charges of their being plastic—as fulfilling expectations" (pp. 191–192). Perhaps in tandem with renegotiating the monolithicity of the term *popular*, we need to unpack—and more considerately repack—concepts like *kitsch*. Indeed, it might be worth doing so here.

According to Clement Greenberg (1957), the origins of kitsch can be traced to the industrial revolution. As a result of urbanization, which for Greenberg includes learning how to read and write, the masses of western Europe and America essentially lost their taste for folk culture. As a result, they

> set up a pressure on society to provide them with a kind of culture fit for their own consumption. To fill the demand of the new market a new commodity was devised: ersatz culture, kitsch, destined for those who, insensible to the values of genuine culture, are hungry nevertheless for the diversion that only culture of some sort can provide. (p. 102)

Hence the mechanical and formulaic nature of kitsch, Greenberg argues, as well as its concentration on "vicarious experience and faked sensations" and its ability to change according to style while also always remaining the same (p. 102). For this reason, he theorizes, kitsch is "the epitome of all that is spurious in the life of our times. Kitsch pretends to demand nothing of its customers except their money—not even their time" (p. 102).

Greenberg's implicit assumption is that all peasants who learned to read and write *could* have inserted themselves easily into the extant cultural circuit. But could levels of reading and writing, synchronous with educational praxes that cognitively induce the higher-order goals associated with high literacy, have actually mattered a great deal more than Greenberg suspects? The fact that kitsch may sometimes be a diluted version of a fully matured cultural tradition (which Greenberg considers "genuine culture") may speak less to commodification-induced *insensibility* than to epistemic *accessibility*. Greenberg's claim that kitsch culture is somehow to the detriment of true culture likewise finds itself appropriately problematized, given that the offshoot of his claim otherwise is that post-industrial truth is solely in the purview of those who are highly literate.

How kitsch intersects with epistemic differentials related to storytelling opens up another compelling avenue for analysis: For, how might *nostalgia* impact the literately inflected individual's engagement with orally inflected texts like the *Ramayan* serial? The saliency of this is in part reflected in one leftist intellectual's admission to Mankekar (1999) that he enjoyed the "gaudy" serial because it reminded him "of the village *Ramlilas* [folk reenactments of Ram's life] he had seen as a child" (p. 191). Interestingly, the disdain for kitsch that Mankekar's more upscale informants exhibited in the early 1990s metamorphosed in the new millennium into a covetous zeal for kitsch—at least according to the weekly magazine *India Today*, which pronounced "Kitsch is in" (Jain, 2000, p. 44). Could this have been owing to the burgeoning of an (often well-educated) upper-middle class who now looked on their own culture's popular traditions with "a twist of irony or irreverence, even a sprinkling of humor" (p. 44), or who analyzed those traditions for, say, "insightful stories about women's status in a patriarchal society" (Melwani, 2001)? What we have here potentially is evidence of a literately inflected second remove from the subject matter, whereby appreciation for kitsch is expressed as a consciousness of kitsch *as kitsch*. Certainly this emphasizes the capability of a single text to be epistemically read on multiple levels and in ways that generate a diversity of experiential and empathic relationships.[3]

---

3. Can we attribute a certain literately inflected attitude, for instance, to *paracinematic* taste? As Jeffrey Sconce explains,

> Paracinematic taste involves a reading strategy that renders the bad into the sublime, the deviant into the defamiliarized and in so doing, calls attention to the aesthetic aberrance and stylistic variety evident but routinely dismissed in the many subgenres of trash cinema. By concentrating on a film's formal bizarreness and stylish eccentricity, the paracinematic audience, *much like the viewer attuned to the innovations of Godard* . . . foregrounds structures of cinematic discourse and artifice so that the material identity of the film ceases to be a structure made invisible in service of the diegesis, but becomes instead the primary focus of textual attention. (cited in Hawkins, 2005, p. 270)

Perhaps this mode of reading reflects exclusively *spectatorially produced* erotic gapes, whereby a more literately inflected attitude toward a text consciously and even artfully (in both senses of the word) *imposes* meaning on that text.

The plot only thickens when one takes into account the latest wave of diasporic Indians who turn to Bollywood films either for cultural sustenance or as a means of (re)negotiating identity. Already we addressed the possibility that NRIs might *privilege* films that retain a certain oral inflection because of the way those films either reflect the genre as nostalgically remembered or help to reinforce a sentimentally held vision of the homeland. Indeed, it has been said that spectators abroad appear less desirous of shifting toward the experimental narration and more credible portraits of contemporary India that Indians in India are beginning to display (N. Joshi, 2006). Is it possible that sometimes our collective attitudes shift—even "regress"—to a more orally inflected mode of narration in times of sociocultural dislocation—and perhaps, by extension, in times of political upheaval, national tragedy, or historical trauma? Under conditions of duress, percipients are possibly subconsciously lured by, or attracted to, structures of feeling that return them to a more orally inflected form of story (and of self).

We might also ask how age, as interpolated by educational factors like reading and writing, affects viewer practices. That theater-going audiences in the United States continue to grow progressively younger cannot help but impact the epistemic register of commercial cinema. By the late 1990s, "50 percent of American movie audiences were between the ages of 12 and 29 years (though they comprised only 30 percent of the national population)" (Gabler, cited in Dixon, 1999, p. 93). Filmic fare that inhabits a space closer to the oral episteme would doubtlessly satisfy a spectatorial body not yet molded by high literacy.[4]

Orality–literacy theory might even assist in expanding on studies of classical Hollywood spectatorship and how such spectatorship intersects with Hollywood's draw on other media. Could the oral episteme, for instance, help to explain the 21st century "cross-pollination (some would say cross-cannibalisation) of Hollywood cinema with cartoons,

---

4. The fact that so many adolescent American viewers who otherwise eschew more literate fare actually liked, even loved, *Pulp Fiction* (1994) warrants some consideration. Despite its titular claims of identification with the more oral "predigested" pulp magazine form, *Pulp Fiction* is structurally and temporally deformed, and employs a steady ironic distancing through comic-book wisecracks and dialogue (which exist for the wisecrack's and dialogue's *sake*). According to Alan Stone (1995) of the *Boston Review*, "Everything Tarantino borrows is a cliché that has been given an original spin," and with a Godardian glibness, he "play[s] with the imaginary world of film, not with reality itself." Even the film's brutal violence is said to exist "in quotation marks" (Howe, 1994). Perhaps it was *Pulp Fiction*'s combination of hip talk, irreverence, and violence especially that rendered the film successful with youth in spite of the film's more literate contours. Its tongue-in-cheek clichéd-ness was perhaps missed altogether, or read as harboring "cool clichés," with its more intellectual, ironical underpinnings gone undetected. To be sure, *Pulp Fiction* muddies in a fascinating way the possibility that a text can be read literately *and* orally— and successfully so—at the same time.

comic-books, television, special effects and theme parks" (Arroyo, 2000, p. 83)? And if, as Varadhan (1985) notes, "non-literates and young children (who are not fully literate) respond with similar thought processes to media like television and film" (p. 125), how might this force an advantageous re-reading of the early American film industry's cross-pollination with dime novels and pulp magazines? The introduction of the oral and literate epistemes to the realm of film exposes, too, the inadequacy of attending to the "reading" positions of spectators alone, given that other readers—as in, directors and screenwriters—have a synergistic hand in shaping the extent of a text's oral-to-literate inflection.

Clearly preferred, and even *ideal,* readings of visual narrative need to make room for a material consideration of *possible*—and even, in some cases, *impossible*—readings.

GENRE STUDIES

No subspecialty within film and media studies perhaps merits scrutiny more in terms of the oral and literate epistemes than that of genre studies. Orality–literacy theory can only inform and expand our understanding of films that are deliberately produced and consumed on the basis of—or against—"a specific generic model" (Altman, 1996, p. 277).

One might ask, for instance, if the limits placed on, or used to circumscribe, a genre's genericalness are in part in deference to an orally inflected predilection for the familiar. In fact, is it possible that the stereotypes and derivative meanings that typically comprise a genre in its incipient stages (Gledhill, 1999) are born of a necessary abstention from the kind of inward turn and noncomformist ideology that literacy has a substantial bearing on stimulating? The general development of genre films in Hollywood may in fact reflect how a primitive genre (with greater ties to orality) *only eventually* becomes literately inflected. As Thomas Schatz (1981) observes, although without citing literacy's sway on genre development, "it seems that those features most often associated with narrative artistry—ambiguity, thematic complexity, irony, formal self-consciousness—rarely are evident in films produced earlier in a genre's development. They tend to work themselves into the formula as it evolves" (p. 41). If indeed "a newborn genre's status as social ritual generally resists any ironic, ambiguous, or overly complex treatment of its narrative message" (p. 41), could this be because a genre in its early stages—even at its heart, we might say—is a comparatively more orally inflected form that only later gets acted on in more literate ways?

Perhaps we even efface or disguise the true epistemic origins for what drives the popularity of particular genres by discounting the more modest B pictures and serials, in favor of the A-level films that have obtained a more canonical status. The real core of a genre like the Western, according to Tom Ryall (2000), "at least in statistical terms, lies in the B Western, the staple series pictures, the Hopalong Cassidy films, the singing-cowboy pictures, and so on" (p. 109). Only there, in that "relatively self-contained world," Ryall argues, are "the norms, the basic conventions, the 'pure' versions of the genre" to be found; the A features, by contrast, are "much more subject to the need to vary the conventions, to break the generic rules, and to conform, in certain respects with the prevalent narrative and stylistic norms of the period" (p. 109).

Perhaps those B texts, and entire cycles of B genres even, offered epistemic respite from classical Hollywood cinema (with its greater devotion to psychologically defined characters). Meanwhile, given the level of variation in A Westerns, compounded by their intentional flouting of the rules, one wonders whether some of the films were operating as a unique type of *mixed cinema*, one that made room for literately derived aspects of novelty and sophistication, but from within a framework that thwarted heavy polysemy and retained connection to certain cherished norms of oral inflection, such as an acquiescence to the status quo.[5]

This of course begs the question: Is it possible to stage highly literately inflected genre films as effectively as orally inflected ones? Schatz's allusion to the irony, ambiguity, and self-consciousness that work their way over time through the generic formula recommends that the answer is a resounding yes. Indeed, we have already addressed melodrama in this fashion, that is, as a characteristic or norm that can be extricated from the reticulate traits that comprise the oral episteme and be worked on as an isolated dramatic form; and to a certain extent we have done the same for the genre of the epic, which may accommodate films that are grand in scale but no longer beholden to other psychodynamic and performative attributes key to the production of oral epic. Genre stories still heavily contoured by oral norms, in other words, exist alongside films that have undergone significant literization. Thus, if Westerns like *The Searchers* (1956), "rather than the singing-cowboy films, are the ones discussed by critics and reviewers, analysed by film scholars, and used as the foundation-stones for the canonic edifice known as the western genre" (Ryall, 2000, p. 109), literate inflection may explain why. The same applies to melodrama, that is, to why a film like Todd Haynes' *Far From Heaven* (2002) affords the kind of intellectually appreciated scrutiny that a fellow melodrama like *Titanic* rarely garners. Steve Neale may be correct in attesting that a genre's conventions "are always *in play* rather

---

5. Here Mikel J. Koven's (2006) elision of the term *popular* or *mass cinema* in favor of *vernacular cinema* seems particularly apt, given that this latter term underscores the "lived experience of the folk for whom [such cinema] is intended" (p. 35).

than being, simply, *re*-played" (cited in Hayward, 2000, p. 169); however, the level or register of that play varies from text to text—and often for epistemic reasons.

How, elaborating on this, might we better position a melodrama like Douglas Sirk's *Imitation of Life* (1959)? The aim here is not to devise some positivistic charting system for all visual narrative; but, as Schatz (1981) pointedly observes, Sirk's reinvigoration of the melodrama genre was largely facilitated by his desire to create an ending for his film that the audience *wouldn't* believe. Such an objective, however, as Schatz himself indicates, calls for a "Brechtian notion of irony and formal distancing. . . . The enforced resolution may provide an upbeat finale, but Sirk's 'narrative attitude' encourages the viewer to consider the characters' plight after the curtain goes down" (p. 258). Anticipating, indeed "hoping," that spectators will figure out the puzzle—play the noetic game, so to speak—runs directly counter to oral expectations apropos storytelling; but, then, that might explain why film academics generally laud *Imitation of Life*.

Is it possible that the gradual literization of a genre also partly facilitates its disintegration? Conceivably, once-loyal viewers are forced to look elsewhere for a storytelling that reflects (or capitalizes on) their contemporaneous social anxieties, while also corresponding to their epistemic needs. In this way, cognizance of the oral and literate epistemes might help to reinvigorate the mutual *in*clusivity of genre films and auterism, while also assisting in more ably untangling how it is that, as Colin MacCabe (1993) remonstrates, the likes of *Klute*, *The Grapes of Wrath*, the Rodgers and Hammerstein musical *The Sound of Music*, Zola's social-realist *L'Assommoir*, and *Toad of Toad Hall* could all get lumped together by scholars under the single rubric of "classic realist text" (p. 58).

We might even propose that the academic need to scrutinize, parse, and categorize films into genres is itself an activity wholly motivated by literacy. Moreover, academia's contemporary dismissal of outmoded Victorian taxonomies of textual operations in favor of less rigid contextual approaches speaks to the new paths of understanding—or "vicinities" as Foucault (1973) would have it—that have been advanced, and even *produced*, by literacy. One could aver, in fact, that much film criticism, most cultural studies, and all literary and film theory—present project included—are inadvertently describing themselves as much as they are their objects or field of study.

Additionally, the oral and literate epistemes make space for a more transnational approach to the study and consideration of genre classification. For instance, how might a more global assessment of the soap opera genre—including Mexican *telenovelas*, Venezuelan *telenovelas*, and Brazilian, Indian, and Canadian soaps—instructively reflect the shifting program of literacy—or of *literacies* as we might prefer? Are there discontinuities and continuities that have, until now, gone unobserved or that have been too facilely subsumed by other explanations? As earlier I noted, scholars have already identified melodrama as the representative dramaturgical form in developing nations (Dissanayake, cited in Vasudevan, 1995, p. 308). Is that perhaps for reasons no less epistemically than psychically driven? We might be well served in addressing oral psychodynamics alongside the usual invocation of melodrama as reflecting the "Third World" spectator's material precariousness and ambivalence about modernizing.

On a related note, could the oral episteme explain the transnational migratory potentials of certain programming, such as the Mexican "developmental" soap opera on which India's own melodramatic series *Humlog* (*We People*, 1984–1985) was modeled[6]? And although the Venezuelan *telenovela* from the 1990s may have derived some of its success from an ideological reversing of "American media hegemony" and an articulation of the Venezuelan nation as a uniquely constituted collection of viewers (Lopez, 1995), might there not be a certain epistemically oral readability factor to the genre, as well, one that might explain its success with non-Latino spectators on continents as disparate as Europe, Asia, Africa, and North America?[7]

Theorists may remain unsuccessful at "producing a coherent map of the system of genres," and "no strictly deductive set of principles" may ever be able to explain genre groupings (Bordwell, 1989, p. 147), but we would be negligent not to explore what the oral and literate epistemes might add to the appraisal of genre production and consumption.

THE POLITICS OF (RE)PRESENTATION

In *Symbolic Narratives/African Cinema*, Ghanain documentarian Kwate Nii Owoo (2000) poses the following with respect to his own continent's filmmaking practices: "how well do we know our audience?; and what are the sociological and psychological implications of the form and content of our films on African audiences?" (p. 228). With a mounting ethical anxiety, he continues:

---

6. Rajadhyaksha and Willemen (1999, p. 28).

7. That there may be a panoply of cultural products worldwide that synchronically spans *multiple* levels of literacy certainly appears tenable as a proposition when one bears in mind how scholars have descriptively differentiated between nations' *telenovelas*. Notwithstanding the legitimacy of culture as a shaper of the genre's conventions, Mexican *telenovelas* are well known for their maudlin, Manichean, ahistorical and amplified projection of the world (Lopez, 1995). Meanwhile, the Brazilian soap opera *Beto Rockefeller* incorporated a realism that allowed the narrative to be situated in the life of the everyday and "within a specifically national reality" (Martín-Barbero, 1995, pp. 279–280). In the case of India, interestingly, it may be that soap-operatic television serials began as a means of shifting away from the *more* orally inflected popular cinema of that nation.

In whose interest do we come together to collaborate? What is the common ground on which we come together to make films? For the sake of art? For personal profit or aggrandizement? or rather to ensure that our joint efforts should result in a product that will have an emancipative and a liberating influence on our people? (p. 229)

Cinematically Speaking's excavation of oral and literate storytelling norms does not make answering these questions any easier. For, how *can* the socially conscious dramatic filmmaker effectively liberate oppressed peoples, given the epistemic pressures that considerably drive narrative content and form? The question is especially germane vis-à-vis one of the more prominent historical movements in emancipatory filmmaking, that of Third Cinema. As an alternative filmmaking practice that arose in the 1960s, Third Cinema espoused a Brechtian version of aesthetics that was notably influenced by Frantz Fanon (Stam, 2003). It distanced itself categorically from First Cinema, or commercial cinema (especially Hollywood), and also from Second Cinema, or auteurist cinema—even as its artists took Godard as their intellectual muse. As Fernando Solanas and Octavio Getino outlined in their pronunciamento, Third Cinema was to be a highly politicized weapon with which filmmakers waged an ideological and ultimately *subversive* battle against the System.

Given the high-literate inflection of Brechtian techniques, however, such revolutionary texts—at least when expressly framed as visual stories[8]—may pose a problem in terms of spectatorial address. Guneratne and Dissanayake's (2003) deft summary of the lacunae in Third Cinema theory hints at this possible impasse, for Third Cinema's insistent address is

to a unitary spectator who is at once disingenuous (requiring lessons in class consciousness and postcolonial development) and sophisticated (capable of appreciating an otherwise *rarified oppositional aesthetics*). Moreover, the suggestion that Third Cinema must resist the illusionistic proclivities of classical narrative harkened back to the Formalist *position of art arising from a process of estrangement or defamiliarization.* . . . Thus, Third Cinema's critical reception and reception at film festivals could seldom be mapped onto the same experiential terrain as those of audiences at popular venues. (p. 181, emphasis added)

---

8. Many Third Cinema films employed narrative modes (e.g., Tomás Alea's *Memories of Underdevelopment* [1968] and Nelson dos Santos' *How Tasty Was My Little Frenchman* [1971]), although Solanas and Getino's film *The Hour of Furnaces* (1968) was a documentary. There may be value in examining the sway of orality and literacy on spectatorial engagement with documentaries and other non-narrative forms, such as "Pamphlet films, didactic films, report films, essay films" (Solanas & Getino, 1976, p. 55). Certainly Varadhan's ethnographic interviews with nonliterate Indian viewers of family-planning instructional films recommend that orality may have significant bearing on comprehension and interpretability of both non-narrative and less traditional narrative forms. Alas, as this project limits itself to visual *story*telling, that vital thread must be left for someone else to pick up.

The authors offer this critique as a segue to introducing alternative approaches and antidotes to Third Cinema's theoretical quandary; but this critique calls precise, if unintended, attention to the *epistemic* quandary grounded in a cinema that wishes to be anti-imperialist and revolutionary—and historical—and experimental—and antimystification—and, by ideological necessity, open-ended.

One might in this way be legitimately inclined to label Third Cinema an agitational extension of Second Cinema. Alas, an artist's narrative tie with reality—contrary to Solanas and Getino's (1976) aims—does not automatically render him more "a part of the people" (p. 58), except insofar as the artist might feel himself to be. This is not to disrespect Third Cinema filmmakers, who can hardly be blamed for being part of the linguistic-semantic system that allows them to *negotiate* the System, even if only to publicly condemn it. Nonetheless, a creative and philosophical schism may exist in the landscape of liberation cinema. Even as directors make laudable use of their own cultural capital in order to reach a downtrodden public, they may fashion stories on the basis of a narrative structure, tone, and orientation that require anterior possession of an analogous cultural capital, of an arduously earned epistemic competence. In fact, could this be why such guerilla films end up being assessed according to the dictates of the very critical traditions from which the artists were initially trying to disassociate themselves? Because of the ways in which these films expand the determinants of literately inflected texts, Third Cinema becomes ironically folded into the art-film canon, assimilated into the very culture that its theorists wished in some sense to decolonize. In this way, Third Cinema could be likened to the French avant-garde of the 1920s, a movement whose experimental, surrealist productions were eventually adopted and extolled by the very system that the films' directors were at the time deliberately subverting.

By the same token, we need ask how any accidental compromise *on behalf* of the oral needs of disenfranchised audiences might sometimes be put into the service of nationalist/state agendas. Consider, for instance, the modifications to narrative that have been historically mandated by the Indian government. Given that the Indian government is directly responsible for censorship guidelines (not to mention, for *censoring*), one wonders if it precipitated the ossification of an orally inflected way of knowing. As film critics and historians often allege, governmental control over film content is at painful variance with the state's parallel and professed constitutional pursuit of freedom, justice, rationality, modernism, development, and progress (Bhowmik, 2002, 2003). Certainly the malicious rape scenes, which served as a veritable motif in 1980s *masala* films, should rouse a kind of ideological caution, in terms of what precisely the Central Board of Censors was protecting—and whom.

Film historians like Someswar Bhowmik (2003) argue that, in the 1990s, censors, in their almost vulgarly patent pursuit of a nationalist agenda, "promote[d] jingoist feature films like *Roja, Gadar, Border* [1997], or *Sarfarosh* [*Fervor*, 1999]" (p. 3151).[9] Meanwhile, in 2001, *Paanch* (*Five*), a film about the psychology of violence—a film touted by *India Today* for being "superbly rendered"—was refused release, presumably because it "glorifie[d] crime, use[d] double-meaning language, depict[ed] the cold-blooded killing of policemen and contain[ed] no positive healthy message" (Unnithan, 2001, p. 45). Perhaps the Board feared a cognitive incapacity on the part of the bulk of the Indian film-going audience to recognize the distinctions between a violent film and a film *about* the psychology of violence. After all, Shyam Benegal's *Nishant*, with its bold and productively troubling open-ended critique of the establishment, was not treated with the same paternalism. No doubt this was because the censors foresaw *Nishant*'s spectatorial appeal as one bound up with a higher stratum of Indian society.[10]

In an uneasy acknowledgment of the difficulty of configuring a national popular cinema that extends to all social classes, even K.A. Abbas—a noted champion of freedom of expression (Bhowmik, 2003)—found something to condone in the government's early exercise of censorship power: "One can imagine the results if an unbridled commercial cinema [had been] allowed to cater to the lowest common denominator of popular taste" (cited in Bhowmik, 2003, p. 3151). Although Abbas' concern was more with cultural values and the "shoddy and vulgar taste" to which producers might otherwise pander (p. 3151), perhaps underpinning it was a philosophical and, indeed, epistemological struggle with how to reach—and, admittedly, socially control—a spectatorial body that lacked sufficient literate inculcation to negotiate texts the way more educated sections of society could.[11]

But to return to a question raised earlier: Could it be that the notion of Nationhood or Indianness that the censor board was imposing *forced* a kind of orally inflected type of narrative? That is, did the government

---

9. Before 1997, Bollywood films—even war films—were not permitted to explicitly name any enemy or opponent. This changed with the release of *Border*, which, as its directors argued, was based on historical events that would be compromised were the filmmakers not allowed to name Pakistan (Ganti, 2004).

10. Bollywood films approved by the censor board can also exhibit marked levels of literate inflection—as the previously discussed *Satya* does—while at the same time "show[ing] 'indiscriminate killing of 'gangsters' at the hands of the police" (Nanda, 2002). Instead of censoring that film, however, the government made it tax free (no doubt because of its ultimate acquiescence to a pro-state ideology).

11. A "double standard" was often applied in the case of foreign-film censorship, too. As Prasad (1998a) explains of the 1969 *Report of the Enquiry Committee on Film Censorship*, "a different code was justified on the basis that audiences for these films were different from the ones for Indian films, with some [committee members] even arguing that this was appropriate since 'foreign pictures cater to a higher stratum of society'" (p. 88).

impede literately inflected advances in storytelling from gracing cinema screens out of a nationalist determination to deter interrogative, open-ended types of storytelling? Gopalan (2002) suggests that filmmakers actually spend "considerable energy in incorporating censorship regulations *during* film-making, in an attempt to pre-empt sweeping cuts" (p. 20). Conceivably, then, censorship in India historically confined some percipients to a movie palace of high-oral inflection—one where, because of arrears in education and literacy training, consciousness *couldn't* replace conformity (in the Horkheimer and Adorno, 1972, conception of things). Interestingly, Egypt's 1947 law precluding any depiction of "poverty, peasant life, calls to revolt, and the questioning of traditional customs" similarly resulted in a proliferation of generic film types, namely Bedouin romances-cum-adventure tales and adaptations of stage melodramas (Armes, 1987, p. 200). That the theatrical style of these films "had the range customary in a Third World commercial industry" (p. 198) suggests as much a link to oral inflection as to the influence censorship regulations imposed on the industry.

Alternatively, one might ask if there has been a *healthy* aspect to the kind of censorship these governments have instituted, given the normative variances that coexist between more orally and more literately inflected citizens. These are of course variances that the published decriers of censorship (who are always literate) may not see or may be less prone to recognize for political reasons. Those critics who navigate censorship's roiling waters, in other words, do so from an epistemic vantage point that may preclude consideration of other epistemic vantage points. They also may presumptuously take as a given people's capacity for abstractly negotiating Enlightenment-type ideals like freedom, justice, rationality, modernism, and so forth. Members of the 1990s Indian Censor Board, on the other hand, were forced to bear in mind, however inarticulably, alternative epistemic states of being. Indeed, we might argue that these censors, in preserving an oral inflection to films, provided a spatial nation—a transnational one, at that—for viewers excluded from other, more theoretical and intangible forms of nation. And if there is paternalism in the censor's speaking "on behalf" of the subaltern, how markedly different is that from the speaking-for that the economist, historian, sociologist, anthropologist, or film theorist engages in?

In some sense, we are asking if subaltern populations are *entitled* to a popular cinema whose contours have been shaped by their own psychic needs and desires. In terms of the recent flourishing of Bollywood, which increasingly takes its inspiration from—and for the sake of—the middle classes, the question opens up a discomfiting space, to be sure. Then again, as a wholesale flip, one might ask if an industry historically anchored in orality constitutes an undemocratic oppression of the masses, given that certain subcategories of percipients, such as dalits (previously known as untouchables), are continually *subjected* in their representation? The same is true of women, whose bodies in *masala* film have historically served as "the prime site of control and regulation in the public sphere" (Gopalan, 2002, p. 21), and who have been forced to exist in a scopic economy that is, in the words of Miriam Hansen (2002), a "patriarchal choreography of vision" (p. 411). How gender representations in the narrative realm are imbricated by oral ways of knowing is, to be sure, an area not only prime but essential for future study.

As if this isn't complicated enough, there is the equally frustrating issue of the political and economic travails that surround a cinema that is highly *literately* inflected. Surely we need to address the irony that art cinema, notwithstanding its capacity to reflect those higher-order skills that literacy fosters, leads a much more tenuous worldly existence. If cinema is indeed an adjunct of capitalism (Vitali & Willemen, 2006, p. 7), those higher-order skills impose a severe restrictiveness in terms of how many can, or will want to, engage with art films—let alone in terms of who will pay for the production of such movies. No doubt this helps to clarify the dual sophistication *and* frailty of art cinema, as well as that cinema's transnational legacy of reliance on state sponsorship.

But what of literacy as a development program? As Terry Eagleton (1976) counsels, "The most efficient form of censorship is, of course, the perpetuation of mass illiteracy" (p. 58). Although academia has in recent decades developed an almost neurotic concern for being politically sensitive to *difference*, sometimes such cultural relativism can be problematically blinding. "Respecting" oral peoples' unique positioning may appear on the surface to be a correct or ethical attitude; but scholars alert to orality and matters pertaining to illiteracy recognize that, given today's sociopolitical landscape, orality is *not* an ideal (Ong, 1982). Literacy, however broadly or narrowly one defines it, is fundamentally necessary in a literate society (Galtung, 1981), that is, in a society where the orientation is already geared toward text and textually based technologies. Indeed, the intellectual dismantling of social hierarchies, which the politically correct academic understandably enjoins, is already completely the byproduct of an already and inherently *privileged* mindset.

The hard truth is that, when devoid of literacy in a literate society, one's lesser positioning in the economic pyramid is almost certainly preordained. As Lippert (2000) reminds us, the interface between high literates and nonliterates is too entirely analogous to a given society's divisions of labor: "The domination of one class by another is maintained not merely through physical possession of industrial plant and material forms of wealth but through what Harold Innis . . . has called 'monopolies of knowledge'" (p. 280). The asymmetrical distribution of epistemic cultural capital, in other words, has effects more pervasive (and more profound) than the "mere" capacity to engage with and be entertained by different types of celluloid stories. The skeptic may be eagerly drawing refutative parallels here between the compulsory recycling exhibited in orally inflected narrative and those college classroom activities that keep literary authors alive through repetition, recitation, and imitation (Smith, 1998, p. 1575). But any claim that these acts closely resemble each other misses the fundamental point: The latter's collectivity is always built on an already exclusivist interaction that promotes and sustains a wholly literate engagement with the world.

One need not rely on the perspectives of (literate) scholars alone. As Varadhan (1985), in her interviews with nonliterate rural Tamils, discovered,

> They [nonliterate parents] all valued education as a goal for their children. . . . All the respondents stated that they turned to literate people to gain knowledge of events on both a local and national level. The ambiance of living in a culture that knows writing and has literate people plays a crucial factor in governing the mind-set of nonliterate people. (p. 96)

As a more personal and intimate example, consider the Afghani woman, who, with the support of her tubercular husband, was learning to read so that her children might not, like her, "grow blind." The idiomatic expression *grow blind* is commonly used by nonliterate women in Afghanistan and "speaks to the confusion and difficulties that [such women] encounter as uneducated members of a society" (Gall, 2002, p. 1). Although one Afghani mother's plight may appear unconvincing or, at best, anecdotal, the reader needs to bear in mind that there are about *774 million* such "blind" adults worldwide (UNESCO, 2009), many of whom, like the women of current Afghanistan, are incapable of deciphering street signs or medical prescriptions, or of understanding notices for public washrooms (Gall, 2002).

My objective here is not to elicit a cheap pathos for the "poor," "suffering," "uneducated" masses. Rather, it is rhetorically to set the stage for what is conceivably a most politically *in*correct question apropos visual narrative, but a question that exposure to the oral and literate epistemes of visual narrative unavoidably gives rise to: If we agree that in the modern setting literacy should be taught (something I think few today would dispute), do we not then acknowledge, however indirectly, the superiority (the pragmatic desirability) of the literate habit of mind and all its cognitive and narrative perquisites? In this sense, it is perhaps debilitating, if not foolish, to purport that no socially inequitable hierarchy exists when it comes to narrative content and form.

DIGITAL TECHNOLOGY—AND BEYOND

Theoretical projects of this sort typically conclude with the author reflecting on political ramifications. That this one doesn't perhaps speaks to my idealism—or maybe only my inclination to end with a narrative-type denouement that looks toward the future—in some sense, toward the possibility of a sequel. It is, alas, a sequel I will never get to write. Although the future may come on ever-swifter heels thanks to the accelerated profusion and advancement of technologies, chances are good that the radical impact of those technologies as they epistemically reconfigure storytelling are not going to manifest for some time. Much as Janet H. Murray (2001) poses in *Hamlet on the Holodeck* (judiciously filtering where we're going through the lens of where we've been), "Can we imagine the future of electronic narrative any more easily than Gutenberg's contemporaries could have imagined *War and Peace . . .* ?" (pp. 66–67). Gutenberg may have invented the printing press, she reminds us, but he did not invent the book as we know it. Many decades of experimentation had to pass before the typefaces, paragraphing, prefaces, chapter divisions, and indices to which we are today so accustomed became routine, and several centuries before we saw the kind of ironic, self-conscious, inner amplitude of the modern novel, which print helped to stimulate. The same will likely be the case for those digital and electronic technologies currently redefining—or, at the least, stoking a kind of theoretical soothsaying about—where literacy is going and what it will *mean*.

These ivory tower prophecies run the gamut: from the utopic to the dystopic, from the promise of a McLuhanesque (1964) extension of our current vision and awareness, to the Birkertsian (1994) certainty that we are steadily eroding as a species. Suffice it to say that the future, technologically speaking, appears at once thrilling and terrifying; promising and dangerous; a sign of our future fragmentation compounded by our restoration into unique collectivities. Scholars are already speculating that we are moving ever closer to what we have always been striving for narratively, and that is to be taken *into* a story's experiential and physical space (G. King, 2000). In part, such theoretical divinations stem from hypertext's ability to generate nonsequential readings, best evidenced perhaps in a reader's ability to navigate through numerous links on the Web. As a result, so experts say, electronic media are certain to reconfigure the function and form of *literature* (R. Fowler, 1994). George Landow, for example, believes hypertext will call into question notions of plot that have been in currency since as far back as Aristotle (cited in Ryan, 2002, p. 588).

This project has limited itself parametrically to the existing cultural landscape and has relied on empirical evidence in order to make its theoretical claims. As such, rather than engaging in conjecture (or, worse, in prophecy) about what the digital future holds, I want to look at how digital technologies have *already* altered the film narrative landscape, and more specifically, whether or not existing academic arguments vis-à-vis their impact are confirmed, redirected, or frustrated when that impact is funneled through the oral and literate epistemes of visual narrative. This means confining myself primarily to theatrically released narratives, as opposed to homegrown digital narratives (which arguably deserve a book of their own).

The perspectives on how digital technologies have refashioned cinema's identity as a storytelling practice are surprisingly in sync. Digital *video* may hold promise for its capacity to democratize filmmaking and wrest it from the "tyranny of the Hollywood industry," but when it comes to *cinema*, as Holly Willis (2005) argues, for many the arrival of digital signals "the 'passing' of real film" (p. 1). More particularly, Constance Balides (2003) argues, "The photographic nature of the cinematic real and the indexical nature of the photographic sign . . . are less appropriate theoretical points of reference for cinema in a digital age" (p. 315). In other words, she envisions the cinematic image as increasingly shifting into the realm of the *artificial*—a migration that of course renders prior theoretical readings, such as those espoused by Bazin, anachronistic. Then again, Thomas Elsaesser (1998) reminds us that tricks to the spectator's eye via special effects have been "practised since Georges Méliès, Fritz Lang's *Die Nibelungen*, Walt Disney and *King Kong*" (p. 201). This leads Elseasser to incisively query, "Are we simply witnessing a new round in the bout between the advocates of 'realism' and the perfectors of 'illusionism'? Or is something more at stake, to do with a major change of cultural metaphor, away from 'representation' to 'simultaneity,' 'telepresence,' 'interactivity,' and 'tele-action'?" (p. 202).

Scholars like Lev Manovich (2001) take a firmer position, suggesting that the mutability of digital data signals a return to *pre*cinematic techniques: Instead of cinema operating as "an indexical media technology," he argues, it functions now as animation, as "a subgenre of painting" (p. 295). The visual realism so embraced by the 20th century was an anomaly, in other words, "an isolated accident in the history of visual representation which has always involved, and now again involves, the manual construction of images" (p. 308).

What orality–literacy theory brings to the fore, however, is that most of these discussions orient themselves exclusively to, and hence invariably overemphasize, the significance of the *image*. In extricating the image from the wider ambit of storytelling, visuality gets privileged at the erroneous expense of the episteme's "totality of relations" (Foucault, 1972, p. 191). Recall, after all, that what permits critics to strip the perceptual image from the interpenetrated network of characteristics that

more broadly and epistemically drive story is *literacy*. Thus in isolating
the image, those critics may be misinterpreting spectatorial engagement.
It might behoove us to think in more global narrative terms and consider
how digital alterations figure into the grander schema of film storytelling. Is it possible, for instance, that modern advances in digital technology have led to an *increase* in films that are more orally inflected? Certainly the recent plethora of animated tales, like *Finding Nemo* (2003) and
Happy Feet (2006), bolsters such a claim, as does the general return of the
old-style Hollywood epic spectaculars (with contemporary ideological
thrust, of course). Here I am thinking of hyperdigital spectacles like
Titanic, Gladiator (2000), and *Troy* (2004). In some sense, these denote a return to a cinema of attractions. Indeed, there even are Bollywood films
that use digital technologies without straying in the least from oral inflection. Movies like *Krrish* (2006) actually employ those technologies in
ways that amplify kinesis and the heaviness of characters—in *Krrish*'s
case, superhumanly, in fact.

Given this, how might orality help us to more fruitfully understand
the increasing production of film tales that, thanks to digital technologies, "explor[e] the idea of being trapped in theme-park, fun-house or
ridelike environments" (Acland, 2003, p. 199)? Perhaps orality no less
than a spectatorial ambition to "take a ride" via an "underdeveloped,
linear narrative structure designed to link a series of elaborate stunts"
(p. 199) has resulted in this shift. Without attempting to undercut valuable readings attentive to cultural imperialism and habits of consumption, we also might consider how orality helps to clarify the tension between a technologically enhanced "Disneyfication" of cinematic fare
and liberal intellectuals who generally loathe that phenomenon. Furthermore, we might ask if the supposed "dumbing down" of American
commercial film culture is really an "opening up," mirroring in some
fashion the post-printing press rise of the reading British public, which
forced editors to appeal more broadly (some said more vulgarly) *across*
educational lines (Milner, 1994). Increased oral inflection may in fact
prove the best means by which to assist spectators in overcoming the
difficulties of technological transition and establishing "stable evaluative criteria" (Young, 2006, p. 233) for strange new technical effects and
applications.

Perhaps this surplus of Disneyfied fare is more the case of a new
technology needing time for directors to discover the idiosyncratic
means by which new technologies can project story more literately. (Recall George Méliès, who in the incipient days of cinema discovered the
magical tricks one could engender in-camera, yet never thought to move
the camera.) Might this usher in the introduction of new kinds of "signature cinema"; that is, might digital technology, in its capacity to splice
away image-making from photographic cinema, eventually rescue ani-

mation from its associations with cartoons or its comparative "con-fine[ment] either to avant-garde forms, such as abstract cinema or video" (Elsaesser, 1998, p. 205)?

Just as debatable is whether or not digital technology's manipula-tions of physical space coincide naturally with more oral storytelling traits and Odyssean-type travels. In fact, what if this is what partly fu-eled the rise of the blockbuster genre, which many scholars assert began with George Lucas' *Star Wars*? That such films, being more epistemically accessible, also are generally more globally *profitable* reminds us that fi-nancial advantage is imbricated heavily with orality as it impacts com-mercial film. For this same reason, one might ask (as I already did in an earlier chapter) if there is an underlying epistemic reason for film's (presumably digitally motivated) predilections for pulling from comic books, graphic novels, and even video games. If a question like this last one insinuates a push toward a more cross-disciplinary/media-ecologi-cal approach to film narrative, it does so for reasons that differ consider-ably from recent calls for such a practice.[12] I am motivated here less by the conviction that various media are coming to inform each other with greater intensity in this new millennium than by the belief that this kind of commingling has *always* been the case. But instruments like the pencil or the written word are so deeply embedded in our culture today that we plumb forget, or no longer believe, that they too are technological ex-tensions that have been shaping other media, not to mention our very psyches, for thousands of years.

Very likely digital cinema, much like the various cinemas that came before it, will evolve in ways that will satisfy epistemic *differentials* apro-pos orality and literacy. In this way, its trajectory will not be unlike that of silent film, which made increasing strides toward more literate inflec-tion (those films Orr calls "modernist"), but alongside a consistent pro-duction of comparatively more oral types of storytelling. The same could be said of the introduction of sound: Although some directors found new modes by which to tell increasingly literate—and ironically *quiet* sound—films, others fashioned tales that led, in recent times, to both the Bollywood *masala* film formula and the Hollywood blockbuster. Art may follow a "drift of consciousness" away from an oral economy,

---

12. Anne Friedberg (2004), for instance, insists that "a singular history of 'the film' without its dovetailing conspirators—the telephone, the radio, the television, the com-puter—provides a too-narrowly constructed geneology" (p. 915). On the other hand, Harold Bloom (1994) vociferously objects to a shift where "what are now called 'Depart-ments of English' will be renamed departments of 'Cultural Studies,' where *Batman* comics, Mormon theme parks, television, movies, and rock will replace Chaucer, Shake-speare, Milton, Wordsworth, and Wallace Stevens" (p. 519). Perhaps were Bloom cognizant of the phylogenetic and ontogenetic journeys that permit literature's existence, he might be more inclined to accept the "culture" in cultural studies.

as Ong (1982, p. 116) contends, but it does so synchronous with other texts *continuing* to pay epistemic commitment to that economy. Narrative digitization is just as grounded in issues of literacy as it is in issues of technology; and for this reason, I agree entirely with Elseaesser (1998) when he proclaims (albeit for different purposes) that cinema in the age of the digital will very likely "remain the same, *and* it will be utterly different" (p. 204).

Scholars animatedly hypothesize that, in the future, cyberdramas with hypertextual possibilities will offer more opportunity for spontaneity and increased audience involvement, and will be more participatory in ways that defy Aristotelian notions of plot. But haven't we already seen this kind of narrative deformation many times over in films by the likes of Ozu, Godard, Resnais? Perhaps we need to configure the argument less on the basis of how narrative in toto will change than on how a new technology will accommodate a novel extension of literately inflected storytelling. Granted, that technology may reconstitute what literate inflection is and where next it will direct our phenomenological attentions. For instance, is it possible that the resultant increased capacity for surfing or speed will stimulate narratives that require a more *outwardly* oriented *immersive* turn on the part of the spectator—the ability, say, to mentally accrue, process, and assemble larger and larger bits of discrete, quickly relayed information? Such a possibility may strike a reader as threatening, as a type of activity destined to "undo" literacy. We might, as an antidote, remind that reader of John Locke's 17th-century anxiety over the discontinuous reading of the Bible that print permitted, and which Locke was sure was going to render people's biblical reading harmfully discontinuous and shallow (J. King & Bracken, personal communication, 2007). Few today, I imagine, would share his phobia about the hazards of *reading*—at least as regards printed text.

Then again, if more persons across the orality–literacy spectrum have increased access in the future to technology, could this not possibly facilitate the production of *more*, rather than less, orally inflected storytelling? Here England's rise of a reading public after the invention of the printing press serves as a worthy comparison, given that the introduction of the press led to a storytelling democratization that inspired the production of *less* sophisticated goods: "No longer were books and periodicals written for the comfortable few; more and more as the century progressed, it was the ill-educated mass audience . . . that called the tune to which writers and editors danced" (Altick, cited in Milner, 1994, p. 121).

Some scholars have theorized that, not far in our future, literacy will be wholly nonessential for survival, a superfluous commodity and "atavistic skill, like quiltmaking, learned and proudly practiced by a few" (Lakoff, 1982, p. 259). But that type of attitude neglects the skills that literacy has already phylogenetically generated. Take the case of interactive cinema. Narrative as a form is generally a "solid structure" one where meaning is "built into the text" (Ryan, 2002, p. 607). Interactive cinema, however, permits a spectator to "intervene actively in the process of the narrative or take over the function of narrator" (Elsaesser, 1998, pp. 216–217). Marie-Laure Ryan (2006) proposes that the external-exploratory interactivity of hypertext de-emphasizes the narrative in favor of the *game*. Texts become "better suited for self-referential fiction than for narrative worlds that hold us under their spell for the sake of what happens in them"; they promote "a metafictional stance, at the expense of immersion in the fictional world. This explains why so many literary hypertexts offer a collage of literary theory and narrative fragments" (p. 109). Her references to collage and fragments—and certainly to the *meta*fictional—seem particularly pertinent when one considers the oral-to-literate pressures placed on storytelling. Yes, such interactive storytelling may appear a liberative and potentially "intriguing compromise between (the 'laws' of) narrative and (the possibilities of) interactivity" (Elsaesser, 1998, p. 218); however, by virtue of its expectation that a participant navigate pockets that patently dissuade or disrupt a clear narrative thread, it also is conceivable that a literacy-influenced mentality is a *precondition* for committed engagement. Certainly Luria's research reminds us of the oral individual's lack of interest in and general aversion to noetic game playing. In the case of narrative especially, such gameplaying distances a participant from the participatory nature of oral inflection; it places too much (and possibly too inconsequential a sort of) problem-solving responsibility on the participant's shoulders. What is the participant becoming democratically "liberated" from, after all?

For reasons like these, I cannot accept that literacy is destined to become superfluous and nonessential. I tend instead to agree with media critic Jay David Bolter (1991) who long ago—by digital era standards, at least—suggested that "What will be lost is not literacy itself, but the literacy of print, for electronic technology offers us a new kind of book and new ways to write and read" (p. 2). All the same, we need to keep in mind that the printing press did not lead to the wholesale evaporation of orally inflected texts. If technological and cultural forces that will radically change the concept of the movies are at work (Schrader, 2006), these forces will only be continuing a mutative process that has been underway since as far back as somebody developed the know-how and initiative (and writing implement) to take Homer's song down. At the same time, privileging the technologies, that is, disentangling them too readily from the epistemic pressures that permit (or disincline) a storytelling's morphology—and here I mean morphology quite literally as the study of morphing—can only lead to an incomplete theorizing of film narrative.

CONCLUDING REMARKS

This book has attempted to expand the collective comprehension of how visual narrative works by drawing attention to epistemic pressures that weigh on storytelling as both a generative act and a viewing practice. It has, once again, taken a highly integrationist approach, committed to the belief that "narrativity, ficitionality, and literariness (or aesthetic appeal) [are] inseparable forces" (Ryan, 2004, p. 4)—or, in less narratological parlance, to the belief that the "what" of film narrative *cannot* be so easily detached from the "how."

There are of course many forces at work when it comes to what shapes the storytelling arts, and, as I have articulated more than once, it would be rash for me to suggest that orality and literacy supersede all the others. (Otherwise wouldn't we all be producing stellar literary and/or cinematic works?) Still, once exposed to the oral and literate epistemes, one is hard-pressed not to recognize their sway on the history of film as an art, and so too on the history of Aesthetics. If the orality–literacy paradigm sheds some light on Hegel's notion of the Aesthetic Ideal,[13] at the same time it warns that we must reject Hegel's teleological position. For, how are we ever to reach the *Ideal*; how can we justifiably speak of an eventual spiritual self-realization, when it is our human interaction with technologies, in tandem with other cultural and social forces, that perpetually re-route where narratives can go? Again—that is, as a second reminder of what Foucault (1972) reminds us—the totality of relations that comprise an episteme are always for, and during, a given time period, and thus that episteme "can never be closed" (p. 191). An episteme can never be "a motionless figure that appeared one day with the mission of effacing all that preceded it: it is a constantly moving set of articulations, shifts, and coincidences that are established, only to give rise to others" (p. 192). In a way, Foucault's description dovetails seamlessly with Ong's (1967) declaration that we need to "revise" our understanding of classical culture "in terms of our new awareness of the role of the media in structuring the human psyche and civilization itself" (p. 18).

---

13. Indeed, it could be argued that Hegel's three-staged representation of the evolving realization of the idea of the beautiful—from the Symbolic Form's mythological externality, to the Classical Form's concentrated individuality, to the Romantic Form's inner subjectivity—traces in some fashion the changing site of beauty *as engendered by an increased literate inflection.*

Once more, my desire is not to repudiate all other critical perspectives, but only to recommend that, no matter the responses or future elaborations to this chapter's miscellany of questions and propositions, orality and literacy as constituents of a hermeneutical framework clearly deserve—as media ecologists argue—a more prominent rank in the fields of cinema and media studies, and indeed in the humanities in general. They belong quite justifiably alongside, and syncretic with, other interpretive models currently in circulation, such as psychoanalytic, Marxist, feminist, deconstructionist, new historicist, and semiotic.

To be sure, this project has had its limitations. I have not been able to—or, perhaps more accurately, I have resisted and been generally unwilling to—judge films qualitatively, either as isolated texts or as reflections of their respective epistemes. Nor have I attempted to speak to the possible aesthetic inferiority or relative superiority of individual texts from within the confines (and contexts) of those texts' own spheres. This is to some degree the ineluctable derivative of the oral and literate epistemes themselves. *How* one judges a film's aesthetic values and virtues, after all, may have as much to do with a percipient's level of literacy as with any socioculturally inculcated notion of storytelling. Were a high-literate viewer to try to identify an oral text that was as crude as a literate text was pretentious, or were she to insist that her choices were right and another person's wrong, would this be because of her better aesthetic sense *separate from* how literacy has shaped her expectations, or because her aesthetic sense has been deeply *informed by* literacy? At the least, awareness of these epistemes helps to counteract the tendency for delimiting interpretive readings of films. "If certain moments or groups," as Staiger (1989) maintains, "evince progressively radical interpretative strategies, the question of what permitted this or supported it or hindered its continuation is one that matters" (p. 364).

This is especially important because judgments, critiques, and evaluations of what constitutes art and aesthetics have been determined almost entirely by literately inflected individuals. How can this not breed a certain, even if unconscious, epistemic complicity? This is not to say that we shouldn't sing the praises of texts which literacy has helped to animate. As Ong (1982) notes, writing *is* "consciousness-raising" (p. 179). Indeed, there are even some scholars, like Jonathon Culler (1975), who maintain that,

> in the final analysis, we are nothing other than our system of reading and writing. We read and understand ourselves as we follow the operations of our understanding and, more important, as we experience the limits of our understanding. To know oneself is to study the intersubjective processes of articulation and interpretation by which we emerge as a part of the world. (p. 264)

What this implies, alas, is that the aesthetic virtues of even orally inflected texts that have made it into a kind of temporary in-perpetuity via
being written about have *always* been based on the readings and evaluations of literately inflected individuals. Hence, aesthetics as a theoretical
and evaluative practice is almost indiscriminately grounded in some
level of literacy, even when the text is *not*. Even if oral individuals were
to have a say, their point of view would probably still be disseminated
through the literate regime. We should remain cognizant of these relations and restrictions apropos human agency.

The oral and literate epistemes also, admittedly, cannot cleanly escape Aristotle's infinite regress when it comes to the interaction between
technology and human. How, or from where, or from whom the next
great epistemic turn or break will arise can hardly be pinpointed. This
project fails, in other words, at being able to answer the questions posed
by Simms (1992) in his study of differing mentalities: "Do creative ge-
niuses originate new ideas in themselves and then impose them on a
more or less receptive society? Or do the very mental or intellectual
structures transform themselves under the external pressures of history,
shifting the centers of hegemonic balance in individuals and classes?"
(p. 60).

These epistemes also expose a major limitation—or reinforce a kind
of division—in terms of what more generally designates the visual arts.
Although they can be readily applied to the novel (or to ancient Greek
tragedy, television romances, India's *Amir Chitra Katha* comic books,
Japanese *anime* . . .), they have less utility in illumining particular ways
of thinking expressed in, and about, the non-narrative plastic arts. This
may seem oxymoronic given the earlier allusion to Hegel, who was writing about arts as inclusive of painting, sculpture, and architecture. But
the visual aspect of narrative film has been plainly shown to be subordinate to structural, psychodynamic, and performative determinants of
storytelling as a sequence of events through time. Thus, too, my relative
incapacity for effectively commenting on those avant-garde films that
lean toward the highly, if not utterly, abstract. (Of course we might propose that, by virtue of their bold departure from situational frames of
reference and self-conservation via storytelling, avant-garde films bespeak an *a priori* form of literate encoding.)

Although I have tried to be cautious about projecting the oral and
the literate epistemes as dichotomous, or of suggesting that they are not
also complexly facilitated by, and intertwined with, other enabling factors (Gough, 1968), the inevitable corollary of several hundred pages of
their discussion is that they have gotten too emphatically emphasized.
That was in large part the purpose of the preceding chapter: to frustrate
any intellectual inclination toward polarization. On the other hand, it
would be a great error, as Jack Goody (1977) argues, "to substitute a dif-

fuse relativism that fails to recognize the differences implicit in the means of communication implied in the terms 'oral' and 'written,' and which fails to take account of other changes in the modes and content of verbal interaction" (p. 26).

Not to recognize that epistemic breaks or discontinuities from the orally inflected narrative stem from events of material import would likewise be reckless. Italian neorealism, for example, was undeniably the aesthetic outgrowth of a specific historical context, one that was responding to a post-war crisis of economy and morale—not to mention, reflecting the need to break decisively with the cultural heritage of Fascism, which had done nothing to reflect the authentic lives of its nation's citizens (Nowell-Smith, 1999). Still, we can conjointly acknowledge that sometimes narrative may not always be available to or coveted by the very citizens whom its directors are trying to reach—as was the case with the neorealist species. At the same time, I have given far less attention than I should have to why it is that orally inflected films are sometimes so vital to, so favored, so cherished—sometimes *fetishistically* so— by literate viewers. Stuart Hall has of course asserted that "[w]e are all, in our heads, several different audiences at once, and can be constituted as such by different programs. We have the capacity to deploy different levels and modes of attention, to mobilize different competencies in our viewing" (cited in Jenkins, 1992, p. 56). Although in many cases this may be true, we must be sensitive, at the least, to percipients who may not deploy as many competencies in viewing, owing to their limited exposure to reading and writing.

Once upon a time (to end on a transpositional note) storytelling was a means of sociocultural self-preservation, of keeping knowledge of one's community perpetually in the communal loop; and it was a purpose and a practice that "could be purchased only at the cost of a total loss of objectivity" (Havelock, 1963, p. 45). Now, with history able to be recorded elsewhere, stories have been released from those ancient requirements. No longer must they be, as oral epic was, a veritable anthology of everything: historical highlights, ethics, polity, the intricacies of battle shields, sexual relations, philosophical musings, altercations with gods. And not unlike the Muses of Ancient Greece, who began as a single goddess of Memory, only later splitting off into three "daughters" (Meditation, Memory, and Song) before divorcing further into nine representatives,[14] stories too have accommodated the sophistication and fragmentation of fields that a social literacy permits.

Hence, stories today have been afforded the capacity to be "mere" entertainment—or, by extension, "mere" art. Where digitization and

---

14. These nine are History, Astronomy, Tragedy, Comedy, Dances to the Gods, Songs to the Gods, Epic Poetry, Love Poetry, and Lyric Poetry (Hamilton, 1942, pp. 39–40).

other burgeoning technologies take narrative in the future, who can say;
but if story-*telling* is ever to become story-*simulating*, it will almost certainly not happen without orality and literacy bearing some responsibility for the means by which we model our relationship to time and space:
how we maneuver through it; where we are capable of traveling because
of it; who we are capable of becoming because of it.

    I only wish I could stick around long enough to witness what epis-
temic changes come next.

Appendix A

Reading Closely: The Orality of *Baazigar*

Given that some readers may not have had exposure to a *masala* film from the period discussed, that is, 1950 to 1990, I provide here a close reading of a single film. The film, *Baazigar* (*Trickster*, 1993), a top-10 hit from 1993 co-directed by brothers Abbas and Mastan Alibhai Burmawalla, garnered four Filmfare Awards, including best actor and best screenplay. The film was also a hit, ranking fourth at the box-office the year of its release (www.boxofficeindia.com). To be frank, my reasons for choosing it are largely born of nostalgia: *Baazigar* was the first Bollywood film that I set out explicitly to study. Nevertheless, there are virtually hundreds of top-10 grossers that I could have used in its place. From the year of *Baazigar*'s release alone, I could have opted instead for *Khalnayak*, *Darr* (*Fear*), *Damini* (*Lightning*), the slapstick comedy *Aankhen* (*Eyes*), or the pseudohistorical *Kshatriya* (*Warrior*).

My intention is to provide readers a comprehensive and chronological experience of the *masala* experience—digressions and repetitions included in order to convey how orally inflected attributes not only permeate but undergird the formula. Although resolved to reading the material, I resist reading *into* it; hence, I provide only occasional analysis and force no conclusions. SMALL CAPS are used to denote traits that bear specific links to the oral characteristics of visual narrative (see Chapter 2). Only occasionally do I expound on these attributes when they appear. Other characteristics—like the film's episodic structure—will hopefully emerge organically out of my idiosyncratic recounting of the tale.

BAAZIGAR, *PART I: FROM* IN MEDIAS RES *TO INTERMISSION*

Baazigar opens with a FLASHBACK: A boy races through a downpour to an urban clinic, urging the doctor to come see his sick mother, who is incapable of making it to the hospital. This opening, abrupt and quickly paced for a movie's start, feels *IN MEDIAS RES*, as if we had entered a picture already in progress. After examining the boy's mother, the doctor informs some concerned locals that the mother has some sort of "setback" that he cannot cure; only medicine will see to her survival.

And so follows a sequence of the boy working menial jobs in order to tend to his mother. He buys her medicine; he feeds her food; he vows with AMPLIFIED FILIAL LOYALTY to take vengeance on the one who has forced them into this situation. In choppy slow motion, he throws into the air a series of unrevealed photographs, as discordant music warns of his vengeance to come. We then cut to flashes of negative images, tonal reversals of blacks and whites, of what we presume to be this boy's nightmare. We are shown his baby sister dead—the baby's funeral—and we hear screams and learn of some horrible, although indistinct, plight that has befallen his family.

And then the boy awakes—only now he is a grown son. We have been catapulted forward in time—to the now, to the AMORPHOUS PRESENT, which will never be dated or given any proper historical context. It will simply be *THIS* AND *EVERY* MOMENT that we are witnessing; and so, modern jeans and sports cars and contact lenses will coexist easily, as we will see, with a mythic imagining of the traditional, the primitive, sometimes even the surreal.

Although Ajay Sharma (Shah Rukh Khan) has escaped his harried childhood, it seems his duties as an adult have hardly altered. His first mission upon rising is to feed his now middle-aged and still brain-afflicted mother (Rakhee Gulzar). She asks sullenly if Ajay has fed his infant sister. With a heartbroken expression, Ajay Sharma answers in the affirmative. Ajay is a son any mother would be proud of, as a lady neighbor at this point verbally informs us. And so, the stage is well set for us to appreciate this lad who has endured all measure of humiliation and hard labor for the sake of his Ma. Upon exiting the house, however, he picks up a coin in the street and tosses it in the air, and issuing once more from the soundtrack is an UNSUBTLE LEITMOTIF to warn and arouse us: REVENGE to come.

En route into the city (Bombay), Ajay hitches a ride with an old school chum, Vicky, who reveals that his parents were killed several years back in an airplane crash. Ajay, we discover through their conversation, is off to meet his girlfriend—and with a rapid cut-to, and then zoom-in, we are transported to that girlfriend's residence (by way of a close-up of her buttocks and, only afterward, her face). She is Seema

Chopra (Shilpa Shetty), and a snippet of ACCOMPANYING MUSIC INFORMS US that she is both lovely and "his." Her father's house is a veritable VILLA-PALACE-MANSION, with lavish, spacious interiors, a fleet of cars, a manmade stream (with waterfall) running through the backyard, and a bevy of uniformed servants. She tells the head domestic that she is off to college campus.

What follows is AN INTERLUDE OF SLAPSTICK DESIGN, led in large part by the domestics of the household: the absent-minded head servant, Babulal (played by prominent comedian Johnny Lever—a customary servant/pal/sidekick in the movies); and his minions, a chauffeur and a portly cook. These characters quite literally WEAR THEIR IDENTITIES ON THEIR SLEEVES: The chauffeur *is* a driver's uniform; the cook *is* a fluffy white chef's hat and rolling pin in hand (not to mention, a dead ringer for Oliver Hardy). Together, they banter, they flex servant muscle, and then Babulal proceeds to mismanage, misinterpret, and then plumb forget a phone call intended for Mr. Chopra (from a plastics businessman who wishes to see Seema engaged to his son). The distended "broken telephone" scene between the two parties possesses all the innocent idiocy and farcical persiflage of Gomer Pyle or a slackened Three Stooges act. To be sure, it has been developed as much for its INDEPENDENT APPEAL as for its relaying of information that will be relevant to the story later on.

We join Seema at her GENERIC, ICONIC SETTING of a college campus, where a girlfriend, Anjali, queries who Seema's mystery man is, and a male classmate, Ravi, agrees to take notes for her (unaware that she is skipping class in order to meet up clandestinely with her boyfriend). When Seema finds Ajay waiting for her in the park, she pouts, she complains. Apparently, he is less interested in her than in a book he is studiously (feigning) reading. Their coy, comical exchanges segue into a COY, COMICAL SONG in which she implores him to "read her face." They prance with choreographed wit about the garden (and through time and space—that is, through an amusement park and into swimming pools and out of changing rooms). The montage is executed with a kind of flat zaniness, except for one sober moment when we see Ravi watching the couple dejectedly from behind a tree. Certainly the musical number, like the situation comedy it follows, is here more for its INDEPENDENT APPEAL than for its forwarding of the plot.[1]

---

1. It is certainly arguable that the musical numbers reduce or constrict the characters to certain types and, thus, force a narrative style that is here being *mistaken* for oral. However, I think it would be more accurate to say that the average spectator's *acceptance* of such types—types that are not at all "real" in the way persons inculcated into literacy understand the term—is precisely what permits the musical numbers. It seems hardly an accident that educated Indians are constantly bemoaning the requirement of song numbers in movies. To them, such interludes signal the "backwardness" of the Hindi cinema as the songs prevent the films from ever being texts in the "classic realist" mode.

Afterward, Seema confesses that she does not like their secret meetings. Ajay, however, insists on them. He is ashamed of his commonplaceness, he tells her, and his ordinary roots, which he is sure would offend her father. (How he has managed, despite his destitution, to appear so modern and *unordinary* is of course of no concern to the film. He is after all the movie's STAR.) Suddenly, Seema has to go, recalling that her sister is returning from her college in Shimla that afternoon.

Our introduction to Seema's sister, Priya (played by Kajol), is through a PARODY OF-CUM-PAEAN TO A PREVIOUS MOVIE. Aping the sequence in *Sholay* in which the enraged villain Gabbar Singh is introduced via his pacing black boots, this scene begins with an extended shot of Priya's high-heeled footwear. Cracking a whip just like her other-movie mentor, Priya strides past her daddy's inept servants lined up in a row, berating them for not having picked her up at the airport. The scene is invested with humor thanks to Babulal's fumbling answers to questions he can never remember. The scolding is interrupted by AGONISTIC squeals of delight as Priya and Seema embrace after such a long separation. Priya's return from school procures further love and affection from her father, Mr. Madan Chopra (Dilip Tahil), who returns from work (where he is portrayed as a somewhat ruthless and inflexible BUSINESS TYCOON) to announce over supper that he will buy Priya a motorcar because she did not get a clothing factory named after her, as her sister did.

To be sure, the relationship between father and daughters is as INFLATED AND OVERRIPE as that between Ajay and his mother, HIGHLY SURFACE IN EXPRESSION—or heavy and flat, as Walter Ong might say. These characters are UNNUANCED. They are NEVER MORE THAN WHAT THEY REVEAL PUBLICLY. At no point, thus, is the spectator expected to infer motive or psychological state, or to "read between the lines." *Being* in the *masala* film means uttering and exposing.

Priya accompanies her father to Madras, to watch him compete in a sports car race. We never see Madras, only the sports car speedway. Indeed, there is little interest generally in these movies in introducing or exhibiting new environs, sometimes even in explaining them. The silent mental gathering of place seems fairly inconsequential. Things move more quickly than that—straight to the ACTION AND TALK. Right away we learn via an attendant that Mr. Chopra has a new rival to fear: a racer named Vicky. Priya pooh-poohs the possibility of any such "Icky-Micky-Licky-Chicky" character posing a genuine threat. That is when we, the audience, get a glimpse of this new contender: It is Ajay (now concealing his true identity and representing himself instead as Vicky Malhotra), who dons his motor racing helmet and proceeds to battle the speedway with Mr. Chopra.

The high-pitched race of crayon-bright, diminutive sports cars takes up some 3 minutes of screen time, with Vicky in the very last leg of the race letting Mr. Chopra win. When Vicky approaches Mr. Chopra afterward, his removal of his helmet is captured in AMPLIFIED slow-motion, as is his shake of his wet hair (the shot comparable to something one might see in a shampoo commercial).

Immediately, we cut to Priya, the camera ZOOMING IN on her lovestruck expression. Love in Bollywood has been generally instantaneous, a cinematic arrow of *amour* discharged as a quick zoom in, or sometimes even as a pulsating repetition of zooms in and out, thus mimicking a heartbeat. Rarely is love revealed or conceptualized as an experience or state of mind that emerges slowly or eventually *through* the interactions of two characters. Of course the logical contention is that this is the narrative outgrowth of a culture in which premarital love has been historically inappropriate. (Quick and sudden love manages to circumvent this otherwise problematic issue; love here becomes fated, a destiny to be fulfilled.) But, given the characteristics of oral narrative, it seems significant that reflected here once again is that propensity for characters to WEAR THEIR IDENTITIES ON THEIR SLEEVES. Even more significant, however, is the way in which this sudden love is visualized: through a LOUDER, MORE THEATRICAL CAMERA WORK than in, say, conventional Hollywood, where we can also find instant-love stories. In effect, what we are witnessing is a visual materialization of the verbomotor culture's OVER-PRACTICING OF RHETORIC, presented here in the form of an AGONISTIC STYLE OF CAMERAWORK. (The preceding mention of Vicky's de-helmeting as resembling something in a shampoo commercial bears relation to this, I think. As commercials must make their point quickly, but memorably, their tendency, too, is to use camerawork that is generally more agonistic and amplified.)

Vicky impresses Priya's father with his deferential ways: He refers to Mr. Chopra as his "guru" and is eager to receive the man's blessings. In fact, it is for these reasons, he explains, that he let the magnate defeat him in the race. Given his passion for sports cars, Vicky generously offers to take Priya car-shopping in Bombay.

Just as Vicky is about to depart, Priya calls him over, wanting to introduce herself; but he already knows who she is. He tells her that he forfeited the race for *her* benefit, so that she wouldn't be disappointed at seeing her father lose. He is, after all, a "*baazigar*," he says, a magician, a trickster with a sleight of hand, and one who was quite willing to lose for the sake of winning later. He makes her repeat the term *baazigar*, and from her smitten whispering of the word, we are TRANSPORTED SUDDENLY to Priya's bedroom, where she prances about in her nightgown with EXCESSIVE GIDDINESS, thinking about her prince-juggler—and foreordaining the upcoming musical number, which is framed as her fantasy.

The MUSICAL NUMBER is as well a compilation of scenes BORROWING (WITHOUT IRONY—without parody, for that matter) from Hollywood, TV commercials, and earlier Bombay films. Vicky, for instance, plays the violin Raj Kapoor made famous in the films of the 1950s. Priya stands by an ocean cliff wearing a flouncy wedding dress, as Vicky arrives on horseback in a black Zorro cape and mask. They croon to each other; they profess their love. Several transformations and costume changes ensue: they are a modern couple vacationing on a yacht; performing Spanish flamenco; trumpet-playing in the aqua waters of a tropical locale. The 5-minute musical number manages to be sexy but warm, sweet but fashionable. So begins, too, the HERO–HEROINE/"ETERNAL LOVERS" ROMANTIC PAIRING OF MALE AND FEMALE STARS (Shah Rukh Khan and Kajol), which Khan and Kajol will repeat in five other mega-hit films over the course of the next decade.

When we return to "reality," Priya (who has also resumed her more girlish demeanor) shrieks gleefully as she races alongside a hotel pool where Seema is ostensibly swimming (posing in a bathing suit would be descriptively more accurate). (As a brief COMIC INTERLUDE, upon trying to reach her sister, Priya steps inadvertently on the back of a wizened lecher lying poolside, resulting in his false teeth popping out, all to VAUDEVILLIAN SOUND EFFECTS.) Both girls announce that they have found love, and they repeat the term in several languages, including Hindi, Urdu, and English. In Indian films, *ishq, pyar, mohabbat, prem* are all perfectly interchangeable. Although this definitely reflects the nomenclature that exists for the word "love" in India, repetition of the terms could also be construed as a kind of COPIA, A THICKENING OR AMPLIFYING OF THE THING ITSELF VIA REPETITION.

Once the sisters agree when to meet so that Seema might be introduced to Vicky, we cut with speed and minimal establishment to Vicky at the helm of a fancy new sports car. (Vicky, it should be added, unlike the more scholarly bespectacled Ajay, dresses like a cool guy—that is, in jeans and a red leather jacket reminiscent of the one Michael Jackson made iconographic.) Vicky is testing out the car on Priya's behalf and won't let her drive. Priya makes a scene, insisting that they stop for ice cream. When Vicky is off satisfying her impulsive demand, she takes off in the vehicle alone. But she finds herself being chased by several motorcycling *goondas* (street thugs). Indeed, they are PROJECTED IMMEDIATELY and clearly as "bad guys" via their demeanor, their Eve-teasing talk, and their darker skin. The DIVERSIONARY SEQUENCE that follows—in which the *goondas* chase Priya by foot, finally to be beaten up by Vicky—ALTERNATES UNSELF-CONSCIOUSLY between moments of suspense, slapstick, and light comedy, before culminating in high serious and bloody revenge.

First, there is a fast-motion chase by the pernicious gang of Priya through a park. Briefly, she evades her pursuers by hiding behind a stranger's umbrella, only to find the stranger is an obese rake (made more rakish by a fish-eye lens). When she disappears into a park tent, one of the *goondas* follows, only to find himself immediately ejected; and then Vicky emerges from the tent, with Priya by his side, both of them comic-casually enjoying a drink of coconut milk. (Some readers unfamiliar with Hindi films may relate to such a scene nonetheless, having witnessed similar slapstick showdowns in Hong Kong movies.)

Several more humorous and CARICATURESQUE scraps follow between Vicky and the gang of four or five, with coconuts knocking bad guys bloody and unconscious, and boxer shorts being exposed, before finally one of the *goondas* pries open his massive pocket knife. The fighting becomes immediately solemn. The cartoon sound effects die away. But it is only when Vicky is wounded—that is, when he wipes blood from his cut wrist, and stares at the thick red fluid emanating from his own being—that the tone of the scene becomes ultra-serious. His eyes grow fierce; he stiffens in outrage, as does the music on the soundtrack. In this way, the moment has a kind of PROVERBIAL RESONANCE. It is as if an unspoken, but collectively understood proviso were being forwarded: To draw blood is to challenge a man's honor and thus to incite his (justifiable) fury. The difference is simply that this "proverb" is told through a series of images and sounds: in this case, through Vicky's touch of the wound, his detecting blood, his trembling with rage.

To literate minds unexposed to these movies, such a sequence will appear highly over the top, even laughable. But its purpose and power stem directly from its READABILITY and FORMULARY REPETITION in Hindi popular film. For, this is a moment that can be found in literally *hundreds* of movies. It is in effect a VISUAL CLICHÉ. The audience knows—predestines, even, with whetted appetite—that now the bad guys must be summarily punished. And of course this is just what happens, with Vicky pulling off his thick leather belt in order to give the knife-wielder a VICIOUS, EVEN VENEMOUS, but ultimately "deserved" LASHING.

At the police station, Priya and Vicky try to make their case against the goons. Fortunately, Priya recognizes one of the policemen, Karan, a kind and softspoken, but slightly lackluster fellow from their college days together. He promises to take care of the situation. Meanwhile, the couple has missed their 1 o'clock meeting with Seema.

From this, we join Seema, who has left to attend her friend Anjali's decidedly Western birthday party. Seema stands out in what can only be described as a yellow and white polka-dotted "party frock," as she dances along with everyone else to the repetitive strains of European pop. (Indeed, most of the major stars' costumes might be justly described as BOLDER, LOUDER, AND CRISPER than those of the other actors, as if TO AUGMENT THEIR SPECIAL STAR VOLTAGE OR LIGHT.)

Present and eager for Seema's advances are several slaphappy Indian nerds (including a diminutive Charlie Chaplin type), who vie for celluloid time as COMIC RECESS. They stumble goofily over each other thinking that Seema is beckoning them, when what she is really doing is signaling Ajay behind them. He has appeared at a window, but refuses to enter the party. The two meet privately in a garden setting afterward and Ajay informs her, with a kind of bratty, infantile playfulness, that he is going home for a few days.

Back at the Chopra household, more BURLESQUE follows, with Babulal announcing to the servants that the plastics businessman (in pursuit of a daughter-in-law) has arrived with his son. As Babulal does not wish to see the Chopra reputation ruined, he has decided to make the tea himself for their guests. He dons a chef hat and begins the task of boiling water with all the cavalier looniness that the FILCHED PINK PANTHER THEME—which now plays on the soundtrack—helps to emphasize. Babulal forgets to insert tea leaves into the water, and by the time Priya furtively informs him of such, it's too late; the businessman and his son are pouring the tea. They drink it anyway; they pretend to enjoy it, calling it "ambrosia." Babulal stands by watching, caught in a protracted, somewhat beleaguered "laughing game" with the plastics businessman. But then Seema returns home and the MOOD TURNS grave (for her—and hence for us). It is a MOOD LARGELY IMPARTED TO US VIA SOUND EFFECTS AND MUSIC, which spring into action on her being told that her engagement to this plastics businessman's son is to be scheduled for the following week. It is in fact a blatant and direct MUSICAL "VERBALIZATION" OF HER STATE. We are not expected to infer her emotional plight; we are TOLD IT BLUNTLY AND OBVIOUSLY, and arguably, by literate standards, artlessly. (Indeed, this type of musical accompaniment occurs incessantly throughout the film.)

Briskly, we shift to a moderately hysterical Seema on the phone with Ajay (his scholarly look intact). He insists he has no position, no status; but finally he relents: they will meet the next day to figure out matters. And so, once again, we join the couple in the park, with Vicky informing Seema that, to remain united, they have but one choice: They must commit suicide together. Seema agrees, declaring she prefers death with Ajay to life without him.

We cut to the couple sitting underneath a tree, READING OUT LOUD TO EACH OTHER from their prepared suicide notes. Seema signs hers, and then Ajay extracts it from her hands, telling her that she has "passed" his test—she has proven her love and faith in him. Tomorrow, he says, they will visit the registrar's office and marry.

With a certain awkwardness (both technically and narratively), we shift from this to a sultry and romantic, if not somewhat voyeuristic, MUSICAL NUMBER set at night, with Ajay and Seema proclaiming themselves in song to be "fellow travelers" and each others' destinies. As some analysts of the Hindi film have astutely theorized, musical numbers like this have come to represent—to *replace*, in fact—explicit sexual liaisons, which, at the time, were highly censored in Hindi popular film. However, it also is important to recognize that music can elicit a kind of INEFFABLE VISCERAL AND EMOTIONAL RESPONSE, a "high" even—in this case, perhaps of romantic relish, or of erotic desire—that would not be easily acquired even through the best dramatic writing. Furthermore, the music does so by using language that, by virtue of RHYME AND TUNE, and the FREQUENT USE OF CLICHÉS, is rendered more ENLIST-ABLE TO THE SPECTATOR'S MIND.

As if it had been some nocturnal dream, the musical number ends, and we fade from black to the sun rising over Bombay amidst the EARSPLITTING SQUAWKING of birds.

Seema retrieves a small heart-shaped pendant from her dresser drawer, and quickly we cut to the eloping couple standing outside the registrar's office, with Seema moaning and gently chiding Ajay because the bureau is closed for lunch. For fear of being seen during their half-hour wait, Ajay suggests they take a walk—and next thing we know they are on the roof of the building. Seema is somewhat alarmed by how high up they are; but she is soon distracted, eager to give Ajay the heart-shaped pendant that contains their pictures. Apparently moved by the gesture, he tells her that she deserves to be "closer to the skies," and so he hoists her up on to the roof's railing. She panics, informing him of her vertigo, but he urges her to trust him. He is sad to be taking her from the world, he confides soberly, but he wants her to know that he is also liberating her from old ties. And with that and a heartfelt apology, he *thrusts her over the roof's edge to her death.*

It is without doubt a shocking and sudden and unanticipated occurrence (provided of course that one is not aware of its having been NARRATIVELY LIFTED FROM A HOLLYWOOD FILM from 1991, *A Kiss Before Dying*). Significantly, in the original Hollywood film noir from which *Baazigar* WAS FREELY ADAPTED, it was *here* that the narrative proper began.[2] That is to say, the original film commenced with the eloping couple's discovery that the registrar's office was closed, leading to their visit to the roof, and the man's hurling the woman over the building's edge for reasons unspoken. Structurally, *A Kiss Before Dying* stays vigilantly true to Freytag's Pyramid, with none of the significant sideline developments regarding romance or family relations (although the "Ajay" character in *A Kiss Before Dying* does have a mother and a later-to-be-revealed "past"). Furthermore, none of the fights and comedy sketches that have thus far punctuated *Baazigar* appear in *A Kiss Before Dying*, which instead maintains a flatly sinister, dark and brooding tone throughout.[3]

---

2. I say "narrative proper" because *A Kiss Before Dying* also begins with a brief flashback episode pertaining to the male lead's distraught childhood, though this childhood is no way given the attention or development that it will receive later on in *Baazigar*.

3. When first released in India, *Baazigar* created a minor stir in the press because of the

Following Seema's homicide, the action moves quickly and in an almost JAGGED FASHION, all to the accompaniment of OVERSTATED ELECTRONIC SOUND EFFECTS and syncopated taps on the steel edge of a drum. Ajay is seen exiting the registrar building, as onlookers rush to examine the bloody victim; not only has she fallen to her death, but she has done so through a glass canopy. Ajay deposits Seema's suicide note in a public mailbox. Back at the scene of the crime, there are sirens and mayhem, signaling a passage of time, before finally an ambulance approaches, and behind it a car carrying Priya—and Ajay, once more masquerading as Vicky. Priya becomes HYSTERICAL at the sight of her dead sister, and Vicky and the timely policeman-college friend Karan, who has also arrived on the scene, must lead her away. The LOGICAL IMPROBABILITY of Ajay-Vicky's character being in two places (as two different people) in such a short span of time is of little consequence to the narrative. In fact, his ability to transform himself with such MAGICAL, SUPRA-HUMAN speed seems almost the point here.

To the melodious and melancholy notes of a reed flute (an instrument whose mood can register for the Indian spectator instantaneous sorrow and loss), we open on the Chopra household's vigil in Seema's honor. The atmosphere is somber, the guests arriving in customary white. The commissioner, accompanied by Karan, arrives as well, asking to speak to Mr. Chopra privately. Taking the immediate family aside, the

---

hero's explicit *villainous* streak. The film had bent one of the cardinal rules of Bollywood, whereby all acts of violence by a hero had to be performed on deserving candidates. Some critics saw Ajay Sharma as reflecting a new narrative strategy, one where heroes, heroines, and villains contained "within themselves more than one—if not many—stereotypical selves" (Doraiswamy, cited in Gokulsing & Dissanayake, 1998, p. 110). Others alleged Ajay was a signal that spectators were maturing and could accept characters that were more complicated and gray. Still others saw the embrace of this unusual protagonist as reflecting the average spectator's contemporaneous lot and life philosophy: The world had become too harsh and corrupt a place for one not to have been rendered morally crippled by it. Ajay Sharma's bad deeds were, in this way, the ugly, dirty, but ultimately digestible, by-product of his heroic attempt to avenge his family's honor and birthright. Of course, that kind of character *wasn't* really new to Bollywood. Rather, he had simply stepped into the foreground. For, a very similar character can be found in the classic *Mother India* (1957). In that film, the protagonist's son, Birjoo, also is warped psychologically by the degradation and injustice he has seen his peasant mother bear. He too tries to seek vengeance in distorted and violent ways; and his rage, too, we are urged to accept, is fueled deeply down by a noble purpose, which is not to see his family's honor bruised or verbally defiled. He is, in effect, good purpose gone awry—but this of course means that he must die in the end, as Ajay Sharma will invariably have to, too. Neither in *Mother India* nor *Baazigar* is the audience expected to envision the son as profoundly evil, as the story's *nemesis*. They both are individuals who have been metaphorically, if not directly, disfigured by the greater evil that exists in the human universe: in the case of *Mother India*, a rapacious village usurer; in the case of *Baazigar*, a rapacious urban business tycoon. We grieve Ajay and Birjoo's demises; we do not celebrate them.

commissioner discloses that Seema's death was a suicide. Karan reveals the evidence, the suicide letter. Once again, these "BIG REVEALS," that is, the announcement of Seema's suicide, the existence of the declarative note, have been PUNCTUATED BY MUSIC that more literate viewers would consider HEAVY-HANDED, even condescendingly INVASIVE. Similarly, the HIGH PITCH and AGONISTIC DELIVERY of Priya's assertions that Seema was happy and could not have taken her own life would strike some as discomfiting. Nevertheless, Priya's claims fall on deaf ears, and Vicky must lead her away, providing silent comfort.

In the now fairly UNIVERSAL, SYNTAGMATIC SYMBOL FOR SIGNALING A COMPRESSION OF TIME, we fade up on a new scene and a brief entr'acte of comedy: The head servant Babulal is in the throes of hammering a nail into the wall, in order to hang up a photograph (more a Bollywood head shot) of Seema. The only problem is that he is trying to insert the nail's flattened head into the wall instead of its tip, and so predictably his attempts at success are for naught. The "wiser" chauffeur informs Babulal of his error: that the nail is meant for *the facing wall*—across the room.

Babulal's handiwork is interrupted by the doorbell and in a PAN-TOMIMED scene reminiscent of SILENT SLAPSTICK, Babulal manages to lose himself and the caller in the revolving front door. The caller, it turns out, is a jeweler who has come to receive payment for Seema's *mangalsu-tra* (a marriage necklace akin in symbolic significance to a wedding ring). When Priya hears this from the vendor, she is quick to confront her father, proposing that Seema's fiancé was somehow involved in Seema's demise and that they should have the case reopened. Here we witness an INFLATED and largely UNPRECIPITATED TURN OF PERSONALITY (except of course for the fact that the actor has PLAYED A SLEW OF SUCH ROLES before, thus FULFILLING AUDIENCE EXPECTATION). That is to say, Madan Chopra refuses. The BILIOUS, ANTAGONISTIC CHARGE of his protestations (engendered by the shame and spoiled reputation that Seema's illicit af-fair would induce were it to become public, and AMPLIFIED by the way the CAMERA SWIRLS DRAMATICALLY around him) certainly suggests to the audience his EVIL UNDERTONES, as does his complete emotional jettison-ing of his dead daughter.[4]

Consequently, we find Priya next on top of the roof of the registrar building, contemplating alone the events of her sister's death. Briefly, as

---

4. This is not to say that a spectator won't identify with Madan Chopra's dilemma (i.e., Chopra's desire to save face; his wish not to spoil the family reputation and hence Priya's chance for marriage). But the IMMODERACY OF THE ACTOR'S DELIVERY, his somewhat MANICHEAN TRANSFORMATION, prevents us from allying ourselves overtly with him in that particular moment. This character type is one that Dilip Tahil has played over and over in films, much as the actress who plays Ajay's "Holy, Victimized Mother," Rakhee Gulzar, is also RE-ENACTING A ROLE THAT SHE HAS PLAYED DOZENS OF TIMES BEFORE.

a kind of remembered proof, we FLASH BACK to Priya on top of a diving board importuning Seema (who stands poolside) to climb up and dive, too; but Seema defers with a panicked air, citing her vertigo and general fear of heights.[5]

Lost in thought, Priya is oblivious to a man (seen exclusively by way of his shoes) advancing toward her; but the "leitmotif" of drum taps that accompanies his approach EXPLICITLY SIGNALS DANGER to us. But then she turns and sees—as we do in full—Karan, the policeman, whom she herself has summoned. Priya informs Karan of the latest particulars of the case, suggesting that Seema's boyfriend had pushed her over the building's edge because he was a cheat. The camera moves around and about the pair with COARSE EXAGGERATION, as Priya rejects Karan's contention that Seema had planned to elope. According to Karan, this is evidenced by the lack of a marriage application having been filed the requisite 1 month in advance. But Priya insists with BOLD, ALMOST MANIC CONVICTION that her sister would never have committed suicide from atop a roof, given her vertigo. Convinced by this information, Karan agrees to help Priya in an unofficial capacity and recommends that she interview anybody with whom her sister may have interacted in her final days.

At the college, Priya interviews Anjali, who mentions Seema's smitten classmate, Ravi. The girls part ways, but the camera lingers behind, turning slowly to a window where we see, to the AURAL DETONATION of drum strikes, Vicky (Ajay, actually, for he appears in the latter's more academic garb). We then cut to Priya who is in the throes of questioning Ravi in the school library. Yes, he acknowledges, he did love Seema—till he saw her in the garden with another boy. When Priya queries as to this other boy's identity, Ravi mentions a photograph he has in his hostel room, one of the boy peering through a window into Anjali's birthday party.

The pair drives to the hostel, followed unwittingly by another car and the REQUISITE CAUTIONARY SOUND EFFECTS. Ravi ascends to his room, locating the photo of Ajay; but no sooner has he done so than hands in surgical gloves fling a rope round his neck. The strangling scene that follows, during which Ajay forces Ravi to sign his name to a blank piece of paper, is LOUD AND FRENZIED, with brisk cuts between the wide eyes of both killer and prey. It is not unlike something one might see in a B-grade Hollywood horror movie. There are flashing lights and electronic music, which assist in AMPLIFYING THE ENERGY AND VIOLENCE OF THE SPECTACLE.

---

5. Seema's fear of heights is nonexistent in the earlier musical numbers, where she can be found dancing with oblivious aplomb across scaffolds and raised stages.

Meanwhile, Priya, who has become impatient with waiting, makes her way into the hostel, past the groggy attendant, and up to Ravi's room. We intercut between her and Ajay, who is now hammering out a note on Ravi's typewriter. There are close-ups of Ajay and of the typewriter, with the camera arcing around them both (although it seems to be highlighting more the miracle of typing). When Priya finally reaches Ravi's door, she opens it to come face to face, not with Ajay, but with Ravi's corpse hanging from the ceiling. Employing a VISUAL SYNTAX THAT IS both BOLD AND OBVIOUS, the camera zooms in on Priya, then on Ravi, then on Priya again, then on Ravi once more, thus expressing explicitly and WITHOUT THE SLIGHTEST HINT OF IRONY the "shock" and "horror" of her discovery.

Outside the hostel later that night, Karan, who has arrived with the police, acknowledges that Priya was right: They have found a suicide note left by Ravi, which verifies that he was Seema's lover—and her killer, too—and that it was for fear of public disclosure that he committed suicide. The camera pans from the conversing pair to Ajay, loitering behind a nearby tree, listening intently. From this, we straightaway join Ajay returning home. As he enters his room, his back menacingly to us, he throws off his jacket and selects a different suit from his closet. The ACCOMPANYING SOUND EFFECTS are akin to attenuated train noises— turning wheels, chugging steam—and they prepare us for the HEIGHTENED CONFESSION AND OATH TO COME.

Ajay stands in front of his bedroom mirror and TALKS OUT LOUD TO HIMSELF. His declarations to his own image are not swift or self-consciously half-mumbled; nor are they presented as the ranting of an unstable mind (as one sees and accepts in a film like *Taxi Driver* (1976), for instance). No, here, Ajay speaks with a kind of UNABASHED ROUTINISM, with a justified ease that does not emerge from sickness or shame, but from the AUDIENCE'S ACCEPTANCE AND EXPECTATION of, and perhaps also the indispensability of, a VOCALIZING SELF. He asks Seema for her forgiveness, as if she were there on the other side of his reflection. Remorsefully, he explains his reasons for betraying her love and killing her: He had to win her father's confidence, which he needs in order now to *destroy Madan Chopra*. But first, Ajay confides (to her, to himself, to the audience) that, as all people who knew "Ajay" are now dead, Ajay too must die. And so in a HIGH MOMENT OF DRAMA, he removes a contact lens case from a drawer and inserts—in SLOW, RELISHING CLOSE-UPS that emphasize their technological marvel and magic—two brown-shaded contacts into his otherwise olive eyes.

EXEGETIC SOLILOQUIES like this one from Ajay are not exclusively owing to an audience's DISCOMFORT WITH AMBIGUITY, with the need to have motives and intentions explicitly spelled out. Such chest baring often does something more. It sets the stage for that FORM OF UTTERANCE that some scholars purport to be the most culturally rootbound; that is, THE AVOWAL OF THE OATH, A VERBALIZED PLEDGE or promise of resistance, or of vengeance or sacrifice. In such a proclamation's being made ALOUD, in its being MADE VISIBLE, it is also rendered *true*. This is precisely what happens in *Baazigar*. With Ajay annihilated, it is Vicky who now turns to the mirror, and in a technically modulated voice that REVERBERATES SUPERNATURALLY LIKE A GOD's, he promises that Chopra's end is near; then he turns to stare directly into the camera, declaring, "Get ready, Madan Chopra! It's time for your downfall!" And in a menacingly cool gesture, Vicky flips his jacket collar upright. In this way, thought is unified with action, such that now action can rightly become destiny. (In the Hindi film, as with much oral narrative, IT IS WITH DESTINY, NOT MYSTERY, THAT ANTICIPATION ARISES.)

BAAZIGAR, *PART II: FROM HERE TO FRATERNITY*

As the cook Fatso (that is what they call him) confirms verbally to a fellow servant, 6 months have elapsed. Babulal enters the kitchen to the sly, SLINKING PINK PANTHER JINGLE that has by now become his PERSONAL LEITMOTIF. Once again in veritable Three Stooges fashion, he tries to exert his influence over the household staff. *SWOOSH! POP!* AND *BOING!* ACOUSTICS pepper the soundtrack as he inspects his men, extracting a half-empty liquor bottle from a pocket, only to be informed that it is his own, handed off the night before.

From this brief exposition, we jump suddenly to Priya at the wheel of a car, driving Vicky to her father's office. Madan Chopra has something to discuss with them, she tells Vicky. And so, we join them as they enter Chopra's MOVIE SET-SPACIOUS OFFICE, its desktop lined with four separate telephones. Chopra begins a speech to the couple, telling of how well Vicky assisted Priya through her grief and how he (Chopra) knows what it was Vicky was after in the way Vicky slowly, slowly came into their lives. Yes, he's understood Vicky's every move, he declares in a somewhat beguiling tone—and the uncertainty of where this address is leading for Vicky (and us) is intensified by a POUNDING, DISCORDANT music and CAMERA WORK THAT IS BEST DESCRIBED AS "IN YOUR FACE."

We (alone) see Vicky take hold of a stone paperweight for fear of having to defend himself. But the next thing Madan Chopra is announcing is "Let's get you engaged." At this, Vicky releases the desk implement-weapon with relief and joy. That is, until Chopra advocates that Vicky call his parents to announce the news.

Once again, the camera moves in on our hero with a DISJOINTED RHYTHM THAT BLUNTLY SIGNALS HIS TRAPPED STATE. (If the telling of this portion of the narrative feels frenetic and insouciantly OSCILLATING IN ITS TONE, then it is accurately conveying the scene.) Vicky FLASHES BACK in memory, as we do in celluloid, to a scene witnessed previously in the movie: of Vicky's old school chum giving him a ride into Bombay, and recounting the tragic death of his parents in a Bangalore airplane accident. Within seconds, we are back to Vicky recounting the same tale to Madan Chopra and his daughter, who are immediately swayed by the poignant story. (Certainly relationship-realpolitik has been WILLINGLY ELIDED here for the sake of IN-THE-MOMENT SUSPENSE. Given the import of family in India, that the Chopras would be absolutely oblivious to Vicky's familial state after 6 months, even a false version of it, seems quite unbelievable.)

Priya's father tells Vicky, more figuratively than literally, to sit in *this*, his own, office chair and become an equal partner in the Chopra empire. Next, the industrialist suggests going out to celebrate, but Vicky declines. He must get to work right away, he insists. The Chopras leave him alone, and fairly immediately Vicky heads to the fancy office chair. WE SEE IT IN HIGH ANGLE, WE SEE IT IN LOW ANGLE. Finally, Vicky grips it; he spins it around—and around—and from various close-ups of this endlessly, "dramatically" revolving chair we are suddenly transported, via an audible explosion of joyous cries, to a LENGTHY FLASHBACK . . .

   . . . It is the colorful spring festival of Holi and Vicky, as a child, is playing with his healthy, wealthy father, as Mrs. Sharma (Vicky's mother) benevolently gives away gifts to the less fortunate. Into this UTOPIAN PICTURE rushes Madan Chopra, dressed in traditional attire (intended here as an OBVIOUS MARKER of his uncouthness, his provincialism, and the 3 years he has just spent in jail). He drags his two young daughters toward Mr. Sharma, PLEADING AND WEEPING IN AN AMPLIFIED MANNER for redemption and a job. "Let me live at your feet," he implores his former boss. But Mr. Sharma, A MAN OF IMPERISHABLE HONESTY AND LOYALTY, stridently reminds Mr. Chopra of Chopra's deceit: how despite being treated "like a brother," Chopra stole funds from Sharma's company. In desperation, and with equal if not greater AGONISTIC DISPLAY, Chopra turns next to Mrs. Sharma and her more forgiving heart, insisting he has reformed, staking his daughters' lives on it. To this, Mrs. Sharma, A WOMAN OF IMPERISHABLE PIETY AND LOYALTY, urges her husband to forgive Chopra, as NO MAN WOULD EVER "MAKE FALSE OATHS IN THE NAME OF HIS CHILDREN." And so, because his noble merciful wife has said so, Sharma takes Chopra back into the business.

   Through a brief montage sequence, we watch Chopra transformed from a country bumpkin into a workaholic businessman. Now he dresses in sharp suits; now he pores over architectural plans. Of course he also smokes cigarettes and conjures up business deals that violate government policy. But unaware of this, and pleased with his employee's diligence and remunerative worth, Sharma allots Chopra 5% of the company. Chopra appears thankful, but when he is left alone, again we find ourselves with a character UNVEXEDLY TALKING TO HIM-SELF. "Five percent!" he rages, exhibiting his pure evil, "I have come for 100%!"

The opportunity arises in the next scene when Sharma, who is packing for a trip to a newly purchased tea plantation, hands his employee a document granting Chopra power of attorney while Sharma is *in absentia*. Once again, when alone, Chopra is IN PARLEY WITH HIMSELF, DECLARING VILLAINOUSLY—for now he has fully ripened into AN ALL-OUT, ALL-BAD, SNEERING, SNARLING NEMESIS—that he has been given not only power of attorney, but, PROVERBIALLY SPEAKING, the land on which the "wheels of Chopra's chair will now rest."

And so, another montage ensues, highlighting the transition of power and land. The "Sharma Group of Companies" sign becomes the "Chopra Group of Companies"; the bronze plaque detailing the array of companies "Sharma Exports, Sharma Textiles, Sharma Sugar, Sharma Pharmacutical [*sic*] . . . " is replaced by "Chopra Exports, Chopra Textiles . . . "; and headlines in Hindi and English newspapers relay the Chopra takeover. One of course DOES NOT LEGITIMATELY NEED TO BE ABLE TO *READ* THE TEXT in order to understand what is happening. The transition of ownership is apparent as much THROUGH VISUAL CUES as written ones—like the ensuing rapid cut to a taxi screeching to a halt outside the "Group of Companies" sign, with Sharma exiting, astounded by what he sees.

Sharma confronts his transgressor, who smokes a cigar with the cool, casual AIR OF A VILLAIN IN A SPAGHETTI WESTERN. Unfazed, Chopra discloses that he was willing to see Sharma murdered for all this, that he had pledged to destroy the man who had put him in prison for having stolen a measly five lakh (500,000) rupees. The scene is peculiarly quiet in terms of dialogic delivery, but there are AMPLE, THICK CLOSE-UPS of Sharma's victimized expression and of Chopra's menacing demeanor as he tells his former boss never to return.

WITHOUT ANY EMOTIONAL OR MATERIAL LET-UP, Mr. Sharma arrives home in time to see his wife and children being locked out of their bungalow, all of their possessions now deemed court property. They are homeless and penniless, Sharma learns from a former employee, because of the massive loan he took (through Madan Chopra) from the bank and never repaid. The QUICK ZOOM IN to Sharma's face ACCENTU-ATES HIS SHOCK—AND HIS VICTIMIZATION.

The Sharmas' helplessness is MILKED TO THE FULLEST when next we see Mrs. Sharma weeping in Madan Chopra's office. In a last, humiliating attempt, she has gone with Vicky to ask for Chopra's aid. What transpires is an INFLATED CONTEST OF WITS, one in which EMOTIONS AND ATTITUDES FLUCTUATE RADICALLY, and THE PAST AND THE PRESENT BEGIN TO BE TELESCOPED TOGETHER via dialogue.

First, Madan Chopra urges her to stop crying, explaining that if the royal nabobs could afford mansions for their courtesans, then certainly he can afford her a flat. After all, as a beautiful woman, he purrs salaciously (his hand moving to touch her), where would she sleep, where would she bathe? She gives him a RESOUNDING SLAP, asserting with the enraged shake of her finger and an ominously cutting tongue that how dare he touch her, that she is the wife of Vishwanath Sharma. In SHRIEK-ING TONES, she LIKENS CHOPRA TO THE VILLAINS OF THE *RAMAYANA* AND THE *MAHABHARATA*, and, clutching young Vicky, VOWS THAT THE "CURSE OF HER CHILDREN" WILL BE ON HIM. "This is a mother's *fatwa*," she screams. But his retort is equally vociferous—and more sinister. Her curses cannot possibly touch him, he bellows, standing resolutely be-hind his desk. After all, he is boss now. And to emphasize the point, he spins his office chair around—and around . . .

. . . Till we are brought back to the present, where adult Vicky, alone in his new office, halts the chair's spinning firmly with one black cowboy boot.

FLAMBOYANT ANGLES follow as Vicky sits and places his legs up on a table, in front of a paper model of a building inscribed "Chopra Empire." From between the V of his boots, he reveals and conceals the miniature empire, then leans back in his chair, closing his eyes.

At this point (we are some 2 hours into the film), you, the reader, have most likely become adjusted to, or at least viscerally cognizant of, the PROTRACTED NATURE OF THE STORYTELLING, the manner in which *Baazigar* ENDLESSLY "PAUSES" TO BASK IN SOME COMEDY OR INDULGE IN FURTIVE ROMANCE; OR NOW AND THEN "REWINDS" ITSELF VIA FLASHBACKS TO PROVIDE INFORMATION OR A TOKEN OF RECOLLECTION, OR TO ELICIT PITY. To literately attuned minds, such devices and interludes may seem to be attenuating the story rather than heightening its energy, rendering it helplessly flat, shallow even, and eroding its narrative tension. Per-haps *Baazigar* up to this point even strikes some as exhibiting the tone and alacrity of the Archie or Superman comic books (or even, more ac-curately, a meeting of the two). EVENTS MUST BE ACTIVE AND ALIVE—SEEN, AND UNAMBIGUOUSLY SO, IN ORDER TO BE REAL AND EFFECTIVE. The *ideas* of loss, or the *symbolic* significance of past events, would be of little aid communicatively to the nonliterate or low-literate viewer.

Concurrently, flashbacks like this one we have just witnessed have the dual effect of BRINGING THE PAST INTO THE PRESENT. After all, if the past exists exclusively within the mind of the oral individual—not as history but as *lived experience*—then it follows that THE PAST FOR OUR PRO-TAGONIST VICKY MUST BE REFLECTED AS AN ASPECT OF HIS PRESENT AND LIVING SELF, as "a resonant resource for renewing awareness of present existence" (Ong, 1982, p. 98). As well, such an incorporation INFLATES (ALMOST THOROUGHLY *INVENTS*, in fact, if one compares *Baazigar* to its Hollywood predecessor) the COMMUNAL-FAMILIAL-INTERGENERATIONAL component of the story.

From Vicky's retributive taking of his office chair, we cut to Priya at a jewelry store, and it is clear some time has passed, as she is trying on an ornate gold necklace. She bumps into Anjali—Seema's best friend from college, whom we met at the film's beginning—and gleefully invites Anjali to her engagement party, which is taking place that very night. Anjali, who works now as a hotel receptionist, regrettably declines because of work. Just then, Vicky appears, urging Priya to hurry up. Priya introduces them, and Anjali swears they have met before. Vicky rebuffs Anjali, declaring the world is a small place. But the ensuing MUSIC AND CLOSE-UP ON ANJALI UNDERSCORES HER UNREMITTING SUSPICION— which is quickly confirmed in the next scene when, reaching her (hotel room) home, she removes a photo album from her suitcase, and to the strains of techno-manic music, locates the very same photograph we saw in Ravi's possession.

Unlike Hollywood thrillers, which frequently milk and distend these types of scenes (scenes of wary encounters, of titillating suspicion), here the NECESSARY PLOT POINTS SEEM ALMOST SECONDARY OR MARGINAL in the way that they are presented briskly and then dismissed. Speaking metaphorically, they are more KNOTS IN A CORD OF EXCITEMENT RATHER THAN THE EXCITEMENT ITSELF. Of course, their PURPOSE AND NARRATIVE RELEVANCY ARE EMPHASIZED by way of several EMPHATIC ZOOMS IN on Anjali's troubled expression, which are punctuated by her two fleeting FLASHBACKS: one to the long-ago birthday party when she espied Seema talking to Ajay/Vicky at the window; and the other to their recent encounter in the jewelry store—their replayed voices (her claim they have met before, his insistence they haven't) rendered a veritable AURAL CLICHÉ in the way they RICOCHET AND REVERBERATE on the soundtrack.

We find ourselves next at Vicky and Priya's OPULENT ENGAGEMENT PARTY, which is being attended by literally HUNDREDS OF GUESTS. Priya's father greets the latest arrivals (including Karan, the policeman), as Babulal, ever the scatterbrain, serves everyone empty glasses, presumably of sherbet. Karan strides quickly up to the young couple to congratulate them; but his privately lovesick expressions, accented by AURAL CUES— melancholy strains of the upcoming song—alert us to his moony state. In this way, the ballad that is about to be sung by "INDIA'S RENOWNED SINGER" in honor of the betrothed couple is identified by us with Karan.

By oral narrative (and film) standards, Karan's is a character too soft and unenergetic—lacking in EPICAL OR HEROIC AGONISM, one might even say, in STAR QUALITY—to merit a heroine's hand; but perhaps that is why we identify with him. Because soon it is he who is singing, floating through the crowd, as if he were a ghost, as if this were his reverie and sole chance to express his unrequited love. His wounded gawks of Vicky and Priya waltzing in each other's arms are intertwined with FLASHBACKS TO HIS COLLEGE DAYS, when in all number of displayed seasons, he eyed Priya adoringly from behind a tree, and contemplated with yearning her name written on his palm.

As the audience honors the balladeer with applause, Babulal answers the ringing telephone. It is Anjali, who implores the head servant that she has information about Seema and must speak right away to Priya. Babulal wends through the party crowd HYPERKINETICALLY (AND COMICALLY) REPEATING HER MESSAGE OUT LOUD to himself for fear of forgetting it. Understandably alarmed, Vicky, who has overheard, quickly interposes himself along Babulal's path, brusquely ordering the servant to get him some ice cream. As a result, by the time Babulal reaches Priya, Anjali's critical message has become completely mangled and incomprehensible: Anarkali has phoned, he tells her, to say it is important to eat ice cream. Madan Chopra rudely dismisses his employee on his daughter's behalf, leading Babulal to turn from the crowd (and toward the camera), PRONOUNCING TO HIMSELF OUT LOUD that sometimes he suspects his master of evildoing.

Meanwhile, Vicky has gone to the telephone and, feigning that he is Madan Chopra, is told by the unwitting girl of Vicky's resemblance to Seema's boyfriend. THE CAMERA LITERALLY FLIES IN on Vicky, the DRUMS AND VIOLINS FURTHER UNDERSCORING his AMPLIFIED DREAD at potential detection. Vicky asks Anjali to say nothing to the police out of respect for the Chopra family's honor. Instead, he asks where she resides, and promises to bring Priya to her. SOUND EFFECTS SWELL PIERCINGLY when Vicky hangs up—because there is Karan, standing at the doorway. But he requests, innocuously, to use the telephone.

What follows next is a comparatively brisk, plot-congested series of scenes—as if these were the indispensable *A-Kiss-Before-Dying* knots the scenario has to get through before reaching events emotively and dramatically more fulfilling (by Indian and oral standards). In cool sunglasses and with an icy demeanor, Vicky makes his way through the hotel's staff quarters and to Anjali's room. In a series of JARRING, INTENSE (AND PROGRESSIVELY SWEATY) CLOSE-UPS, Vicky chokes the young woman to death, then locates with DRAMATIC, ALMOST CAVALIER FLAIR from within her suitcase the photo album and incriminating picture of himself as Ajay. This, he rips into pieces and eats. Next, he drags the heavy (Anjali-containing) suitcase through the lobby—next brakes his automobile to a screeching halt on a bridge, from which he throws the suitcase into the water. WITHOUT ANY ADO, we cut immediately to that repeated AURAL AND VISUAL CLICHÉ of braking tires. It is Karan, who has come to the Chopras' estate to inform Priya that Anjali is missing. Priya questions Babulal about the alleged phone call the night of the engagement and, to his SIGNATURE PINK PANTHER MUSICAL THEME, he struggles PROTRACTEDLY AND FARCICALLY to remember, finally having to query whose engagement she's referring to before smacking his head doggedly in an attempt to recall.

Meanwhile, foretold by another automotive slam on the brakes, Vicky arrives; and when our privately apprehensive protagonist (dressed in pure and immaculate white) is informed of the reason for Karan's presence, Babulal's memory is jogged. He jumps for joy; he squeals with delight, recollecting now how someone stopped him at the party. What ensues is another ODD, CAPTAIN CLOUSEAU-ESQUE OMELET OF BUFFOON-ERY AND TENSION, of comedic and edgy sound effects, as Babulal scruti-nizes their faces for clues, Vicky's especially, only to find that his mem-ory has once again dimmed.

Prior to departing, Karan queries as to whom Vicky was speaking the night of his engagement. In order to deflect from the truth, Vicky pounces on Karan with a THEATRICALLY COCKY TONGUE LASHING. It was Madan Chopra's daughter married that day, not some ordinary per-son, he avers pompously, putting the lowly inspector in his place. Vicky's arrogant hostility is contritely accepted by Karan (and the au-dience), given THE GREATER STATUS, THE INFLATED IMPORTANCE OF THE FAMILY'S (AND BY EXTENSION HIS) PROFESSIONAL AND DOMESTIC UNI-VERSE. Privately—once he has indirectly dismissed Karan—Vicky coun-ters Priya's rekindled suspicion regarding Seema's case, contending that this is how the police make their money: off excavating the dead. All Vicky wants, he tells her before walking off, is for her grief to be erased. But the emphatic, discordant pounding of an electronic key-board as we hold on Priya's face ANNOUNCES BALDLY TO US that she has not given up.

The next time we see Vicky, he is in his plush corporate digs, waking from a nap in order to take an interoffice phone call from Madan Chopra. Chopra asks to see his future son-in-law straightaway, revealing to his assistants that he plans to give his future son-in-law power of attorney. Vicky stops in the bathroom in order first to wash up and discovers with horror upon wiping his face that he has lost one of his contact lenses. As he searches with CRAZED DESPERATION for the colored piece of plastic— and the scene, quite sincerely, is as HIGH-PITCHED AND AGONISTICALLY FILMED as even the preceding homicides, conspicuously AMPLIFYING BOTH THRILL AND DREAD—Chopra appears in search of his delayed em-ployee. But just before Chopra opens the bathroom door, Vicky locates the lens and manages to re-insert it over his telltale olive pupil.

When Vicky is told of Madan Chopra's imminent business trip to Europe and of Chopra's consequent delivery to Vicky of power of attor-ney, Vicky thoughtfully informs his boss of his need to get to the airport. In this way, Vicky is left alone in the office and so is given the opportu-nity to MAKE HIS FUTURE PROSPECTS FOR VENGEANCE ORALLY MANIFEST. In language that is HIGHLY APHORISTIC, HE DECLARES ALOUD that what he has been given is not only power of attorney, but a blank piece of paper on which he will now write Chopra's downfall. That Vicky here is in some way REPRISING A PERFORMANCE ALREADY DELIVERED by Madan Chopra (i.e., the "5%!" denunciation witnessed in Vicky's flashback) is of course no accident. What we have in such AN AURAL AND CINEMATIC REPRISE IS AN UPDATED "TAKING OF THE THRONE," SO TO SPEAK—THE USURPING OF ANOTHER'S POSITION THROUGH MANNERED, CEREMONIAL RE-ENACTMENT.

Building on this are two brief scenes: of Vicky reprimanding a dissenting employee, followed by his signing of documents that return the empire to ITS RIGHTFUL FAMILY. Immediately on the heels of this come several pithy scenes that drive the plot quickly forward and toward THE INEVITABLE TRYST WITH DESTINY (BETWEEN GOOD AND EVIL, BETWEEN COMMUNAL CORRECTNESS AND ITS AUTONOMOUSLY RAPACIOUS, ANTI-STATUS QUO ENEMY).

First, a man and his pet dog discover along Chowpatty Beach the tide-deposited suitcase containing Anjali. This is followed by Priya, in A BAROQUELY FAUX-FURNISHED DEN-CUM-PARLOR, hearing on the morning's television news that the body of Anjali has been discovered. (As in the Hollywood version, she drops her china mug in shock.) Next, she is on the phone with Karan, who is at the police station. She stresses that she wants neither Vicky nor her father to know of her continued interest in the case and arranges to meet Karan at a hotel café. Upon hanging up, she is noticeably startled by Vicky's sudden (coincidental) appearance, and he questions her about the phone call. She insists that she was only talking to a girlfriend, whom she is now on her way to see. But Priya's lie is exposed when, upon her departure from the room, Vicky notices her forgotten telephone index, splayed open to a page with a single entry: Karan's name (in Roman letters).

At the hotel café, Karan and Priya discuss what kind of killer they are dealing with. Someone extremely clever, Karan acknowledges, for the man ridded himself of the only two parties who could have possibly identified him.

When Priya returns home that night, Vicky is waiting in the yard (furrowing his brow, tapping his fingers). With DECLAMATORY PUFFINESS, he berates her for lying, for being so secretive. Offended, she throws it right back at him, telling him that it was his and her father's disinterest in the case that led to her being so secretive—especially given that Seema's killer is alive! She enters the house in tears, wholly upset by Vicky's insinuations that she might be amorously involved with Karan.

Vicky comes to her contritely, expressing with ROMANTIC FULSOME-NESS that his suspicions were born of his fear of losing her, and that she is not only his love, but also his *junoon*, his obsession. "I am yours, only yours," she assures him, to which he responds, "Then let tonight be dedicated to our love," propelling us thus toward a musical number. For suddenly we are with the young couple as they head into an ersatz (studio-set) nightclub (its walls papered in aluminum foil). Vicky joins the genie-costumed dancers on the stage, singing with mirth and abandon about his fiancée's arousing looks and her graceful walk; and soon Priya is up on the stage with him to sweat out the PLAYFUL, FRISKY DISCO DANCE NUMBER. Halfway through the song, however, unbeknownst to them, the *real* Vicky walks in (the one with whom Ajay once hitched a ride). While at the bar ordering a drink, the real Vicky espies his old school chum on the dance floor. And so, when the musical number is through, the real Vicky elatedly waves and shouts to his friend (who from hereon in we shall re-christen Ajay).

CYMBALS CLASH on the soundtrack, and the KEYBOARD MIMICS AJAY'S TREPIDATION as he sees his old pal and so tries to hustle Priya out of the club. But the real Vicky stops the fake Vicky en route. When the real Vicky becomes FLAGRANTLY ANGRY at Ajay's disavowal of his own identity, Priya explains that her partner's name is not Ajay, but Vicky Malhotra. To this, the friend grows even more inflamed, telling her that that's *his* name and conjecturing somewhat libidinously that it is for the sake of being with this girl that Ajay has given a false name. The affront to Priya enrages Ajay, and there is a BRIEF, NECK-CHOKING TUSSLE between the two men before others split them apart. When finally Ajay is able to lead Priya out of the club, they are pursued by OUT-OF-PROPORTION SHOUTS from the real Vicky of "I am Vicky Malhotra! He has forgotten our friendship!"

What follows are shots of each member of the engaged couple alone in contemplation. First, there is Priya, whose suspicions are made manifest to us not only through the image of her in her dark sitting room, fearfully mulling over the preceding events, but also by way of a MATERIALIZATION OF HER THOUGHTS IN THE FORM OF VOICEOVERS AND FLASHBACKS. There is a VISUAL RECAPITULATION of Ajay's explanation to her father about how his parents died in the Bangalore airplane crash, and then an aural one of the real Vicky Malhotra's vociferous contentions regarding his name. These are in a sense INFORMATIONAL BACKLOOPS that concretize for us what Priya is thinking, while also serving to KEEP US NARRATIVELY ON TRACK.

Next, we join Ajay in his darkened office, where he is unexpectedly visited by an invisible presence—that is, BY HIS OWN ECHOING VOICE (ON THE SOUNDTRACK) ACTUALLY *SPEAKING* TO HIM. It reminds him in STENTORIAN TONES that the acquisition of Priya's love is nothing more than a sad coincidence. Besides, once she discovers his past deeds, she will most certainly detest him. In this way, the voice admonishes that REVENGE IS HIS ONLY GOAL.

Now, we shift quickly to Ajay's revenge being played out in a BRISK, UNBRIDLED FLURRY OF SHOTS: a plane lands; a car screeches to the closed gates of the business empire; Chopra dashes out of the vehicle, his shock and horror at the takeover accentuated by rapid zooms in on the now Sharma-oriented business banner and bronze plaque. "Vicky!" he bellows in rage; and with that we are transported inside, to Ajay who,

sporting cool sunglasses, spins around once in the ICONIC CEO chair—
but around again, and again, and again because THE ACTION IS DISJOINT-
EDLY REPEATED FOUR TIMES IN A SERIES OF ZOOMS-IN, TRACKS, AND TILTS.

Chopra enters and vociferously accosts Ajay, who maintains a com-
posure that is, for lack of a better term, CARTOONISHLY SUPERCILIOUS.
When Chopra demands whom Ajay has betrayed him for, Ajay gives an
extended cackle. He informs his former boss that birds can talk about
flying, but not men like Chopra, who are without feathers.

Indeed, from hereon in, the dialogue will manifest A HIGH RELIANCE
ON PROVERBS, the consequence being that the dialogic tone becomes
more ORACULAR AND TRIUMPHAL. This is by no means an idiosyncrasy of
Baazigar; the same is true of virtually every contemporaneous *masala*
films. Morally inscribed truths and the absolutist discrimination between right and wrong—between those who protect community relations and those who destroy community relations—are best packaged
and intellectually digested in the form of PROVERBS. So, with regularity,
Bombay films take on this attribute as they near resolution.

Not only do such proverbs allow for the information to be more easily etched into the consciousness of the audience, though; by the very
dint of proverbs being communal in nature, the segue into such rhetoric
serves as well to BIND AUDIENCE MEMBERS AS A GROUP AND TO THEIR
COMMON PAST. The ethical and moral interplay between Ajay and
Madan Chopra becomes much more of a shared event, "modulated into
group evaluation," as Ong (1982) states, "and then handled in terms of
expected reactions from others" (p. 55).

Ajay reminds Chopra of their competition at the speedway a year
ago, disclosing that his goal that day was not a racing trophy, but the
eventual reclamation of the CEO chair. "Time has come to a standstill,"
he declares. "EVERYTHING IS REPEATING AS IT DID 15 YEARS BEFORE." And
so Ajay announces that he is the son of Viswanath Sharma.

To great CLASHING AND PULSATING SOUND EFFECTS, Ajay removes his
sunglasses, the camera zooming in tightly to reveal his fair eyes. A COPI-
OUS DISPLAY OF EMOTION follows on Ajay's part, with him facilely vacil-
lating during his speech from melodramatic weeping to venomous
anger. First, with tears in his eyes, Ajay reminds Madan Chopra of the
dissolute way Chopra treated Ajay's mother all those years ago. Ajay
holds up his hands, remarking of the life of struggle that ensued. Then,
with wrath, he announces that today the Chopra name has been
stamped out with his own. He grabs his adversary's collar, proclaiming
spitefully (and with proverbial sway), "This time your condition is
handicapped. You are like a man who needs a crutch with which to
walk, but has no hands." Thereupon Ajay's superciliousness returns,
and with a smug smile, he snaps his fingers and orders Madan Chopra
out of his office.

Priya, meanwhile, is at the Indian Airlines office, and we join her as she requests from a computer operator the address of the Malhotras who died in the Bangalore air crash. Immediately, she is on the steps of said home, ringing the doorbell; and of course it is the *real* Vicky Malhotra who answers. The aggressive chap tells her that now she knows who the real Vicky is. In slighted tones, he castigates Ajay for having insulted him publicly, for having lied to an old friend to whom Ajay should have felt obligated. After all, in childhood Vicky had helped Ajay with all his schoolwork. "He is a liar!" the real Vicky finally barks, and tells Priya that if she doesn't believe him, she should go visit Ajay's mother.

Of course that is precisely what Priya does. She exits her car in front of the Sharmas' home. Significantly, THIS HOME IS LOCATED OUTSIDE THE CITY, REMOVED FROM ANY URBAN LANDSCAPE (although this fact was not visually patent in the movie's opening scenes). Now we see that it is a home surrounded by wilderness, by jungle. In this way, the rest of the film (for we will not leave these environs, except via flashback) is EXTRACTED FROM ANY MEASURABLE PRESENT. The story enters A REALM THAT IS SOMEWHAT MYTHIC AND TIMELESS.

Priya enters the house in search of Mrs. Sharma only to find herself face to face with a photograph of Ajay. She searches about the room, locating the newspaper that we witnessed previously in a flashback, and which announces (in Hindi) Chopra's long ago usurping of the group of companies; she finds a poster of a sports car; she opens a suitcase to discover pictures of Ajay and his mother, of their respective fathers, and even of herself and her sister as kids. And then she comes upon the heart-shaped locket containing Ajay and Seema's pictures.

Violins on the soundtrack amplify her despair, as tears roll down her cheeks. When she stands, she notices Ajay—who has appeared almost artistically via his reflection, which merges with the poster of himself on the wall. Priya turns on him angrily, demanding what name she should call him, APHORISTICALLY DECLARING that changing one's name doesn't change the human or one's face. In an intensely ORATORICAL DELIVERY, she lambastes him for killing his sister and feigning love, for turning on her father who did so much for him.

Now, it is he who is enraged, and with EQUAL AMPLITUDE AND GREATER FLATULENCE, he protests that the wealth belongs rightfully to him, that he knows where her father really comes from. And so Ajay chronicles for Priya the vile conduct of her father and the heartless victimization of the benevolent Sharma clan. He tells of his family being forced out onto the street, and of witnessing as an innocent child his own good mother accosted by Madan Chopra. "You have only seen the crown on his head," he declares to Priya APHORISTICALLY, "Look under the thief's sleeve and you will find blood." And in between all this, there are shots of Priya, with commiserative tears streaming liberally down her

face. With Ajay's admission that "Even now I remember the night of your
father's atrocious blows," we FLASH BACK to 15 years ago . . .

. . . Like the exterior locale of the scene that precedes it, the flashback that
follows is also situated in A SPACE THAT IS ALMOST LIMINAL, A META-
PHORIC ADJOINING OF "15 YEARS AGO" TO MYTH. Furthermore, there are
FEW MATERIAL MARKERS OF THE CONTEMPORARY ERA during the sequence, as if to accentuate the very preserved permanence of ideals: of
duty, of sacrifice. This, in other words, is THE ARENA OF "THAT WHICH
HAS ALWAYS BEEN AND WILL ALWAYS CONTINUE TO BE." And here "that" is
played with an extremely COMPRESSED, THICK, ALMOST GLUTINOUS LEVEL
OF MELODRAMA (at least to literate minds unaccustomed to such films).

In the dark, one-room shack that, thanks to Madan Chopra's business manipulations, is now the Sharmas' pathetic home, Ajay and his
mother inspect Ajay's tiny sister, whose body is limp and sick with
fever. Mr. Sharma rises from his cot, saying he will go get medicine.
Mrs. Sharma reminds her husband that, as per the doctor's orders, he
requires rest. But Mr. Sharma laments PROVERBIALLY that for the man
who has so many problems as he does, rest can only be an affliction. As
he heads out the door (and into a violent downpour), Mrs. Sharma un-
does her wedding *mangalsutra* from around her neck, depositing it in
his hands. Take this, she says, because it will pay for our daughter's
medicine. From this, we cut to Ajay (still clasping his ill sister) solemnly
watching his parents, the sad necessity of his mother's sacrificial act
burning into his memory.

Mr. Sharma exits into the deluge and, within a matter of seconds,
he is clenching at his heart and dropping to the ground. A distraught
Mrs. Sharma runs after him, followed by Ajay still carrying the infant.
As the rain beats down on the sinister, evacuated streets, Mrs. Sharma
places her husband on a long wooden pushcart. She wheels him back
toward the shack, but a bump results in his sliding off. She tries to lift
him, but it is too late. His releasing of the *mangalsutra* signals that he is
already dead. Ajay who is standing nearby suddenly calls out "Ma?"
because the baby in his arms has also died. FOUR TIMES, THEN, THE CAM-
ERA ZOOMS IN on Mrs. Sharma cradling her dead husband, staring at
her dead baby. And then the camera turns to Ajay, freezing on his van-
quished expression.

What follows are scenes equally girdled by darkness, PROJECTED
THUS AS PART OF A MYTHIC NETHERWORLD—as the "horror" of the story.
We see the funeral procession for Viswanath Sharma, which includes
Ajay carrying his sister's shrouded corpse. Ajay walks past a miniature
shrine to Shiva, and the white marble icon of the god is brightly lit, almost incandescent against the darkness. With an implacable need for
answers, Ajay stares at the deity, at THAT GREATER FORCE THAT HAS FOR
GENERATIONS BOUND THE COLLECTIVE. Then he continues along with the
procession.[6]

---

6. This could be read as Ajay's turning his back on faith and rejecting any resigned expectation that revenge will be appropriately exacted by and through the gods. However,

With his father's lit funeral pyre in the background, Ajay buries his sister (infants are buried, not cremated, according to Hindu custom), weeping profusely as he performs this last rite . . .

. . . We EXIT THE FLASHBACK, returning to (grown) Ajay's mien, and to his eyes particularly, which billow with tears. He tells Priya in a wavering, sob-stifled voice that he carries his father's pyre and his sister's grave in his eyes, as well as a profound sadness. "You've only been pricked with a thorn," he alleges with PROVERBIAL ACUITY. "I have been wounded with a complete trident." As proof of his great unhealable wounds, Ajay takes Priya into the adjacent room, where he kneels down beside his mother, touching her face and waking her. "This is my Ma," he says, acknowledging that she does not always remember him, that consequently he's lived his life without ever receiving her love.

At this, Priya's tears of pity for her betrothed become more profuse. To be sure, there is NO AMBIGUITY here as to with whom Priya's emotional allegiances lie, whether her father or her lover. Her sympathies rest quite blatantly (as do the audience's) with Ajay. And as if to highlight this, there is suddenly the rattle of approaching car engines, before roughly we cut to cars screeching outside, followed by a messy web of feet exiting the vehicles and marching up to the bungalow.

Ajay rises from his mother's side and enters the adjoining room—just as Madan Chopra, encircled by seven *goondas*, enters and abruptly shoots Ajay in the shoulder. Ajay PITCHES DRAMATICALLY THROUGH THE AIR, slamming against the wall, then onto his face. And so, we begin A VERY SPIRITED 12-MINUTE SHOWDOWN OF GROSS PHYSICAL VIOLENCE between Ajay, Madan Chopra, and Chopra's posse, with even Mrs. Sharma briefly inserting herself for a momentary plea of justice.

When Ajay lands wounded on the floor, victim to Madan Chopra's impromptu resorting to WEAPONRY AND FULL-FLEDGED CARICATURED INSIDIOUSNESS, Chopra barks menacingly at his daughter to move away from Ajay, whom he calls a thief. But Priya insists with EQUAL AURAL ARDOR that it is her own father, not Ajay, who is the liar and thief. For this, she receives a VICIOUS AND RESOUNDING SLAP ACROSS THE FACE, her father next instructing the thugs to take her outside. "Chopra!" comes a RESOUNDING, WARLIKE CRY from Ajay, and at hearing Madan Chopra's name, Mrs. Sharma begins to regain her memory—all while A BLOODY FIST-FEST PROGRESSES—with the thugs slamming Ajay with full-blown kicks to the gut—blood soaking his white business shirt—Ajay GRIPPING HIS WOUNDED ARM LIKE A COURAGEOUS MARTYR.

Blood pours liberally from his mouth, as he endures the agony of heels being thrust into his chest, his face, and lastly into his bleeding

---

that later HE *TAKES ON* THE PERSONA OF A GOD indubitably confirms his faith in the supernatural power.

shoulder. When Chopra pronounces fierily that the wealth is his, a horrified look crosses Mrs. Sharma's face, and she FLASHES BACK to that time in his office when Chopra tried to touch her and in response she whacked him across the face. With that, we return to the present—and to a close up of her eyes—as sentience returns and she recalls who Chopra is.

She approaches Chopra, but then sees her son IMMERSED IN BLOWS from the *goondas*. With astounding, SUDDEN, SUPERHUMAN STRENGTH, Mrs. Sharma manages to cast the three or four henchmen who are attacking him to the wayside. "Madan Chopra! How could you dare hurt my son?" she demands, clutching Ajay in her arms.

At Chopra's threatening demand for his property and his promise to tear Ajay to pieces should Ajay refuse, Mrs. Sharma advances toward Chopra. With PROVERBIAL RESONANCE, she informs him that "A mother picks a future for her son, not the pieces of his body." Mrs. Sharma shakes Chopra by the collar, promising shrilly that she will make pieces of his body should he touch her son. Crudely Madan Chopra thrusts her away, and she FALLS WITH SLOW-MOTION GRACELESSNESS INTO A FREESTANDING PIECE OF GLASS.

"Ma . . . Ma . . . !" Ajay groans with childlike anguish, cradling his injured mother. And then, at the sight of the blood that is now flowing from her wounds, at a careful inspection of the viscous sap smearing his fingers, Ajay's fury incrementally and no doubt gratifyingly (for the spectator) grows. For, as we witnessed in a scene much earlier, the sight of red staining the fingers initiates a viewer's anticipation of what is inevitably to come. Then again, this is his *mother's* blood that has been drawn, not his own—which induces an even more charged scenario. LIKE THE VERBALIZING OF AN OATH, SUCH A SCENE TAKES ON A SPECIAL ICONOGRAPHIC SACREDNESS.

And so, slowly, Ajay stands; he raises one fist in a revenge-will-be-mine gesture; his lower lip quivers wrathfully. A BREEZE APPEARS OUT OF NOWHERE, blowing his hair (and only his) from his face; and the voice that emerges from his throat is deep, reverberating and unearthly, in essence a voice not his own alone. It is, thanks to the technical aid of a post-production sound studio, the VOICE OF THE GODS SPEAKING THROUGH HIM, with him, their intentions commingling with his own. He has taken on, or rather been SUFFUSED WITH, THE POWER OF A DEIFIC FIERCE ASPECT, inadvertently summoned by the horrific transgression (and indeed Hindi film CLICHÉ) of an enemy having drawn the blood of one's own family members. And in a declaration that is less proverbial than PROPHETIC, LINKING HIM THUS TO HIS ANCESTORS, TO THE IDEA OF LINEAGE, AND HENCE TO GOD AND TO THE SACRED, Ajay intones, "Fifteen years ago, the blood was flowing from my mother's tears. Now, you have opened the floodgates. Now there will be a flood."

With a NEWFOUND SUPERHUMAN STRENGTH, and blood gushing from his mouth, Ajay leaps through the air and onto his foe, catapulting them both out of the house and onto the porch. Fists and bodies (in "appealing" close-up) glide ominously through the air (for everything now is captured with SLOW-MOTION GUSTO), as Ajay is forced into battling Chopra between sadistic bouts with the assorted ruffians who intervene. Ajay manages to throw one of them into a mirror, once, twice, the camera pausing delectably on the face of Ajay's victim to take in the large shards of mirror piercing his flesh.

The punches continue. The BODIES SOAR IN AND OUT OF FRAME, as Ajay makes his way back to Chopra, kicking his adversary with RIGID KUNG-FU BLOWS, holding his own wounded arm so that he can direct its punches effectively at Chopra, and then, afterward, knock unconscious an intervening hood.

Ajay picks up a large fish tank and releases it over the hood's supine body (all still in slow motion). The tank smashes into bits over the man's face, and again we are given a privileged close-up of the triangular pieces of glass wedging into the man's fleshy countenance. With Chopra's henchmen momentarily defeated through a tad more battering and one more choking scene, Ajay now concentrates his efforts on Chopra.

Ajay drags his opponent out into the yard, where an AURAL CLICHÉ OF HOWLING WIND AMPLIFIES, INDEED SANCTIFIES, THE EXECUTION OF A WILD AND HOLY WRATH. Ajay thrusts Chopra's head through a car window and then drags him across the ground, pausing momentarily to thrash and brutally twist with an explosive crack the neck of a *goonda* who springs on him unexpectedly. When Chopra lunges desperately for a gun he's spotted on the ground, Ajay SOARS WITH BRUCE LEE AGILITY INTO THE AIR, his foot landing on Chopra's arm, which is caught between the pickets of a fence. Chopra cries out in pain as his elbow snaps, his forearm bending 90 degrees backward—the wrong way—behind him. Ajay clutches Chopra's head, castigating him fiercely, "That was the hand you raised to my mother!" A large thug flies out of the house, ambushing Ajay with a wide cutlass, but Ajay manages to thrust the weapon into the assailant's own belly. Ajay pulls the blade out, with the thug falling backward into a shed, which topples over him. With ANOTHER WAR CRY OF HIS NEMESIS' NAME WHILE BRANDISHING THE BLOODY DAGGER in the air, Ajay leaps across a series of parked cars and runs down the pathway along which Chopra has escaped.

We cut from pursuer to pursued as nine electronic keyboard notes are pounded over and over, and the chase moves deeper and deeper into the jungle, the shots a blur of emerald green foliage and Ajay's cherry red (bloody) shirt.

Meanwhile, Karan, escorted by Priya, drives up to the house in Karan's police jeep. Priya hastens to Mrs. Sharma's side, for the disoriented woman is making her way feebly along the porch, calling for her son. But Ajay is nowhere near, the jungle path having led him into the OVERGROWN RUINS OF AN ANCIENT FORT.

The lush primevalness of this setting is embellished by the piercing sounds of chattering monkeys, and the echoing resonance of our protagonist's summoning of Chopra. Here, then, is our full immersion into a UNIVERSE WHERE THE PRESENT IS TELESCOPED WITH THE ETERNAL, where the past is not a historical has-been, but part and parcel of the continuing present. Indeed, the hero's noble display of familial loyalty (or duty or revenge) is highlighted as such, perhaps even becomes so, because it occurs in environs that signal a continuity with the past, and hence A PRESERVATION OF THE COMMUNAL SELF. Through this righteous, motivated hero (even if his methods are wrong), it is in effect WE WHO ARE BEING TELESCOPED TOGETHER WITH COMMUNITY AND GOD. For, we do not exist independently, but rather as a collective, and as such seek in the *masala* film to be reconstituted into a communal subjectivity—one that is sanctified by, if not inclusive of, the Supreme. Thus *Baazigar*, in culminating in a mythically charged and familiar setting, becomes for us a CONTINUATION OF THE MYRIAD STORIES THAT PRECEDED IT. We are witnessing, after all, A MOMENTOUS BATTLE between Fealty and Greed, between Duty to one's family (to one's ancestors) and a Rebuff of the same, which has been handed down through the ages, through tales as ancient (and alive) as the *Mahabharata*. So, even though a movie may allude frankly to its narrative predecessors, it is also in this way coterminous with such tales.

But, alas, because of our hero's warped methods, which are not part and parcel of the existing social structure, Ajay is doomed. Although his deeper mission may be to return what is rightfully his to his own, to exterminate the villain responsible for severing the Sharmas' generational ties (via a mother who does not remember her son), his methods have rendered him in effect unreconstitutable. THERE IS NO PLACE FOR HIM IN THE TRADITIONAL ORDER THAT (BECAUSE OF THE NEEDS OF ORALITY) MUST BE RESTORED BY THE MOVIE'S END. Hence, it is inevitable that he be "sacrificed." But of course Chopra, too, must be destroyed, for there is similarly no place for him.

But Ajay is unable to find Chopra in the derelict bones of the ancient fort, and he collapses to the ground, frustrated, angry, and exhausted. From a stronghold wall above, we see Chopra's face appear, looking smugly down on his opponent—until drops of his blood land on Ajay's extended arm, giving Madan Chopra's whereabouts away.

Ajay sprints up the fort stairs after Chopra (to the uniform electronic motif), just as Karan, Mrs. Sharma, and Priya appear below in a jeep.

Ajay chases his nemesis along a parapet and finally, soaring through the air, onto the roof of an enclosed turret. His archenemy finally cornered, Ajay raises his scarlet-stained cutlass, ready to slice off Chopra's head. But Karan shouts out from the grounds below, "Stop! In the name of your Mother!"

The wind wails, and monkeys screech from their invisible perches, as the camera frames with a SPAGHETTI-WESTERN FLAVOR both Ajay's deliberating expression and Chopra's on-tenterhooks scowl. And then, in slow motion, blood-soaked Ajay casts away the weapon and walks off.

Immediately, and with enterprising depravity, Chopra pulls out a long, stiff metal rod (from somewhere unclear) and PLUNGES IT THROUGH AJAY'S GUT. Ajay groans and moans in amplified agony (thanks to the art of dubbing), before finally rearing his head to take in Chopra's demonic expression and his equally demonic laugh, which echoes hyena-like on the soundtrack.

But then Ajay also begins to laugh—a laugh of matching MISPLACED HYSTERIA AND OTHERWORLDLINESS. Chopra falters, worriedly—and for good reason; for, Ajay charges now straight into his nemesis, thrusting the rod impaled in his stomach straight into Chopra's own. The skewered business rivals tumble off the rooftop and plunge to the earth below. Ajay manages to extricate himself from his foe, who thereafter dies.

CRYING OUT FOR HIS "MA" (WHOSE NAME HE WILL REPEAT 22 TIMES in this final encounter), Ajay runs his half-broken body over to her, collapsing in her arms. She holds him in her lap as Karan and Priya stand by, watching with an admixture of horror and pathos. With the tone and sentiment of a dim-witted child—in a kind of baby talk, in fact—Ajay caresses his mother's face and announces that he has gotten back what was theirs; HE HAS "ENDED THE STORM" that rendered them helpless, thereby ending her difficulties. To this, Mrs. Sharma replies, "What can be more difficult for a mother than to hold in her lap her wounded son for whom she can do nothing?" The MELODRAMATIC AND OVERLY RIPE INTERACTION continues with Ajay revealing between his final painful gasps that, for the first time in many years, he finds it soothing to be in her embrace.

"Envelop me in your arms," Ajay implores her. "I've been yearning for your love since childhood." She holds him tightly to her and, in close-up, we witness our dying hero calmly declare, "Now I can sleep peacefully. I can sleep peacefully." "Yes, sleep in my lap," she urges him, only to realize moments later that he is gone.

Gently, as Ajay's mother intones her son's name and wipes his lifeless face with her sari, Priya approaches, kneeling beside her dead fiancé and fighting sobs. With TRANSPARENT INTENTION, strains of a song heard earlier fill the soundtrack: "Don't think I am a wandering cloud," Ajay croons, "Your name has been engraved on my heart"—all while the camera pulls out from the despairing scene.

Despairing, perhaps, but also desired. The spectator is, after all, permitted departure from the theatre and the cinematic experience WITH-OUT ANY RESIDUAL ANXIETY, FREE OF ANY MORAL QUANDARY OR ETHICAL DILEMMA that might arise were our protagonist Ajay to live. For what would we do with such a righteous (but malfeasant) individual were he still to be haunting the metaphoric streets of our minds? Would we in all likelihood be able to admire him? Would we be able to reconcile our admiration of his retributive drives with his less savory murderous impulses? Do we need a Comeuppance Imperative to ensure that our collective moral fiber is not ripped asunder?

Our hero has transgressed in a way that cannot be socially forgiven and so, ultimately, he must be exterminated. In this way, we as viewers, who may feel similar impulses for retribution, for destroying our enemies, do not leave the theatre intent on spirited imitation. Ajay has done it for us—and within the safe confines of a celluloid universe where RE-TURN TO THE TRADITIONAL ORDER IS A *SINE QUA NON*. Scholars and critics of the Hindi popular film habitually lambaste the industry for buttressing the status quo in this way, for purposely generating a docile and politically sedentary viewing body through the provision of comfortable, resolutionary endings; but, of course the justification for such endings may go deeper and be more ancient than that. For in both Hindi film and orally transmitted narrative, we must leave our story with a sense of THE EXISTING SOCIAL STRUCTURE RESTORED AND INTACT. Although our hearts may be pulled and swayed by an anti-hero, it is inevitably the Ajays of the world who must die, while the Karans of the world persist. The film's resolution must be MORALLY SEAMLESS. After all, if as communal individuals and the landlords of the collective soul, we live in a world that is not the right one, what then?

Appendix B

Titanic as American Orally Inflected Cinema Nonpareil

Although more linear (not to mention, more costly) than the standard Hindi popular film, James Cameron's *Titanic* (1997) also is American orally inflected cinema nonpareil. Perhaps this explains why, despite winning the Academy Award for Best Picture, the film has been frequently dismissed, even excoriated, by academic intellectuals. Consider the acerbic tone of the following scholarly appraisal (I quote it here at length because of the way it simultaneously offers a refresher on the plot):

> Cameron's *Titanic* offers spectacle in the place of substance and cynically attempts to capture the audience's attention through the use of an epistemic Romeo and Juliet "star cross'd lovers" conceit. . . . *Titanic* strives to live up to its title, and indeed, in budget, length (195 minutes), and sheer aural/visual spectacle, it certainly does so, but Cameron simultaneously reduces the human element of tragedy to a series of schematic caricatures. Jack is entirely true and brave; Rose is a misunderstood rich girl who adores Picasso and Monet; Cal is a ruthless, sneering villain, straight out of a Victorian melodrama. The music cues relentlessly attempt to manipulate our emotions (now you should cry; now you're scared), the dialogue is astonishingly wooden (when the Titanic first hits the iceberg, Jack declares solemnly, "This is bad"), and every other character in the film (with the possible exception of Kathy Bates as Molly Brown) is marginalized by a foredoomed attempt to focus our attentions solely on the young lovers, to the expense of all other passengers. (Dixon, 1999, pp. 3–4)

Even critics' reviews from the period, says Matthew Bernstein (1999), make clear that "*Titanic*'s popularity arose not from its aesthetic coherence but, in part, from the sheer diversity of its elements" (p. 15). But were the elements really that diverse? Bernstein and the other essayists represented in *Titanic: Anatomy of a Blockbuster,* claim so, pointing to what the anthology's editors handily summarize as the film's "narrative framing device linking the past and the present, the interpenetration of a cross-class romance in a disaster picture, the star appeal of Leonardo Di-Caprio, James Cameron's visual style, and the nostalgic appeal of the film's evocation of classic Hollywood" (Sandler & Studlar, 1999, p. 7). These will surely sound familiar to readers now cognizant of the oral norms of storytelling—and not just as reflective of an incoherent assemblage of traits, but as a *pattern* with its own particular coherency.

Vivian Sobchack (1999) expands on the movie's critical reception, making note of the frequent attacks *Titanic* garnered for its "superficial historicism, its ludicrous dialogue, and over-the-top melodrama" (p. 191). She cites these as a prelude to theorizing that the film's emotional force is located in its "absolutely crucial *frame story*, which . . . narratively encircles the irreversibility of the historical past" (p. 191). (Flashbacks, in other words.) Furthermore, the film's potency, she argues, derives from its "*resonant imagery,* which functions as a quite literal 'medium of exchange' between the film's two temporal registers of present and past and its two spatial registers of vast and small" (p. 191). (In other words, an amplified and unambiguous plenitude.) Through these, she continues, *Titanic* is able to provide a type of hermetic shelter, inside which a spectator can experience a historically "authentic experience" as filtered through *bathos* (p. 191). (Or melodrama, as it is sometimes termed.) What her analysis inadvertently underscores, in other words—especially when read in light of *Titanic*'s "emotional clarity . . . undampened by the murky ambivalence of contemporary irony"; its "*ahistorical* form of poesis"; and its use of the gigantic as a metaphor for 'the abstract authority of the state' and 'the collective, public life'"[1] (pp. 191, 195–196, 202)—is the extent to which the film is tied to the oral episteme of visual narrative.

Add to these the manner in which our alliances in the film are forged straightaway: We root for (free, virtuous) Jack and (imprisoned, thoughtful) Rose and snub Rose's (elitist, shrewd, conniving) fiancé and her (avaricious) mother. That our convictions can be set in stone right from the start and never stray attests to the film's general lack of psychological complexity. These characters are flat, even frontal—much like the film's thematic conflicts, which are obvious and unsubtle, playing as they do "on the basic opposition between 'decadence' and 'over-civiliza-

---

1. This she borrows from Susan Stewart (1984).

tion'" and between the notion of free spirit as versus the society that im-
prisons" (G. King, 2000, p. 57). Additionally, there is the lavish world of
wealth ("We are royalty," as one character proclaims with oral straight-
forwardness), which is pitted against the impecunious (but earthy
singing and dancing) world of the peasants who bunk in the ship's dark
belly. In the end, it is the common man who will be celebrated (Jack is a
martyr; Rose forgoes her patrician lifestyle), but of course it has all been
accomplished *through* elegance and extravagance, for that makes the
story memorable—as in, unforgettable.

The fact that the entire tale of the ship's sinking is told in a narrated
flashback establishes a sense of community, Sobchack (1999) sagaciously
suggests (although without awareness of this norm's oral etiology). She
adds that, through the "bathyspheric nature" of its framing, the film conveniently provides an *erasure* of the historical past in deference to a temporally and spatially ahistorical world (p. 202). One should not forget
that, from an orality perspective, such a diachronic conflation also gives
important emphasis to the *continuity between the generations*. For, although Rose's mother may be obsessed with assets and nasty to the
point of deserving (and hence receiving) rejection, the binding ancestral
presence (i.e., that which reflects the communal self carried through
time) is underscored by the elderly Rose, who is narrating the entire
story of the *Titanic*'s tragic journey—and with her faithful grand-niece
permanently by her side, no less. In this way, the past is linked to the
present: *this* time to *that* time; who we are *now* to what we *have been*. The
entire story is thus "told," a repetition of events concerned less with
what's going to happen unbeknownst to us than with how an already
known calamity of the ship's going down is going to be dramatically,
even melodramatically, *re-enacted*.

Could it be only accidental that the year of its release *Titanic* was the
No. 1 film in India? One could find many jocular assertions on the Inter-
net that *Titanic* was in fact a Hindi film in Western wear. But of course its
epical excess and operation as a "public collection" (Sobchack, 1999) are
what made the film as accessible in India as in the United States—and
in Japan and Brazil, and even in Afghanistan, where it lived a popular
bootlegged existence (Farrell, 2001).

Bibliography

Acland, Charles R. *Screen Traffic: Movies, Multiplexes, and Global Culture*. Durham: Duke University Press, 2003.

Aiyar, Shankkar and Sandeep Unnithan. "The World's a Stage." *India Today International*. 13 January 2003: 40–42.

Altman, Rick. "Cinema and Genre." *The Oxford History of World Cinema*. Ed. Geoffrey Nowell-Smith. Oxford: Oxford University Press, 1996: 276–285.

Anderson, Benedict. *Imagined Communities: Reflections on the Origin and Spread of Nationalism*. London: Verso, 1991.

Andrew, Dudley. *Concepts in Film Theory*. Oxford: Oxford University Press, 1984a.

———. *Film in the Aura of Art*. Princeton: Princeton University Press, 1984b.

Appadurai, Arjun and Carol A. Breckenridge. "Why Public Culture?" *Public Culture* 1 (1988): 5–9.

Aristotle. *The Poetics*. Trans. Gerald F. Else. Ann Arbor: University of Michigan Press, 1967.

Armbrust, Walter. *Mass Culture and Modernism in Egypt*. Cambridge: Cambridge University Press, 1996.

Armes, Roy. *Third World Film Making and the West*. Berkeley: University of California Press, 1987.

Arroyo, José, ed. *Action/Spectacle Cinema: A Sight and Sound Reader*. London: BFI Publishing, 2000.

Aumont, Jacques, Alain Bergala, Michel Marie, and Marc Vernet. *Aesthetics of Film*. Trans. Richard Neupert. Austin: University of Texas Press, 1992.

Baazigar. Dir. Abbas Burmawalla and Mastan Burmawalla. Perf. Shahrukh Khan, Kajol. Eros. 1993. Film.

215

Balides, Constance. "Immersion in the Virtual Ornament: Contemporary 'Movie Ride' Films." *Rethinking Media Change: The Aesthetics of Transition*. Eds. David Thorburn and Henry Jenkins. Cambridge, MA: MIT Press, 2003: 315–336.

Banerjea, Koushik. "'Fight Club': Aesthetics, Hybridization and the Construction of Rogue Masculinities in *Sholay* and *Deewar*." *Bollyworld: Popular Indian Cinema through a Transnational Lens*. Eds. Raminder Kaur and Ajay J. Sinha. New Delhi: Sage, 2005: 163–185.

Barthes, Roland. *The Pleasure of the Text*. New York: Farrar, Strauss & Giroux, 1975.

Bazin, André. "An Aesthetic of Reality: Neorealism (Cinematic Realism and the Italian School of the Liberation)." *Post-War Cinema and Modernity*. Eds. John Orr and Olga Taxidou. New York: New York University Press, 2001: 5–12.

———. *What is Cinema?* Vol. I. Trans. Hugh Gray. Berkeley: University of California Press, 1967.

———. "From *What Is Cinema?*" (Vol. 2). In *Film Theory and Criticism*. 5th ed. Eds. Leo Braudy and Marshall Cohen. Oxford: Oxford University Press, 1999: 195–211.

Bernstein, Matthew. "'Floating Triumphantly': The American Critics on *Titanic*." *Titanic: Anatomy of a Blockbuster*. Eds. Kevin S. Sandler and Gaylyn Studlar. New Brunswick: Rutgers University Press, 1999: 14–28.

Bhattacharya, Mihir. "He Was Everyman's Film-Maker." *The Hindu* 23.18 (2006). www.hinduonnet.com.

Bhowmik, Someswar. "From Coercion to Power Relations: Film Censorship in Post-Colonial India." *Economic and Political Weekly*. July 26, 2003: 3148–3152.

———. "Politics of Film Censorship: Limits of Tolerance." *Economic and Political Weekly*. August 31, 2002: 3574–3577.

Binford, Mira Reym. "Innovation and Imitation in the Contemporary Indian Cinema." *Cinema and Cultural Identity: Reflections on Films from Japan, India, and China*. Ed. Wimal Dissanayake. Lanham: University Press of America, 1988: 77–92.

Birkerts, Sven. *The Gutenberg Elegies: The Fate of Reading in an Electronic Age*. Boston: Faber and Faber, 1994.

Bloom, Benjamin S., ed. *Taxonomy of Educational Objectives: The Classification of Educational Goals, Handbook I, The Cognitive Domain*. New York: Longmans, Green, 1956.

Bloom, Harold. The *Anxiety of Influence: A Theory of Poetry*. New York: Oxford University Press, 1997.

———. *The Western Canon: The Books and Schools of the Ages*. New York: Harcourt, Brace, 1994.

Bogue, Ronald. *Deleuze on Cinema*. New York: Routledge, 2003.

Bolter, Jay David. *Writing Space: The Computer, Hypertext, and the History of Writing*. Hillsdale, NJ: Lawrence Erlbaum, 1991.

Bordwell, David. *Making Meaning: Inference and Rhetoric in the Interpretation of Cinema*. Cambridge, MA: Harvard University Press, 1989.

———. *Narration in the Fiction Film*. Madison: University of Wisconsin Press, 1985.

———. *Planet Hong Kong: Popular Cinema and the Art of Entertainment*. Cambridge: Harvard University Press, 2000.

——— and Noël Carroll, eds. *Post-Theory: Reconstructing Film Studies*. Madison: The University of Wisconsin Press, 1996.

Bourdieu, Pierre. *Distinction: A Social Critique of the Judgement of Taste*. Trans. Richard Nice. Cambridge, MA: Harvard University Press, 1984.

———. *The Field of Cultural Production: Essays on Art and Literature*. Ed. Randal Johnson. New York: Columbia University Press, 1993.

Branigan, Edward. *Narrative Comprehension and the Fiction Film*. London: Routledge, 1992.

Brecht, Bertolt. *Brecht on Theatre: The Development of an Aesthetic*. Trans. John Willett. London: Methuen & Co., 1964.

Brooks, Peter. *The Melodramatic Imagination: Balzac, Henry James, Melodrama, and the Mode of Excess*. New York: Columbia University Press, 1985.

Calinescu, Matei. "Orality in Literacy: Some Historical Paradoxes of Reading." *Yale Journal of Criticism* 6.2 (1993): 175–190.

"Cannes Is Not My Goal." *The Hindu*. April 12, 2002. 29 October 2006. www.hindu.com.

Carpenter, Edmund. *Oh, What a Blow That Phantom Gave Me!* New York: Holt, Rinehart and Winston, 1972.

Carroll, Noël. *Mystifying Movies: Fads & Fallacies in Contemporary Film Theory*. New York: Columbia University Press, 1988.

———. *A Philosophy of Mass Art*. Oxford: Clarendon Press, 1998.

Chakravarty, Sumita S. *National Identity in Indian Popular Cinema, 1947–1987*. Delhi: Oxford University Press, 1996.

Chatman, Seymour. *Story and Discourse: Narrative Structure in Fiction and Film*. Ithaca: Cornell University Press, 1978.

Chatterjee, Partha. "The End." *Hard News*. November 29, 2006. www.hardnewsmedia.com.

Cheng, Khoo Gaik. *Reclaiming Adat: Contemporary Malaysian Film and Literature*. Vancouver: University of British Columbia, 2006.

Chion, Michel. *The Voice in the Cinema*. Ed. and Trans. Claudia Gorbman. New York: Columbia University Press, 1999.

Chirol, Marie-Magdeleine. "The Missing Narrative in *Wend Kuuni* (Time and Space)." *Research in African Literatures* 26.3 (1995): 49–57.

Chopra, Anupama. *Dilwale Dulhania Le Jayenge (The Brave-hearted Will Take the Bride)*. London: BFI Publishing, 2002.

———. "Can Bollywood Please All the People, All the Time?" *The New York Times*. October 29, 2006. 3 November 2006. www.nytimes.com.

———. "New Age Baddies." *India Today International*. September 25, 2001: 44–46.

Cole, Michael. "Cognitive Development and Formal Schooling: The Evidence from Cross-Cultural Research." *Vygotsky and Education: Instructional Implications and Applications of Sociohistorical Psychology*. Ed. Luis C. Moll. Cambridge, UK: Cambridge University Press, 1990: 89–110.

———. "Foreword." *Cognitive Development and Its Social Foundations*. By A.R. Luria. Trans. Martin Lopez-Morillas and Lynn Solotaroff. Ed. Michael Cole. Cambridge, MA: Harvard University Press, 1976: xi–xvi.

Coleman, Joyce. *Public Reading and the Reading Public in Late Medieval England and France.* Cambridge, UK: Cambridge University Press, 1996.

Cook, Pam and Mieke Bernink, eds. *The Cinema Book.* London: BFI Publishing, 1999.

Corliss, Richard. "Going Bollywood." *Time Asia.* 160.2 (2002). 22 July 2002 www.time/com/asia/magazine. 3 pp.

Crick, Malcolm. *Explorations in Language and Meaning: Towards a Semantic Anthropology.* New York: John Wiley, 1976.

Culler, Jonathon. *Structuralist Poetics: Structuralism, Linguistics and the Study of Literature.* Ithaca: Cornell University Press, 1975.

Currie, Gregory. "Unreliability Refigured: Narrative in Literature in Film." *Philosophy of Film and Motion Pictures: An Anthology.* Eds. Noël Carroll and Jinhee Choi. Malden, MA: Blackwell Publishing, 2006: 200–210.

Datta, Sangeeta. *Shyam Benegal.* London: BFI Publishing, 2002.

Deleuze, Gilles. *Cinema 1: The Movement-Image.* London: The Athlone Press, 1986a.

———. *Cinema 2: The Time-Image.* Minneapolis: University of Minnesota Press, 1986b.

———. "Beyond the Movement Image." *Post-War Cinema and Modernity.* Eds. John Orr and Olga Taxidou. New York: New York University Press, 2001: 89–102.

Desai, Jigna. "Bombay Boys and Girls: The Gender and Sexual Politics of Transnationality in the New Indian Cinema in English." *South Asian Popular Culture* 1.1 (2003): 45–61.

Desai, Lord Meghnad. "Bollywood Needs to Change Its Act." *The Hindu.* November 25, 2007. http://www.thehindu.com/thehindu/mag/2007/11/25/stories/2007112550030100.htm.

Desphande, Sudhanva. "The Consumable Hero of Globalised India." *Bollyworld: Popular Indian Cinema through a Transnational Lens.* Eds. Raminder Kaur and Ajay J. Sinha. New Delhi: Sage, 2005: 186–206.

Diawara, Manthia. "Oral Literature and African Film: Narratology in *Wend Kuuni.*" *Questions of Third Cinema.* Eds. Jim Pines and Paul Willemen. London: BFI Publishing, 1989: 199–211.

———. "Popular Culture and Oral Traditions in African Film." *African Experiences in Film.* Eds. Imruh Bakari and Mbye B. Cham. London: BFI Publishing, 1996: 209–219.

Dickey, Sara. *Cinema and the Urban Poor in South India.* Cambridge, UK: Cambridge University Press, 1993.

———. "Opposing Faces: Film Star Fan Clubs and the Construction of Class Identities in South India." *Pleasure and the Nation: The History, Politics and Consumption of Public Culture in India.* Eds. Rachel Dwyer and Christopher Pinney. Delhi: Oxford University Press, 2001: 212–246.

Dissanayake, Wimal and Malti Sahai. *Sholay: A Cultural Reading.* New Delhi: Wiley Eastern Limited, 1992.

Dixon, Wheeler Winston. *Disaster and Memory: Celebrity Culture and the Crisis of Hollywood Cinema.* New York: Columbia University Press, 1999.

Dudrah, Rajinder Kumar. *Sociology Goes to the Movies.* New Delhi: Sage, 2006.

Dwyer, Rachel and Divia Patel. *Cinema India: The Visual Culture of Hindi Film.* New Brunswick: Rutgers University Press, 2002.

—— and Christopher Pinney, eds. *Pleasure and the Nation: The History, Politics and Consumption of Public Culture in India*. Delhi: Oxford University Press, 2001.

——. *Filming the Gods: Religion and Indian Cinema*. London: Routledge, 2006.

Dyer, Richard. "Entertainment and Utopia." *Movies and Methods: Vol. II*. Ed. Bill Nichols. Berkeley: University of California Press, 1985: 220–232.

Eagleton, Terry. *Criticism and Ideology: A Study in Marxist Literary Theory*. London: NLB, 1976.

Easthope, Anthony. *Literary into Cultural Studies*. London: Routledge, 1991.

Eco, Umberto. *The Role of the Reader: Explorations in the Semiotics of Texts*. Bloomington: Indiana University Press, 1979.

Eisenstein, Elizabeth L. *The Printing Revolution in Early Modern Europe*. Cambridge, UK: Cambridge University Press, 1983.

Elsaesser, Thomas. "Digital Cinema: Delivery, Event, Time." *Cinema Futures: Cain, Abel, or Cable?: The Screen Arts in the Digital Age*. Eds. Thomas Elsaesser and Kay Hoffmann. Amsterdam: Amsterdam University Press, 1998: 201–222.

Fabe, Marilyn. *Closely Watched Films: An Introduction to the Art*. Berkeley: University of California Press, 2004.

Farrell, Stephen. "Movies Return to Kabul." *The Montreal Gazette*. November 20, 2001: B1.

Finnegan, Ruth. *Literacy and Orality: Studies in the Technology of Communication*. Oxford: Basil Blackwell, 1988.

Fiske, John and John Hartley. *Reading Television*. London: Methuen & Co., 1978.

Foley, John Miles. *How to Read an Oral Poem*. Urbana: University of Illinois Press, 2002.

Foucault, Michel. *The Archaeology of Knowledge*. Trans. A.M. Sheridan Smith. New York: Pantheon Books, 1972.

——. *The Order of Things: An Archaeology of the Human Sciences*. New York: Vintage Books, 1973.

——. *Power/Knowledge: Selected Interviews and Other Writings, 1972–1977*. Ed. Colin Gordon. Trans. Colin Gordon, Leo Marshall, John Mepham, and Kate Soper. New York: Pantheon Books, 1977.

Fowler, Bridget. "True to Me Always: An Analysis of Women's Magazine Fiction." *Popular Fiction and Social Change*. Ed. Christopher Pawling. New York: St. Martin's Press, 1984: 99–126.

Freeland, Cynthia. "The Sublime in Cinema." *Passionate Views: Film, Cognition, and Emotion*. Eds. Carl Plantinga and Greg M. Smith. Baltimore: The Johns Hopkins University Press, 1999: 65–83.

Friedberg, Anne. "The End of Cinema: Multimedia and Technological Change." *Film Theory and Criticism*. 6th ed. Eds. Leo Braudy and Marshall Cohen. New York: Oxford University Press, 2004: 914–926.

Gall, Carlotta. "Long in Dark, Afghan Women Say to Read Is Finally to See." *The New York Times*. September 22, 2002: 1.

Galtung, Johan. "Literacy, Education, and Schooling—For What?" *Literacy and Social Development in the West: A Reader*. Ed. Harvey J. Graff. Cambridge, UK: Cambridge University Press, 1981: 271–285.

Ganti, Tejaswini. *Bollywood: A Guide Book to Popular Hindi Cinema*. New York: Routledge, 2004.

Garga, B.D. *So Many Cinemas: The Motion Picture in India*. Mumbai: Eminence Designs Pvt. Ltd., 1996.

Geertz, Clifford. 1973. *The Interpretation of Cultures*. New York: Basic Books, 1973.

Gledhill, Christine. "History of Genre Criticism." *The Cinema Book*. 2nd ed. Eds. Pam Cook and Mieke Bernink. London: BFI Publishing, 1999: 137–147.

Godzich, Wlad. *The Culture of Literacy*. Cambridge, MA: Harvard University Press, 1994.

Gokulsing, K. Moti and Wimal Dissanayake. *Indian Popular Cinema: A Narrative of Cultural Change*. Hyderabad: Orient Longman, 1998.

Goodenough, Jerry. "Introduction I: A Philosopher Goes to the Cinema." *Film as Philosophy: Essays in Cinema After Wittgenstein and Cavell*. Eds. Rupert Read and Jerrry Goodenough. Basingstoke: Palgrave Macmillan, 2005: 1–28.

Goody, Jack. *The Domestication of the Savage Mind*. Cambridge, UK: Cambridge University Press, 1977.

——— and Ian Watt. "The Consequences of Literacy." *Literacy in Traditional Societies*. Ed. Jack Goody. Cambridge, UK: Cambridge University Press, 1968: 27–68.

Gopalakrishnan, Amulya. "The Benegal Oeuvre." Rev. of *Shyam Benegal*, by Sangeeta Datta. *Frontline*. 20.20 (2003). www.hinduonnet.com/flonnet.com /fl2020/stories/20031010000407300.htm.

Gopalan, Lalitha. *Cinema of Interruptions: Action Genres in Contemporary Indian Cinema*. London: BFI Publishing, 2002.

Gough, Kathleen. "Implications of Literacy in Traditional China and India." *Literacy in Traditional Societies*. Ed. Jack Goody. Cambridge, UK: Cambridge University Press, 1968: 70–84.

Gozzi, Jr., Raymond and W. Lance Haynes. "Electric Media and Electric Epistemology: Empathy at a Distance." *Critical Studies in Mass Communication* 9.3 (1991): 217–228.

Graff, Harvey J. *The Literacy Myth: Literacy and Social Structure in the Nineteenth-Century City*. New York: Academic Press, 1979.

Green, J.R. *Theatre in Ancient Greek Society*. London: Routledge, 1994.

Greenberg, Clement. "Avant-Garde and Kitsch." *Mass Culture*. Eds. B. Rosenberg and D.M. White. Glencoe: The Free Press, 1957: 98–107.

Guillory, John. *Cultural Capital: The Problems of Literary Canon Formation*. Chicago: University of Chicago Press, 1993.

Guneratne, Anthony and Wimal Dissanayake. "Receiving/retrieving Third (World) Cinema: Alternative Approaches to Spectator Studies and Critical History." *Rethinking Third Cinema*. Eds. Anthony Guneratne and Wimal Dissanayake. London: Routledge, 2003: 181–182.

Gunning, Tom. "The Cinema of Attraction: Early Film, Its Spectator and the Avant-Garde." *Wide Angle* 8.3/4 (1986): 63–70.

Haina, M.L. "'I'm All Right Jack': Packaged Pleasures of the Middle Cinema." *Journal of Popular Culture* 20.2 (1986): 131–142.

Hamilton, Edith. *Mythology*. Boston: Little, Brown, 1942.

Hansen, Miriam. "Chameleon and Catalyst: The Cinema as an Alternative Public Sphere." *The Film Cultures Reader*. Ed. Graeme Turner. London: Routledge, 2002: 390–419.

Hansen, Thomas Blom. "In Search of the Diasporic Self." *Bollyworld: Popular Indian Cinema through a Transnational Lens.* Eds. Raminder Kaur and Ajay J. Sinha. New Delhi: Sage, 2005: 239–260.

Harindrinath, Ramaswami. "Ethnicity and Cultural Difference: Some Thematic and Political Issues on Global Audience Research." *Participations* 2.2 (2005). Online. 26 January 2007. www.participations.org/volume%202/issue%202/2_02_harindranath.htm.

Havelock, Eric A. *The Literate Revolution in Greece and Its Cultural Consequences.* Princeton: Princeton University Press, 1982.

———. "The Oral–Literate Equation: A Formula for the Modern Mind." *Literacy and Orality.* Eds. David Olson and Nancy Torrance. Cambridge, UK: Cambridge University Press, 1991: 12–27.

———. *The Muse Learns to Write: Reflections on Orality and Literacy from Antiquity to the Present.* New Haven: Yale University Press, 1986.

———. *Preface to Plato.* Cambridge, MA: The Belknap Press of Harvard University Press, 1963.

———. "Some Elements of the Homeric Fantasy." *Homer's The Iliad.* Ed. Harold Bloom. New York: Chelsea House Publishers, 1987: 93–109.

Hawkins, Joan. "Sleaze Mania, Euro-Trash Art: The Place of European Art Films in American Low Culture." *Popular Culture: A Reader.* Eds. Raiford Guins and Omayra Zaragoza Cruz. London: Sage Publications, 2005: 263–278.

Hayward, Susan. *Cinema Studies: The Key Concepts.* London: Routledge, 2000.

Hegel, Georg Wilhelm Friedrich. "Lectures on Aesthetics: Selections from Hegel's Lectures on Aesthetics, by B. Bosanquet and W.M. Bryant, 1905." 20 October 2006. http://humanum.arts.cuhk.edu.hk/.

Heifetz, Hank. "Mixed Music: In Memory of Satyajit Ray." *Cineaste* 19.4 (1993): 72–73.

Henderson, Brian. "Toward a Non-Bourgeois Camera Style." *Film Quarterly* 24.2 (1970–1971): 2–14.

Herman, David, ed. *Narratologies: New Perspectives on Narrative Analysis.* Columbus: Ohio State University Press, 1999.

Higgins, Lynn A. *New Novel, New Wave, New Politics: Fiction and Representation of History in Postwar France.* Lincoln: University of Nebraska Press, 1996.

Hiltebeitel, Alf. *Rethinking India's Oral and Classical Epics: Draupadi among Rajputs, Muslims and Dalits.* Chicago: University of Chicago Press, 1999.

Homer. *The Odyssey.* Trans. Robert Fagles. New York: Penguin Books, 1996.

Horkheimer, Max and Theodor W. Adorno. *Dialectic of Enlightenment.* New York: Herder and Herder, 1972.

Howe, Desson. Rev. of *Pulp Fiction. Washington Post.* 14 October 1994. www.washingtonpost.com.

Illich, Ivan and Barry Sanders. *ABC: The Alphabetization of the Popular Mind.* San Francisco: North Point Press, 1988.

India International Centre Quarterly, 8.1 (1981).

Jacob, Preminda. "From Co-Star to Deity: Popular Representations of Jayalalitha Jayaram." *Representing the Body: Gender Issues in Indian Art.* Ed. Vidya Dehejia. Delhi: Kali for Women, 1997: 140–165.

Jaikumar, Priya. "Bollywood Spectaculars." *World Literature Today* 77.3/4 (2003): 24–29.

Jain, Kajri. "Figures of Locality and Tradition: Commercial Cinema and the Networks of Visual Print Capitalism in Maharashtra." *Bollyworld: Popular Indian Cinema through a Transnational Lens.* Eds. Raminder Kaur and Ajay J. Sinha. New Delhi: Sage, 2005: 70–89.

Jain, Madhu. "Kitsch-ri." *India Today International.* May 15, 2000: 44–47.

Jameson, Fredric. "Third-World Literature in the Era of Multinational Capitalism." *Social Text* 15 (1986): 65–88.

Jenkins, Henry. *Textual Poachers: Television Fans & Participatory Culture.* New York: Routledge, 1992.

Joshi, Lalit Mohan. "Shyam Benegal." *Indian Summer: Films, Filmmakers and Stars between Ray and Bollywood.* Ed. Italo Spinelli. Milan: Edizioni Olivares, 2002: 118–122.

Joshi, Namrata. "Bole To . . . It's Dhoomtime." *Outlook.* 4 December 2006: 74–80.

Kadapa-Bose, Surekha. "A Time of Reckoning for Bollywood." *Dawn.com.* 23 August 2009. www.dawn.com/wps/wcm/connect/dawn-content-library/dawn.

Kahler, Erich. *The Inward Turn of the Narrative.* Princeton: Princeton University Press, 1973.

Kakar, Sudhir. "The Ties that Bind: Family Relationships in the Mythology of Hindi Cinema." *India International Centre Quarterly* 8.1 (1981): 11–22.

Katz, Ephraim. *The Film Encyclopedia.* New York: Perigree Books, 1979.

Kaur, Raminder and Ajay J. Sinha, eds. *Bollyworld: Popular Indian Cinema through a Transnational Lens.* New Delhi: Sage, 2005.

Kaur, Ravinder. "Viewing the West through Bollywood: A Celluloid Occident in the Making." *Contemporary South Asia* 11.2 (2002): 100–209.

Kavoori, Anandam and Aswin Punathambekar, eds. *Global Bollywood.* New York: New York University Press, 2008.

Kawin, Bruce F. *Mindscreen: Bergman, Godard, and First-Person Film.* Princeton: Princeton University Press, 1978.

Kazmi, Fareed. *The Politics of India's Conventional Cinema: Imaging a Universe, Subverting a Multiverse.* New Delhi: Sage, 1999.

Kemp, Philip. "Ingmar Bergman." *The Oxford History of World Cinema.* Ed. Geoffrey Nowell-Smith. Oxford: Oxford University Press, 1996: 572–573.

Kenrick, Donald and Colin Clark. *Moving On: The Gypsies and Travellers in Britain.* Hatfield: University of Hertfordshire Press, 1999.

King, Geoff. *Spectacular Narratives: Hollywood in the Age of the Blockbuster.* London: I.B. Tauris Publishers, 2000.

King, John N. and James K. Bracken. Personal communication. February 2007.

King, Rob. "'Made for the Masses with an Appeal to the Classes': The Triangle Film Corporation and the Failure of Highbrow Film Culture." *Cinema Journal.* 44.2 (2005): 3–33.

Kolker, Robert Phillip. *The Altering Eye: Contemporary International Cinema.* Oxford: Oxford University Press, 1983.

Koven, Mikel J. *La Dolce Morte: Vernacular Cinema and the Italian Giallo Film.* Lanham, MD: Scarecrow Press, 2006.

Kristeva, Julia. *Revolution in Poetic Language.* New York: Columbia University Press, 1984.

Lagny, Michèle. "Popular Taste: The Peplum." *Popular European Cinema*. Eds. Richard Dyer and Ginette Vincendeau. London: Routledge, 1992: 163–180.

Lakoff, Robin Tolmach. "Some of My Favorite Writers Are Literate: The Mingling of Oral and Literate Strategies in Written Communication." *Spoken and Written Language: Exploring Orality and Literacy*. Ed. Deborah Tannen. Norwood, NJ: Ablex, 1982: 239–260.

Lal, Vinay. "The Impossibility of the Outsider in the Modern Hindi Film." *The Secret Politics of our Desires: Innocence, Culpability and Indian Popular Cinema*. Ed. Ashis Nandy. London: Zed, 1998: 228–259.

Langer, Judith A., ed. *Language, Literacy, and Culture: Issues of Society and Schooling*. Norwood, NJ: Ablex, 1987.

Langer, Susanne K. *Feeling and Form: A Theory of Art*. New York: Charles Scribner's Sons, 1942.

Larkin, Brian. "Bandiri Music, Globalisation and Urban Experience in Nigeria." *Bollyworld: Popular Indian Cinema through a Transnational Lens*. Eds. Raminder Kaur and Ajay J. Sinha. New Delhi: Sage, 2005: 284–308.

———. "Bollywood Comes to Nigeria." *Samar* 8 (1997a). 26 July 2002. www.samarmagazine.org.

———. "Indian Films and Nigerian Lovers: Media and the Creation of Parallel Modernities." *Africa* 67.3 (1997b): 406–440.

Lévi-Strauss, Claude. *Structural Anthropology*. Trans. Clair Jacobson and Brooke Grundfest Schoepf. New York: Basic Books, 1963.

Liehm, Mira. *Passion and Defiance: Film in Italy from 1942 to the Present*. Berkeley: University of California Press, 1984.

Lippert, Paul. "Cinematic Representations of Cyberspace." *Communication and Cyberspace: Social Interactions in an Electronic Environment*. Eds. Lance Strate, Ronald Jacobson, Stephanie B. Gibson. Cresskill: Hampton Press, 1996: 261–269.

———. "Commodity Fetishism: Symbolic Form, Social Class, and the Division of Knowledge in Society." *Critical Studies in Media Commercialism*. Eds. Robin Andersen and Lance Strate. Oxford: Oxford University Press, 2000: 276–286.

Lopez, Ana M. "Our Welcomed Guests." *To Be Continued . . . : Soap Operas Around the World*. Ed. Robert C. Allen. London: Routledge, 1995: 256–275.

Luria, A.R. *Cognitive Development and Its Social Foundations*. Trans. Martin Lopez-Morillas and Lynn Solotaroff. Ed. Michael Cole. Cambridge, MA: Harvard University Press, 1976.

Lutze, Lothar. "From Bharata to Bombay: Change and Continuity in Film Aesthetics." *The Hindi Film: Agent and Re-Agent of Cultural Change*. Eds. Beatrix Pfleiderer and Lothar Lutze. Delhi: Manohar Publications, 1985.

Lyotard, Jean-François. "Acinema." *Narrative, Apparatus, Ideology: A Film Theory Reader*. Ed. Philip Rosen. New York: Columbia University Press, 1986: 349–359.

MacCabe, Colin. "Realism and the Cinema: Notes on Some Brechtian Theses." *Contemporary Film Theory*. Ed. Anthony Easthope. London: Longman, 1993.

McDonald, Paul. "Star Studies." *Approaches to Popular Film*. Eds. Joanne Hollows and Mark Janovich. Manchester: Manchester University Press, 1995: 79–98.

McLuhan, Marshall. *The Gutenberg Galaxy: The Making of Typographic Man*. Toronto: University of Toronto Press, 1962.

————. *Understanding Media: The Extensions of Man.* New York: McGraw-Hill Book Company, 1964.

Macdonell, Diane. *Theories of Discourse: An Introduction.* Oxford: Basil Blackwell, 1986.

Macey, David. *The Penguin Dictionary of Critical Theory.* London: Penguin Books, 2000.

Malhotra, Sheena and Alagh Tavishi. "Dreaming the Nation: Domestic Dramas in Hindi Films Post-1990s." *South Asian Popular Culture* 2.1 (2004): 19–37.

Mankekar, Purnima. *Screening Culture, Viewing Politics: An Ethnography of Television, Womanhood, and Nation in Postcolonial India.* Durham: Duke University Press, 1999.

Manovich, Lev. *The Language of New Media.* Cambridge, MA: M.I.T. Press, 2001.

Margulies, Ivone. "Bodies Too Much." *Rites of Realism: Essays on Corporeal Cinema.* Ed. Ivone Margulies. Durham: Duke University Press, 2003: 1–26.

Martin, Henri-Jean. *The History and Power of Writing.* Trans. Lydia G. Cochrane. Chicago: The University of Chicago Press, 1994.

Martín-Barbero, Jesús. "Memory and Form in the Latin American Soap Opera." *To Be Continued . . . : Soap Operas Around the World.* Ed. Robert C. Allen. London: Routledge, 1995: 276–284.

Marx, Karl and Frederick Engels. *Literature and Art: Selections from Their Writings.* New York: International Publishers, 1947.

Melwani, Lavina. "Pin-Up Icons." *India Today International.* November 26, 2001. North American Special: The Arts. www.indiatoday.com/itoday/20011126/na-arts.shtml.

Metz, Christian. *Film Language: A Semiotics of the Cinema.* Trans. Michael Taylor. New York: Oxford University Press, 1974a.

————. *Language and Cinema.* Trans. Donna Jean Umiker-Sebeok. The Hague: Mouton, 1974b.

————. *The Imaginary Signifier: Psychoanalysis and the Cinema.* Trans. Celia Britton, Annwyl Williams, Ben Brewster, and Alfred Guzzetti. Bloomington: Indian University Press, 1982.

Mills, Sara. *Discourse.* London: Routledge, 2004.

Milner, Andrew. *Contemporary Cultural Theory: An Introduction.* London: University College London Press, 1994.

Mishra, Vijay. *Bollywood Cinema: Temples of Desire.* London: Routledge, 2002.

————. "Decentering History: Some Versions of Bombay Cinema." *East–West Film Journal* 6.1 (1992): 111–155.

———— and Peter Jeffery, and Brian Shoesmith. "The Actor as Parallel Text in Bombay Cinema." *Quarterly Review of Film and Video* 11 (1989): 49–67.

Moretti, Franco. "Planet Hollywood." *New Left Review* 9 (2001): 90–102.

Morrissey, Lee, ed. *Debating the Canon: A Reader from Addison to Nafisi.* New York: Palgrave Macmillan, 2005.

Mukherjee, Meenakshi. *Realism and Reality: The Novel and Society in India.* Delhi: Oxford University Press, 1985.

Murray, Janet H. *Hamlet on the Holodeck: The Future of Narrative in Cyberspace.* Cambridge, MA: MIT Press, 2001.

Naficy, Hamid. "Theorizing 'Third World' Film Spectatorship." *Rethinking Third Cinema*. Eds. Anthony R. Guneratne and Wimal Dissanayake. New York: Routledge, 2003: 183–201.

Nanda, Shammi. "Censorship and Indian Cinema." *Bright Lights Film Journal* 38 (2002). 2 February 2007. www.brightlightsfilm.com/38/indiacensor.htm.

Nandy, Ashis. "The Popular Hindi Film: Ideology and First Principles." *India International Centre Quarterly* 8.1 (1981): 89–96.

———. *The Savage Freud and Other Essays on Possible and Retrievable Selves*. Princeton: Princeton University Press, 1995.

———, ed. *The Secret Politics of our Desires: Innocence, Culpability and Indian Popular Cinema*. London: Zed, 1998.

Narasimhan, Chakravarthi V. *The Mahābhārata: An English Version Based on Selected Verses*. New York: Columbia University Press, 1965.

Narasimhan, R. "Literacy: Its Characterization and Implications." *Literacy and Orality*. Eds. David Olson and Nancy Torrance. Cambridge, UK: Cambridge University Press, 1991: 177–197.

The Nātyaśāstra. Trans. Adya Rangacharya. Delhi: Munshiram Manoharlal Publishers, 1996.

Nayar, Sheila J. "Cinematically Speaking: The Impact of Orality on Indian Popular Film." *Visual Anthropology* 14.2 (2001): 121–153.

———. "Dis-Orientalizing Bollywood: Incorporating Indian Popular Cinema into a Survey Film Course." *New Review of Film and Television Studies* 3.1 (2005): 59–74.

———. "Dreams, *Dharma*, and *Mrs. Doubtfire*: Exploring Hindi Popular Cinema via Its 'Chutneyed' Western Scripts." *Journal of Popular Film & Television* 31.2 (Summer 2003): 73–82.

———. "*Écriture* Aesthetics: Mapping the Literate Episteme of Visual Narrative. *PMLA* 123.1 (2008): 140–155.

———. "Invisible Representation: The Oral Contours of a National Popular Cinema." *Film Quarterly* 57.3 (2004): 13–23.

———. "Seeing Voices: Oral Pragmatics and the Silent Cinema." *Early Popular Visual Culture* 7.2 (July 2009): 145–165.

———. "The Values of Fantasy: Indian Popular Cinema through Western Scripts." *Journal of Popular Culture* 31.1 (Summer 1997): 73–90.

Neupert, Richard. *The End: Narration and Closure in the Cinema*. Detroit: Wayne State University Press, 1995.

———. *A History of the French New Wave Cinema*. Madison: University of Wisconsin Press, 2002.

Nowell-Smith, Geoffrey. *The Oxford History of World Cinema*. Oxford: Oxford University Press, 1996.

———. "Italian Neo-Realism." *The Cinema Book*. 2nd ed. Eds. Pam Cook and Mieke Bernink. London: BFI Publishing, 1999: 76–78.

Nyce, Ben. *Satyajit Ray: A Study of His Films*. New York: Praeger, 1988.

Okpewho, Isidore. *The Epic in Africa: Toward a Poetics of the Oral Performance*. New York: Columbia University Press, 1979.

Olson, David R. *The World on Paper: The Conceptual and Cognitive Implications of Writing and Reading*. Cambridge, UK: Cambridge University Press, 1994.

————, and Nancy Torrance. "Conceptualizing Literacy as a Personal Skill and as a Social Practice." *The Making of Literate Societies*. Eds. David R. Olson and Nancy Torrance. London: Blackwell, 2001: 3–18.

Öncü, Ayşe. "The Banal and the Subversive: Politics of Language on Turkish Television." *European Journal of Cultural Studies* 3.3 (2000): 296–318.

Ong, Walter, J. *Interfaces of the Word: Studies in the Evolution of Consciousness and Culture*. Ithaca: Cornell University Press, 1977.

————. "Oral Residue in Tudor Prose Style." *PMLA* 80.3, 1965: 145–154.

————. *Orality and Literacy: The Technologizing of the Word*. London and New York: Methuen, 1982.

————. *The Presence of the Word: Some Prolegomena for Cultural and Religious History*. Minneapolis: University of Minnesota Press, 1967.

————. "Reading, Technology, and the Nature of Man." *The Yearbook of English Studies* 10 (1980): 132–149.

————. *Rhetoric, Romance, and Technology: Studies in the Interaction of Expression and Culture*. Ithaca: Cornell University Press, 1971.

Orr, John. *Cinema and Modernity*. Cambridge, UK: Polity Press, 1993.

Owoo, Kwate Nii. "Audiences and the Critical Appreciation of Cinema in Africa: Respondents." *Symbolic Narratives/African Cinema: Audiences, Theory and the Moving Image*. Ed. June Givanni. London: BFI Publishing, 2000.

Parziale, Jim and Kurt W. Fischer. "The Practical Use of Skill Theory in the Classroom." *Intelligence, Instruction, and Assessment: Theory into Practice*. Eds. Robert J. Sternberg and Wendy M. Williams. Mahway, NJ: Erlbaum Associates, 1998: 95–110.

Pasolini, Pier Paolo. "The 'Cinema of Poetry.'" *Post-War Cinema and Modernity*. Eds. John Orr and Olga Taxidou. New York: New York University Press, 2001: 37–53.

Patnaik, Priyadarshi. *Rasa in Aesthetics: An Application of Rasa Theory to Modern Western Literature*. New Delhi: D.K. Printworld, 1997.

Pfleiderer, Beatrix, and Lothar Lutze. *The Hindi Film: Agent and Re-Agent of Cultural Change*. New Delhi: Manohar, 1985.

Postman, Neil. *The Disapperance of Childhood*. New York: Random House, 1982.

————. "The Humanism of Media Ecology." *Proceedings of the Media Ecology Association* 1 (2000): 10–16.

Power, Carla and Sudip Mazumdar. "Bollywood Goes Global." *Newsweek*. February 28, 2000. 26 July 2002. http://discuss.washingtonpost.com/nw-srv/printed/int/socu/a16653-2000feb21.htm.

Prakash, Sanjeev. "Music, Dance and the Popular Films: Indian Fantasies, Indian Repressions." *Indian Cinema Superbazaar*. Eds. Aruna Vasudev and Philippe Lenglet. Delhi: Vikas Publishing House, 1983: 114–118.

Prasad, M. Madhava. *Ideology of the Hindi Film: A Historical Construction*. New Delhi: Oxford University Press, 1998a.

————. "The State in/of Cinema." *Wages of Freedom: Fifty Years of the Indian Nation-State*. Ed. Partha Chatterjee. Delhi: Oxford University Press, 1998b: 123–146.

Price, Leah. "Introduction: Reading Matter." *PMLA* 121.1 (January 2006): 9–16.

Radway, Janice. *Reading the Romance: Women, Patriarchy, and Popular Literature*. Chapel Hill: The University of North Carolina Press, 1984.

Raina, M.L. "'I'm All Right Jack': Packaged Pleasures of the Middle Cinema." *Journal of Popular Culture* 20.2 (1986): 131–141.

Rajadhyaksha, Ashish. "India: Filming the Nation." *The Oxford History of World Cinema*. Ed. Geoffrey Nowell-Smith. Oxford: Oxford University Press, 1996: 678–689.

———. "Neo-Traditionalism: Film as Popular Art in India." *Framework* 2.33 (1987): 20–67.

——— and Paul Willemen. *Encyclopaedia of Indian Cinema*. New Delhi: Oxford University Press, 1999.

Ray, Satyajit. *Our Films, Their Films*. New York: Hyperion, 1994.

Resnick, Lauren B. *Education and Learning to Think*. Washington DC: National Academy Press, 1987. 17 August 2002. www.nap.edu.

Restivo, Angelo. "Into the Breach: Between *The Movement-Image* and *The Time-Image*." *The Brain Is the Screen: Deleuze and the Philosophy of Cinema*. Ed. Gregory Flaxman. Minneapolis: University of Minnesota Press, 2000: 171–192.

Robinson, Andrew. *Satyajit Ray: The Inner Eye*. Berkeley: University of California Press, 1989.

Ross, Andrew. *No Respect: Intellectuals and Popular Culture*. London: Routledge, 1989.

Ryall, Tom. "Genre and Hollywood." *American Cinema and Hollywood: Critical Approaches*. Eds. John Hill and Pamela Church Gibson. Oxford: Oxford University Press, 2000: 101–112.

Ryan, Marie-Laure. *Avatars of Story*. Minneapolis: University of Minnesota Press, 2006.

———. "Beyond Myth and Metaphor: Narrative in Digital Media." *Poetics Today* 23.4 (2002): 581–609.

———. *Narrative Across Media: The Languages of Storytelling*. Ed. Marie-Laure Ryan. Lincoln: University of Nebraska Press, 2004.

Salomon, Gavriel and David N. Perkins. "Rocky Roads to Transfer: Rethinking Mechanisms of a Neglected Phenomenon." *Educational Psychologist* 24.2 (1989): 113–142.

Sandler, Kevin S. and Gaylyn Studlar, eds. *Titanic: Anatomy of a Blockbuster*. New Brunswick: Rutgers University Press, 1999.

Sarkar, Bhaskar. "Hong Kong Hysteria," *At Full Speed: Hong Kong Cinema in a Borderless World*. Ed. Esther C.M. Yau. Minneapolis: University of Minnesota Press, 2001: 159–176.

Saxena, Poonam. "Gadar: The Potboiler's Revenge." *Hindustan Times*. August 5, 2001. www.hindustantimes.com

Schatz, Thomas. *Hollywood Genres: Formulas, Filmmaking, and the Studio System*. Boston: McGraw-Hill, 1981.

Scholes, Robert and Robert Kellogg. *The Nature of Narrative*. New York: Oxford University Press, 1966.

Schrader, Paul. "Bresson." *Post-War Cinema and Modernity*. Eds. John Orr and Olga Taxidou. New York: New York University Press, 2001: 298–306.

———. "The Film Canon." *Film Comment* 42.5 (2006): 33–49.

———. *Transcendental Style in Film: Ozu, Bresson, Dreyer*. Berkeley: Da Capo Press, 1988.

Scribner, Sylvia and Michael Cole. *The Psychology of Literacy*. Cambridge, MA: Harvard University Press, 1981.

Sekhon, Joti. *Modern India*. New York: McGraw-Hill, 2000.

Shafik, Viola. "Egyptian Cinema." *Companion Encyclopedia of Middle Eastern and North African Film*. Ed. Oliver Leaman. London: Routledge, 2001: 23–129.

Shedde, Meenakshi. "Bollywood Cinema: Making Elephants Fly." *Cineaste* 31.3 (2006): 24–29.

Simms, Norman. *The Humming Tree: A Study in the History of Mentalities*. Urbana: University of Illinois Press, 1992.

Singer, Ben. *Melodrama and Modernity: Early Sensational Cinema and Its Contexts*. New York: Columbia University Press, 2001.

Smith, Barbara Herrnstein. "Contingencies of Value." *The Critical Tradition: Classic Texts and Contemporary Trends*. Ed. David H. Richter. Boston: Bedford/St. Martin's, 1998: 1552–1575.

Sobchack, Vivian. "'Surge and Splendor': A Phenomenology of the Hollywood Historical Epic." *Film Genre Reader II*. Ed. Barry Keith Grant. Austin: University of Texas Press, 1995.

———. "Bathos and Bathysphere: On Submersion, Longing, and History in *Titanic*." *Titanic: Anatomy of a Blockbuster*. Eds. Kevin S. Sandler and Gaylyn Studlar. New Brunswick: Rutgers University Press, 1999: 189–204.

Solanas, Fernando and Octavio Getino. "Towards a Third Cinema." *Movies and Methods*, Vol. I. Ed. Bill Nichols. Berkeley: University of California Press, 1976: 44–64.

Sontag, Susan. *Against Interpretation and Other Essays*. New York: Farrar, Straus & Giroux, 1961.

———. "Godard." *Post-War Cinema and Modernity*. Eds. John Orr and Olga Taxidou. New York: New York University Press, 2001: 307–317.

Sorlin, Pierre. *Italian National Cinema 1896–1996*. London: Routledge, 1996.

Srinivas, S.V. "Kung Fu Hustle: A Note on the Local." *Inter-Asia Cultural Studies* 6.2 (2005): 289–295.

Staiger, Janet. *Interpreting Films: Studies in the Historical Reception of American Cinema*. Princeton: Princeton University Press, 1992.

———. "Reception Studies: The Death of the Reader." *The Cinematic Text: Methods and Approaches*. Ed. R. Barton Palmer. New York: AMS Press, 1989: 353–368.

Stam, Robert. "Beyond Third Cinema." *Rethinking Third Cinema*. Eds. Anthony R. Guneratne and Wimal Dissanayake. New York: Routledge, 2003: 31–48.

Steimatsky, Noa. "Pasolini on *Terra Sancta*: Towards a Theology of Film." *Rites of Realism: Essays on Corporeal Cinema*. Ed. Ivone Margulies. Durham: Duke University Press, 2003: 245–269.

Stewart, Susan. *On Longing: Narrative of the Miniature, the Gigantic, the Souvenir, the Collection*. Baltimore: Johns Hopkins University Press, 1984.

Stock, Brian. *Listening for the Text: On the Uses of the Past*. Philadelphia: University of Pennsylvania Press, 1996.

Stone, Alan. "Pulp Fiction." *Boston Review*. April/May 1995. http://bostonreview.mit.edu/BR20.2/stone.html.

Strate, Lance. *Echoes and Reflections: On Media Ecology as a Field of Study*. Cresskill, NJ: Hampton Press, 2006.

Street, Brian V. *Literacy in Theory and Practice*. Cambridge, UK: Cambridge University Press, 1984.

Tannen, Deborah. "The Orality of Literature and the Literacy of Conversation." *Language, Literacy, and Culture: Issues of Society and Schooling*. Ed. Judith A. Langer. Norwood, NJ: Ablex, 1987: 67–88.

Telotte, J.P. "*Noir* Narration." *Post-War Cinema and Modernity*. Eds. John Orr and Olga Taxidou. New York: New York University Press, 2001: 25–36.

Thomas, Rosie. "Melodrama and the Negotiation of Morality in Mainstream Hindi Film." *Consuming Modernity: Public Culture in a South Asian World*. Ed. Carol A. Breckenridge. Minneapolis: University of Minnesota Press, 1995: 157–182.

———. "Indian Cinema: Pleasures and Popularity." *Screen* 26.3–4 (1985): 116–131.

Thoraval, Yves. *The Cinema of India, 1896–2000*. New Delhi: Macmillan India Limited, 2000.

Thorburn, David. "Television as an Aesthetic Medium." *Critical Studies in Mass Communication* 4 (1987): 161–173.

Titanic. Dir. James Cameron. Perf. Leonardo DiCaprio, Kate Winslet. Twentieth Century-Fox Film Corporation. 1997. Film.

Todorov, Tzvetan. *Introduction to Poetics: Theory and History of Literature, Vol. I*. Minneapolis: University of Minnesota Press, 1981.

Tomaselli, Keyan G., Arnold Shepperson, and Maureen Eke. "Towards a Theory of Orality in African Cinema." *Research in African Literature* 26.3 (1995): 18–35.

Uberoi, Patricia. "Imagining the Family: An Ethnography of Viewing *Hum Aapke Hain Koun . . . !*" *Pleasure and the Nation: The History, Politics and Consumption of Public Culture in India*. Eds. Rachel Dwyer and Christopher Pinney. Delhi: Oxford University Press, 2001: 309–351.

UNESCO Institute for Statistics. Based on April 2009 release date. 26 November 2009. http://www.uis.unesco.org/ev_en.php.

Unnithan, Sandeep. "Total Recall." *India Today International*. October 22, 2001: 45.

Valicha, Kishore. *The Moving Image: A Study of Indian Cinema*. Bombay: Orient Longman, 1988.

Varadhan, Vasundara. "The Impact of Indian Government Family Planning Instructional Films on Non-Literate Rural Audiences: A Case Study 1983–1984." Diss. New York University, 1985.

Vasudev, Aruna. *The New Indian Cinema*. Delhi: Macmillan India Limited, 1986.

Vasudevan, Ravi S. "Addressing the Spectator of a 'Third World' National Cinema: The Bombay 'Social' Film of the 1940s and 1950s." *Screen* 36.4 (1995): 305–324.

———. "The Cultural Space of a Film Narrative." *Indian Economic and Social History Review* 28.2 (1991): 171–185.

———, ed. *Making Meaning in Indian Cinema*. New Delhi: Oxford University Press, 2000.

Vazzana, Gene. "Indian Films." *Films in Review* 45.3–4 (March–April 1994): 46–51.

Virdi, Jyotika. *The Cinematic ImagiNation: Indian Popular Films as Social History*. New Brunswick: Rutgers University Press, 2003.

Vitali, Valentina. *Hindi Action Cinema: Industries, Narratives, Bodies*. Oxford: Oxford University Press, 2008.

Vitali, Valentina and Paul Willemen, eds. *Theorising National Cinema*. London: BFI Publishing, 2006

Volga. "To Censor or Not to Censor: Film and Public Policy." *Economic and Political Weekly*. April 29, 2000: WS-18-20.

Wagstaff, Christopher. "A Forkful of Westerns: Industry, Audiences and the Italian Western." *Popular European Cinema*. Eds. Richard Dyer and Ginette Vincendeau. London: Routledge, 1992: 245–261.

Walunjkar, Somashukla Sinha. "Bollywood Expands Big Time Overseas." *The Financial Express*. October 17, 2006. www.financialexpress.com.

Watt, Ian. *The Rise of the Novel: Studies in Defoe, Richardson and Fielding*. Berkeley: University of California Press, 1957.

Wellek, René and Austin Warren. *Theory of Literature*. New York: Harcourt, Brace & World. 1956.

Willis, Holly. *New Digital Cinema: Reinventing the Moving Image*. London: Wallflower Press, 2005.

Wolpert, Stanley. *India*. Berkeley: University of California Press, 1991.

Yaeger, Patricia. "Editor's Column: My Name is Blue—A Map of Ottoman Baghdad." *PMLA* 123.1 (January 2008): 9–19.

Young, Paul. *The Cinema Dreams Its Rivals*. Minneapolis: University of Minnesota Press, 2006.

Zavattini, Cesare. "Some Ideas on the Cinema." *Sight and Sound*, 1953: 64–49. Rpt. in *An Introduction to World Cinema*. Comp. and author Aristides Gazetas. Jefferson: McFarland & Company, Inc., 2000: 143–150.

Author Index

231

Subject Index

CPSIA information can be obtained
at www.ICGtesting.com
Printed in the USA
FFOW03n1255090414
4779FF